Legends in their Spare Time

(Volume One)

by

Shane O'Donoghue

A Niche Publication

Published by
Primary ABC,
Abercorn House,
57 Charleston Road,
Dublin 6, Ireland.

Telephone: +353 1 269 5008
Email: primaryabc@eircom.net
Web: www.primaryabc.ie

ISBN: 978-0-9556972-0-3

Origination & Layout: CRM Design & Print Ltd.

Printing: Betaprint, Dublin.

CONTENTS

Wilson Staff
Bank of Irela

FOREWORD

In winning the Open Championship at Carnoustie in July 2007, I realised one of my golfing dreams. It was one of the most special weeks of my life and in my quieter moments of reflection, it gives me a great sense of pride to become the first Irish golfer since the late, great Fred Daly, sixty years before, to claim the title of Champion Golfer of the Year.

I am so proud to have succeeded in a sport to which Ireland has contributed so much. The week of the Open highlighted this more than ever. Before the Championship got underway, it was announced that Joe Carr was to be inducted into the World Golf Hall of Fame, meaning that his amazing achievements and immense contributions to golf were deservedly recognised. The Open week concluded with my own victory and Rory McIlroy's Silver Medal winning performance as leading amateur. The past, present and future of Irish golf all had something very special to celebrate.

"Legends in Their Spare Time" is also a celebration and a reminder to us all of so many of those great Irish amateurs who have contributed immeasurably to the rich heritage of golfing excellence that exists in the four provinces of Ireland. So many talented men and women have helped pave the way for future generations to follow and carry on a wonderful tradition of success, in this great sport. Enjoy the stories, the recollections and those priceless photos.

Padraig Harrington

Padraig Harrington, 2007 Open Champion

September 2007

ACKNOWLEDGEMENTS

This book would not have come together without the help of so many wonderful people, in particular Jody Fanagan, Noel Fogarty, Philomena Garvey, Garth McGimpsey, Mary McKenna, Arthur Pierse and David Sheahan, who all gave generously of their time.

I'm extremely grateful to the family members of our "Legends" for their support and invaluable help: Mary, John and Roddy Carr; Nell Bruen; Alison, Rhona and Joe Fanagan; Bella Fogarty; Peter McKenna; Margaret Pierse; Phil Rooney and Maureen Sheahan.

To Dr. Gerry Owens Junior for providing me with such incredible footage of Joe Carr and Jimmy Bruen, all taken in the fifties by his late father Gerry, the former Irish champion and former GUI President.

To Shay Keenan who brought me out to meet Noel Fogarty for a memorable first meeting in December 2004, which really got the ball rolling.

I would also like to thank the following people for their generosity of spirit in assisting this ambitious project.

The Professionals: Padraig Harrington, Jack Nicklaus, Arnold Palmer, Gary Player, Christy O'Connor, Peter Thomson, David Feherty, John O'Leary, Ted Higgins, Philip Walton, Paul McGinley, Darren Clarke, Norman Drew, Deane Beman, Peter Alliss, John Jacobs, Laura Davies, Trish Johnson, Warren Humphreys, Philip Parkin, Denis Hutchinson, Maureen Madill, Alex Hay, Luke Donald, Justin Rose and Noel Fox.

Michael Bonallack, Peter McEvoy and the late Michael Lunt at the R & A.

Bob Lewis, Ellen McMahon & Corinne Felice at the USGA.

To all at the GUI, in particular George Crosbie, Mark Gannon and former Presidents Fred Perry, Michael Fitzpatrick and Ian Bamford.

To all at the ILGU, in particular Centenary President Anne Tunney, the late Pat Turvey, Claire Dowling (née Hourihane), Ita Butler, Ann Heskin, Elaine Bradshaw, Kitty MacCann, Clarrie Reddan (RIP), Vivienne Singleton and Eileen Rose Power (née McDaid).

At the Ladies Golf Union: Susan Simpson, Angela Bonallack, Tegwen Matthews, Ann Irvine and Belle Robertson.

To Richard Hills, Mark MacDiarmid and Scott Crockett at the European Tour.

Marie Holeva at PGA Tour HQ.

Guy Kinnings, Adrian Mitchell, Rob Alter, Katie Powell and Jane Brooks at IMG and James Green at IMG Creative. Andrew (Chubby) Chandler and Suzanne De La Perelle at ISM.

Amateurs with impressive memories included: Dick Lord, Bruce Critchley, Brian Hoey, Vincent Nevin, Eoghan

O'Connell, Declan Branigan, Scott MacDonald, John Morris (jnr), Padraig Slattery, and Eddie Power. A very special thanks to Barry Reddan, who arranged a memorable meeting for me with his late, great mother Clarrie in October 2005, in addition to providing me with crucial reference material.

Special thanks also to Scott Tolley, Doc Giffin and Marc Player for their invaluable help regarding the 'Big Three' and to my good friend Cameron Morfit at Golf Magazine for his encouragement and help. Rossa McDermott was particularly helpful as the momentum built in early 2007. Special mention goes to my cousin Colin Hackett, who helped enormously in transcribing many a lengthy interview for me. It's very handy to have a stenographer in the family! Thank you all.

It goes without saying that the photographs in this book play a massive role in enhancing the stories of these magnificent men and women. The 'Legends' and their families have been incredibly kind in sharing so many precious photos that I can't thank them enough. Special thanks also to the Irish Examiner, Irish Independent, Irish Times, Irish Press Archive, Getty Images, Sportsfile, Owen O'Connor, Matt Browne and also Michael Delaney at Baltray Golf Club.

To my publisher and editor Brian Gilsenan, thanks for immediately recognising the potential for this project and of course, for your all-important commitment, it has been an exciting journey. My friend Gary Moran assisted in editing some early drafts and to Richard, Mark and Christy at CRM, thank you for your excellent work with the layout.

Last but by no means least, to my wife Clare Louise (who first turned my head at 'the East' at Baltray in the year 2000 - the GUI's loss was certainly my gain!). I can't thank you enough for all your love and support and indeed patience, when it came to getting this written, ironically, in my spare time, and for giving us such a beautiful daughter Giselle. To my parents Denis and Helen, thank you both so much, in particular for the cut-down four-iron when I was eight and for introducing me to Dermot Gilleece's 'Golfing Log' in the Irish Times every Saturday! Caddying for my mother in various Senior Scratch Cups in the eighties assisted in no small way in allowing the golfing bug to bite. Here's to Volume Two.

Shane O'Donoghue

November 2007

To Clare Louise, Giselle, Helen and Kay
(my favourite ladies fourball)

Jimmy Bruen

Courtesy of a unique looping swing, this insurance broker from Cork hit the ball prodigious distances. Such was his amazing talent, he was installed as one of the favourites for the British Open at St Andrews in 1939, even though he had only just turned nineteen.

"Jimmy Bruen was THE most outstanding player. He had the most wonderful pair of hands I have ever seen on a golf club. I gave him a lesson one time believe it or not. He came to me at Royal Dublin in the early sixties and was having trouble with his game. His wrists were beginning to act up, but he was so good, he went out and just took a seven iron with him. He sent the caddy up the practice ground and the caddy didn't have to move at all, he was just picking the ball up to his left and right, Jimmy was that accurate."

CHRISTY O'CONNOR speaking exclusively for '*Legends in their Spare Time*' in September 2005.

The 'Boy Wonder' gets ready to tame St Andrews during trials for the 1938 Walker Cup

Irish Golf's First Superstar

Now in his nineties, Dick Lord's memory of the first day he met the great Jimmy Bruen remains vivid. It occurred while on holiday in Killarney in 1933 and Jimmy was the talk of the Parknasilla Hotel in Co. Kerry, having just shot 29 over the hotel's nine-hole course... Jimmy was only thirteen!

"I was two years older than Jimmy and our families knew each other well. After my brother was killed in an accident in China in 1931, my mother would never stay at home at Christmas or Easter, so we spent those holidays at Parknasilla and that's where I first came across Jimmy, who was there with his parents James and Margaret."

Lord, speaking from his holiday home in Dooks, has been a member of Cork Golf Club (Little Island) for over seventy years, having joined at the age of seventeen, in 1935. Lord was then a promising seven handicapper playing out of Douglas Golf Club when he was accepted for membership at Little Island club, in the same year as young Jimmy was looking to leave! Jimmy had just turned fifteen and the club wasn't being very helpful when it came to assisting young Bruen's lofty ambitions.

"Jimmy had to leave Cork Golf Club in 1935 because his mother wanted him to play in the British Boys Championship and to do that, he needed a full handicap, which Cork weren't prepared to give him at the time, so his father got him into Muskerry Golf Club."

As a consequence, Jimmy Bruen always represented Muskerry in the various Championships that he contested as an individual from that day forward. However, in club competitions like the prestigious Senior Cup and Barton Shield, he represented Cork. "Cork was a very old club in those days; Jimmy and myself were the two youngest members until the likes of George Crosbie came along and we started to get younger members."

Dick Lord played foursomes alongside Jimmy in the Barton Shield and was a team-mate of his in the Senior Cup. "Jimmy was the best thing I ever met! In my opinion, he didn't realise how much better than everybody else he was - he could really do things with a golf club. Whereas most of us think we can shape a shot, Jimmy could actually do it. He was absolutely magic!"

As a consequence, Jimmy Bruen always represented Muskerry in the various Championships that he contested as an individual from that day forward.

Genius

Irish golf has been blessed with prodigious talents in the last quarter century like Ronan Rafferty and Rory McIlroy, but for sheer fascination and wonderment, no Irish golfer has ever quite captured the imagination of the sporting public quite like James O'Grady Bruen.

He was born in Belfast to James and Margaret Bruen on the 8th of May, 1920. James Bruen senior worked at the time for the Munster and Leinster Bank there, but the family returned home to the southern capital not long after their only child's birth, when James Senior took up a prominent managerial position with Dwyers Sunbeam Wolsey, who were one of the biggest employers in Cork City and specialised in ladies hosiery.

Within 18 years, 'Bruen the Bear' became famous the world over by virtue of his exceptional golfing talent and record breaking performances in the most illustrious of company.

His is an astonishing tale of golfing success; before he was twenty, he had not only earned the respect of Britain's greatest ever professional golfer Henry Cotton, but spectators gathered in their thousands to catch a glimpse of the youngster as he equalled the feats of the great Bobby Jones around St Andrews. The world's press heaped praise on the Irish prodigy, whose all-round game was quite simply breathtaking.

His record in amateur golf remains outstanding and when he did choose to mix it with the best professionals in the world, he could more than hold his own. Yet in many ways Bruen under-achieved.

In fairness, it's wrong to suggest that he never capitalised on his amazing talent. He did. It's just that the crowd wanted more than he was willing to give. The Second World War and a crippling wrist injury also played their own crucial part in the brevity of his golfing career.

The famous Bruen Loop.

Attempting to give a flavour of the great Corkman's achievements in one short chapter is difficult. Jimmy Bruen won the British Boys Championship, played number one for Britain and Ireland in the historic Walker Cup triumph at St Andrews in 1938 and was

Within 18 years, the young Jimmy became famous the world over by virtue of his exceptional golfing talent and record breaking performances in the most illustrious of company.

installed as a favourite for the British Open, also at the home of golf. All this by the time he was 19 years of age! We are dealing with a very rare and special talent indeed.

With the assistance of people like Dick Lord and in particular George Crosbie, who penned the best-selling archive of Bruen's golfing career, 'The Bruen Loop' in 1995, it has been possible to bring Bruen's short-lived time at the pinnacle of the game to life. Speaking with many other professional and amateur golfers who have cherished memories of playing and socialising with him, have come rich illustrations of what set him apart.

A Legend is Born (not made)

Had he been born twenty years later, one can only dream of how much he could have achieved. Jimmy's first introduction to the game came while on holiday as an eleven year-old at Rosapenna in Donegal. He caddied for his father one day when he played alongside a Dr. Cremin from Dublin, who had brought along his young daughter Nell to pull his bag. In the one day, Jimmy had not only struck his first golf ball, but he had also met the girl who would become his wife twelve years later!

The clearest indication that Bruen was a boy prodigy came when he reached the quarter-finals of the Irish Amateur Championship at his first attempt, aged just 15 at Castlerock in County Derry

Bruen's rate of improvement was swift upon returning home to Cork. His parents secured junior membership for their boy at the Alister Mackenzie-designed Cork Golf Club at Little Island. While attending Presentation Brothers School in Cork, he played most sports but undoubtedly, his days on the school hurling team contributed to that famous loop in his swing. Bruen's participation in both hurling and rugby were sidelined at an early stage however, when an injury on the playing field led him to favour golf exclusively.

When he joined Muskerry Golf Club in 1935, his starting handicap of six was reduced to scratch within weeks after winning all around him and his outrageous length off the tee, allied to a silky short game, saw him beat par practically every time he played 18 holes!

The Bruen's enjoyed a very comfortable lifestyle; when it came to their son's undoubted potential at golf and more importantly, his own desire to compete and improve, their support was significant. The clearest indication that Bruen was a boy prodigy came when he reached the quarter-finals of the Irish Amateur Championship at his first attempt, aged just 15, at Castlerock in County Derry. His opponent was the legendary John Burke of Lahinch. Burke had been a Walker Cup player three years earlier and would go on to amass 25 major amateur titles in his own storied career. He was quoted as saying that he 'took no chances' in the match against the Cork whiz-kid and had 'been all-out from the start' in order to win.

Bruen had announced his arrival in no uncertain terms, and being so young, it was only natural that he wanted to test his skills against the very best of his contemporaries, in the British Boys Championship. He was by this time playing off a handicap of plus one and was in the fortunate position of having parents who could afford the cost of sending their talented son to Balgowrie in Scotland for a tilt at the prestigious title. There was no such tournament in Ireland at the time - surprisingly, there would not be an Irish Boys Championship for another 48 years.

That fateful trip to Scotland proved to be a valuable lesson. Losing in the second round of matchplay, to an older boy from Falkirk, Bruen's appetite for success was well and truly whetted - he came away determined to return and win the premier Boy's tournament before he was 18. It was also costing his parents a pretty penny and he vowed to make good their investment. At fifteen, time was obviously on his side, but little did he know that exactly twelve months later, his chance would come over one of Lancashire's most famous links.

Again, James and Margaret decided to enter Jimmy in the British Boys Championship in 1936 and mother and son took the ferry across the Irish Sea to Liverpool, a week in advance of the Championship being held that year at Royal Birkdale, near Southport.

Having picked up a new set of clubs from Fred Smyth, the renowned club-maker at Royal Dublin the previous week, Bruen was in high spirits in advance of the Championship that he had been dreaming about winning for a whole year.

Speaking in 2005, Christy O'Connor, who took over the professional duties at Royal Dublin himself in 1959, recalled with great pleasure the story of Jimmy's build-up to that Championship at Birkdale:
"When Jimmy went over there to play in the Boys', his mother tried to get Bobby Halsall, who was a pro there and subsequently a friend of mine, to give him a lesson. Halsall was too busy, as he was trying to make a few bob in the shop. She asked several times before Bobby relented and agreed to have a look at the youngster. He says 'take a five-iron with you, son'. So Jimmy went out with a five-iron and a four-wood and Halsall threw down a few balls and said 'hit them there.' Jimmy did his whirly swing and he hit the ball - wonderfully of course.

Halsall says to him, 'lad, hit a few woods there and I will have a good look at you'. 'Sir', says Jimmy, 'I might send it over that hedge.' Don't be telling me that, you couldn't possibly do that,' claimed Halsall.

So young Jimmy threw the balls down, took a few swings and I guarantee you, it was like spitting fuel flying over the range, going clean on over the fence. 'Sir', he said, 'I told you I'd do that!' 'Lad, come on with me quick,' said Halsall and with all the magnificence that he'd just witnessed there, he immediately invited Bruen to play nine holes with him; Bobby's attitude had now changed completely!

At that time when money was very scarce, you could get an awful lot of things for a fiver. Halsall went in, he rang his bookie immediately and asked 'what price is Bruen? The bookie had never heard of him, so Halsall said, 'Well, what price will you give me?' so the bookie gave him 100/1. Halsall immediately placed a fiver, at those odds, on Bruen to win the British Boys Championship. They then went out to play nine holes and the youngster began by driving the par four tenth. He won the nine-hole match easily. Halsall again rang up the bookie to see if Bruen's odds had changed in the last couple of hours, but they remained at 100 to 1, so Halsall said that he'd have another 'tenner' on him! The bookie, smelling a rat, asked him to come clean and tell him about the youngster, to which Halsall replied, 'I will tell you, this is the best thing I have ever seen. He is a boy of young age and the talent is oozing out of him. Every department is great, a huge hitter and a great putter, with superb touch around the greens, he is a real find!' recalled O'Connor.

A real find indeed. Bruen had no equal in that famous Championship and having cruised to the final, he completely outplayed his opponent, another 16 year-

Jimmy announces his arrival on to the world stage with an emphatic win at the British Boys' Open Amateur Championship at Royal Birkdale, 1936.

"So young Jimmy threw the balls down, took a few swings and I guarantee you, it was like spitting fuel flying over the range, going clean on over the fence."

old called William Innes of Lanark in Scotland. The score of 10 and 9 over 36 holes included two eagles, the second one occurring at what turned out to be the closing hole of the match, the par five ninth. Holing from 15 yards for a three and the win, he was carried shoulder high to the clubhouse. The dream had been realised and Jimmy Bruen's rich potential at that point had been fulfilled.

The Golden Years

The Cork youngster was now the most talked about golfer on these islands and he was not yet seventeen! While continuing to support his clubs (Little Island and Muskerry), he also began an assault on the biggest Championships in Ireland and further afield. In 1937, he helped Cork Golf Club to win the coveted Barton Shield. As one of the top club competitions in Ireland, the Shield finals were held in the run up to the Irish Amateur Close Championship that year at Ballybunion.

With a growing reputation, he was clearly one of the pre-Championship favourites and justified those expectations by making it to the final, where he again came up against John Burke. Having grown immeasurably in confidence in the intervening twelve months since Burke had beaten him in the last eight, Bruen produced a flawless performance to usurp the defending champion by 3 & 2 over thirty-six holes. Not only was his length the subject of much awe, it was primarily his prowess with the wedge and putter that proved the difference between the pair.

Jimmy, a strapping fifteen-stone 17 year-old claims his first 'major' on Irish soil at the Irish Close at Ballybunion in 1937.

James Bruen was now the most talked about golfer on these islands and he was not yet seventeen!

He went on to finish sixth behind Bert Gadd in the Irish Open Championship at Portrush that July and finished leading Irish player (pro or amateur). After a debut in the Home Internationals at Portmarnock, the seventeen year-old played in the Mackesy Cup at Muskerry and shot a course record 65. The round included nine threes; he was playing off a handicap of plus two and carded a nett 67, only to lose by two shots!

Jeffrey Simpson of the Daily Mail wrote a piece at the end of that year about the prospects of two rising stars of the amateur game, South Africa's Bobby Locke and Australia's Jim Ferrier. Acknowledging that they were future stars, he made a point to include the claims of the Irishman: "Dominion Golfers claim that Locke and Ferrier are the world's outstanding amateurs...but I fancy the seventeen year-old Irish boy, James Bruen, younger by two years, would give him (Locke) a fight any time."

Henry Cotton, that year's Open Champion at Carnoustie watched Bruen for the first time that summer in the British Amateur Championship at Sandwich, which was eventually won by the American playboy Bobby Sweeny (remember the name!). Cotton was impressed by the Corkman's power, but encouraged a change of style: "I should like to see him develop a smoother swing. If he is wise, Bruen will concentrate on cultivating an easier style. One encouraging feature of his play in my opinion is his capacity for hard work, but he will be well advised not to overdo it."

The Bruen Loop in practise for the Walker Cup trials at St Andrews

Prophetic words indeed from the great champion. Cotton also predicted that Bruen would be selected for the Walker Cup team the following year, and again he was proven to be absolutely right. In May of 1938, Bruen was one of twenty four players selected to take part in trials for the team that would play the Americans that June over the Old Course at St Andrews.

This was a decisive move by the R&A to encourage greater team spirit amongst the top players of the home countries, having witnessed some notable thrashings in the past. By bringing them together at the time of the R&A spring meeting, the hope was that the ten men eventually chosen would have had a unique opportunity to bond as a unit, in advance of the Walker Cup matches. It had the desired affect.

What followed over that famous week was an astonishing display from the boy Bruen, that saw him heralded as the next big star of world golf (and he had yet to finish school at Presentation College in Cork!)

After impressive displays during practice ahead of the trials, Bruen knew that he was in the form of his life, carding two rounds of 71 over the par 73 course (the 'Road Hole' at number seventeen was at that time a par five). When the trials began in earnest, Bruen belied his youthful years by showing the course no mercy and equalling the course record by carding a five under par 68. Gordon Greenwood, the famed Daily Telegraph correspondent wrote of this historic performance in gushing tones:

"James Bruen, an Irish boy of seventeen from Cork, was the hero of the Walker Cup trial matches which were begun on the Championship course here today. He accomplished an electrifying round of 68 which equals Bobby Jones' amateur record for the course. Bruen is the greatest discovery of modern times in British golf and his selection for the British team to meet America in the international match at St Andrews next month is now an absolute certainty. No golfer of his age has ever played for either country. Even Bobby Jones was nineteen when he first came to England to play for America."

Bruen followed that round with a 71 and the next day, in a match against fellow triallist Gordon Peters, he produced figures of 73 and 71 to win his match by seven holes. Thus, in shooting 283 for four rounds over the Old Course, Bruen had beaten the winning total of Bobby Jones when he won the Open there eleven years before, by two shots! A day before his eighteenth birthday, he had guaranteed his place on the ten-man team and was the talk of the 'Old Grey Toon'.

What followed over that famous week was an astonishing display from the boy Bruen that saw him heralded as the next big star of world golf

"I don't drink or smoke in the ordinary way, although if I do well in a tournament maybe I'll have a glass of champagne...it does you good, and it certainly makes you feel good"
- 17 year-old Jimmy Bruen charming the press at St Andrews.

Cotton, who was by then an unofficial advisor to the British and Irish team was wholesome in his praise of Bruen, whom he had now studied up close and at great length.

"I have not seen a player do such scores, no matter what his age. Here was a mere boy playing it (St Andrews) with a wise head and a technique that left everybody gasping. Bruen has indeed set a standard for all golfers."

Curiously, Bruen decided not to enter the British Amateur Championship at Troon, which was held the week before the Walker Cup matches at St Andrews. He explained to Percy 'Laddie' Lucas after the trials:

"I am going to concentrate on the Walker Cup match and shall not be competing. If I did well in this I would be dead tired for the Walker Cup match. What is the good of playing for your country if you do not give yourself up to do all you can to reach your peak when the match comes along?" So while fellow team-mate Cecil Ewing of County Sligo made it all the way to the final, losing to the Atlantan Charlie Yates by 3 & 2, Bruen chose to spend the week practising around the Old Course, in readiness for his much heralded debut.

There was, by then, massive speculation about whether Bruen would play number one on the team in the singles matches, as many felt he deserved to, given his dominance in the trials. It was also felt, that because of his reputation that he would have a talismanic role and could inspire his team-mates, who were beginning to feel like more of a unit. It worked.

The great performances of many of the team at the British Amateur Championship at Troon (and that of Ewing in particular) gave a great boost to the home side. In addition, Bruen had become the subject of much speculation amongst the American team. He had taken on an almost mythical status and there was, by then, great curiosity amongst them regarding his precocious talent.

WALKER CUP, St Andrews 1938

The Walker Cup in those days consisted of one series of foursomes and one series of singles. All matches were played over thirty-six holes and over two days. A marathon indeed.

In the opening foursomes match, Bruen played alongside Harry Bentley and they never fired on all cylinders. Clearly the enormity of the occasion had an affect on the youngster, but the pair battled hard. Although playing in front of an expectant first day

Jimmy and his foursomes partner for the first day's 36-hole match, Harry Bentley.

crowd of about 10,000, the home pairing produced a gallant comeback, having been 3 down at the 18-hole halfway mark against former US Open Champion Johnny Fischer and short game wizard Charles Kocsis.

They contrived to reduce the deficit to just level after Bruen lamped a brassie (3 wood) onto the then par five Road Hole. Bentley downed a twenty yard putt and all of a sudden the home supporters could sense a victory all the way up the eighteenth. Decades later, team-mate Leonard Crawley, by then the golf correspondent with the Daily Telegraph, recalled the conclusion to Bruen's debut in the Walker Cup: "Having been one time a long way down and almost a lost cause, Bruen had a putt of 20 feet across that innocent looking treacherous slope on the last green to win the match. One may well imagine Bentley's feelings, having nursed his youthful sick partner through a long day and desperately important match, when he heard him whisper, 'Harry I think I can hole it'. His reply was firm and immediate: 'No, you can't, putt the booger dead.' "

And so he did. Their match ended in a share of the spoils, with a half point apiece, but it was the start of a successful first day's play for the British and Irish boys, ending with two foursomes wins and one loss.

GB & I: 2½ USA: 1½

The following day, Bruen came up against the recently-crowned British Amateur Champion Charlie Yates, a twenty four year-old Georgian, who had learned the game by studying Bobby Jones at the famous East Lake Golf Club outside Atlanta.

Almost sixty years later, Yates revealed (in a letter which is contained in George Crosbie's book *"The Bruen Loop"*) that he was delighted when captain Francis Ouimet named him at number one to face 'Bruen the Bear' as he was known. A win over the Cork teenager would add greatly to the status of his

The Illustrated
SPORTING
and DRAMATIC News

Registered for Transmission in the United Kingdom.
PRICE ONE SHILLING

Boy Golf Prodigy—James Bruen of Ireland

Jimmy Bruen is front page news in June 1938.

victory in the Amateur, where some observers felt that his success was a hollow one, due to Bruen's self-enforced absence from Troon.

Both gladiators went at it from the gun on that famous morning, the fourth of June. The standard of golf was exceptionally high and while Yates was the

"What I think of mainly when I am playing or practising is my left hand. If I am using that hand well, I can be pretty sure that my game will be fairly good, but as soon as I start getting my left hand too much over the shaft, and pulling it in instead of letting it go out after the ball, I know I will go wrong." - Bruen explains his 'feel' for his unique swing.

steadier, Bruen did not disappoint - his long driving and sublime short game were in good order. However, having shot 34 for the opening nine, he found himself one down. His putter began to let him down on the back nine when he missed a short putt for a win at the 13th and similarly on the fourteenth for a half, falling two behind, eventually finishing the first eighteen three down.

Despite a courageous fight in the afternoon Bruen never clawed back enough of the deficit and the match concluded on the 17th by a scoreline of 2/1. His very participation was a source of clear inspiration to his team-mates, with five out of eight victories going to the home side, including a terrific win by Cecil Ewing in the singles against Ray Billows, who had been runner-up at the previous year's US Amateur Championship. History was made...the Walker Cup had been won by the British and Irish team for the first time in the event's nine match history.

GB & I: 7 USA: 4

Purple Patch

After finishing school in June, Jimmy's good form on the golf course didn't let up. That month, he posted a round of 62 in a club competition at Cork Golf Club, going out in 30 shots and back in 32! Only days later, he travelled to the Castle Golf Club in Dublin to represent Cork G.C. in the Barton Shield final, which they won after disposing of Holywood Golf Club (the club that produced Bruen's heir, Rory McIlroy seven decades later) in the final. Although losing the Senior Cup final to Portmarnock, Bruen was the hot favourite to retain his Irish Close title in the following days which he duly did, defeating his friend and fellow Cork member Redmond Simcox by 5 & 4 in the final.

It was turning into a golden summer and all thoughts were now focussed on making a run at the biggest prize of all, the Open Championship.

Royal St George's was the venue and given his growing reputation, the 18 year-old sensation received plenty of coverage in the newspapers. The Cork

"I would not turn professional unless I thought it would be worth my while to do so: and I'd have to win an Open Championship before that."
- 18 year-old Jimmy Bruen thinks big after the Walker Cup trials.

318 THE ILLUSTRATED SPORTING AND DRAMATIC NEWS May 13, 1938

May 13, 1938 THE ILLUSTRATED SPORTING AND DR

The series produced above are exclusive action photographs taken by "The Sporting and Dramatic," and we believe that they are the first series of this player published in England. As you can see, Bruen is a large, upstanding youth with any amount of strength. In the address (1) the stance is slightly pigeon-toed, but the whole poise of the body is delightfully easy. The grip is overlapping and the left hand a shade over the shaft. The take-up (2) of the club suggests the wide arc covered by the club-head. The left arm is extending with the centrifugal force of that head and the firmness of the left hip and the grip of the feet indicate that the blow will be delivered from a firm base. In (3) the ball on its way. Note the firm bracing of the left leg, the firm support of the left hand and particularly the turn forward of the right hand, indicative of the enormous punch delivered. An instant later (4) the follow-through begins, the hands are preparing a scissors-like movement, the right side is coming after the ball, but the head is immovably fixed. The follow-through (5) is exceptionally high. Note the delicate hold of the fingers and the splendid balance of the whole body. The expression of the player is presumably owing to the fact that the sun is in his eyes.

Having just turned 18, Bruen's ability to strike a golf ball attracts widespread coverage.

On a momentous day at the Castle GC, Jimmy accepts the Irish Close Championship Trophy for a second successive year. He is pictured alongside Redmond Simcox, the runner-up from Cork Golf Club. Immediately behind the pair are George Crosbie Snr, the President of the Golfing Union of Ireland that year and his wife Maureen. All four were members at Little Island. However, Jimmy represented Muskerry GC, as he did throughout his Championship career.

Examiner reported that Bruen shot a 64 in practice, but after the first round, he was world news once more, as he opened up with a round of 70 and emulated Bobby Jones as the only amateur to lead the Open in more than a decade. Laurie Pignon was then a rising journalist (who would soon be imprisoned for nearly five years by the Germans in the subsequent World War), who wrote in the Daily Mail of Bruen's nonchalance after his first eighteen: "When he walked from the eighteenth green through the applauding gallery, all he said was, 'that will do', for he is a dour, reticent young man who always expects to do well, and donning his school blazer, went out to watch Henry Cotton, the holder. Bruen's golf was as different from Cotton's as can be imagined. He attacked the hole with every shot within his reach. His youthful courage was sometimes a handicap rather than an asset for he was occasionally too strong. But his great short approaches and his very sound putting counteracted that..."

However, the expectation and high hopes gave way very quickly to bitter disappointment, as Bruen followed up with a calamitous second round of 80. His total of 150 saw him miss the halfway cut, which came at 148. Edward Deane, writing in the Irish Tatler and Sketch brought a bit of realism to the situation, when reacting to some headlines suggesting that Bruen had 'Blown Up!': "In the very crudity of the pronouncement, there lies a subtle compliment. Is it not flattering to advertise his failure in the Open? Does it not imply that everybody expected him to win and his failure consequently became 'hot news?'

Later that month, Jimmy bounced back in style and became the first Irishman since Lionel Munn in 1911 to win the Irish Close and Irish Open Amateur Championships in the same season, when he defeated medical student Jim Mahon, of County Sligo and later Portmarnock, by 9 & 8 in the 36-hole final.

The Irish team that contested the Home Internationals at Royal Porthcawl in 1938.
Back Row l-r: Gerry Owens (Skerries), John Neill (Cliftonville), Clifford McMullen (Knock), Cecil Ewing (Co.Sligo), Billy O'Sullivan (Killarney), Bertie Briscoe (Castlebar), John Burke (Lahinch).
Front Row l-r: John Fitzsimmons (Royal Portrush), Jimmy Bruen (Muskerry), Redmond Simcox (Cork), Jim Mahon (Co.Sligo), Joe Brown (Tramore).

Later that month, Jimmy bounced back in style and became the first Irishman since Lionel Munn in 1911 to win the Irish Close and Irish Open Amateur Championships in the same season

1939 - A Changing World

Bruen was now at the peak of his powers. He was also about two stone lighter after taking the advice of Cotton, and working on a better diet and training regimen. It had the desired effect. He was breaking course records at the drop of a hat, shooting 61 around Muskerry. In carding a 64 at Cork Golf Club, off a handicap of plus four, he signed for a nett 68 which was good enough to win by two shots!

Hoylake was the venue for that year's British Amateur Championship in May and just weeks after his nineteenth birthday, he was the runaway favourite. However, Jimmy's moment would not come to pass, following a disappointing ending to his quarter-final encounter with Alex Kyle of Scotland, who had been a Walker Cup team-mate of his the previous year.

All square playing the last, Bruen made it on to the green in two shots, leaving a definite chance of a birdie. Kyle, who was bunkered in two, played out of the sand and the ball finished between Bruen's ball and the hole. The Corkman was stymied. With no chance to hole his putt, he was forced to concede the match, one down.

"for all due respect to the winner, I have to confess that I shared the general opinion that Bruen stood head and shoulders above them all, British or American..."
- Henry Longhurst

Henry Longhurst, the famed BBC commentator, was quoted as saying, "with all due respect to the winner, I have to confess that I shared the general opinion that Bruen stood head and shoulders above them all, British or American. For myself I should rate Bruen in the highest professional class and shall not be in the least surprised if he wins the Open."

Henry Cotton, who was also disappointed to see Bruen's exit from the Amateur, was himself gushing in his praise of the Corkman's talent:
"To my mind he is a golf genius and will be a danger at St Andrews in the Open. Besides being an improved golfer, he likes the course and he is the only man who plays the old Course in a new way, disregarding old traditions and precedents - this applies to almost all of his game."

The case for outlawing the stymie was never more prevalent, but it would take a few more years to happen. Serious world events were about to put everything on hold for quite some time.

Although disappointed not to claim the Amateur, Jimmy was more determined than ever to test his game against the very best, and before heading back to Britain for the Open, he made his way to Rosses Point in County Sligo to defend his Irish title and try to make it an historic three-in-a-row. After some great early play, Bruen's bid came to an abrupt end in the quarter-finals, when he was outplayed by Gerry Owens of Skerries, who won four of the last eight holes to defeat the hot favourite on the seventeenth by three and one. Owens was a deserving winner. He needed to shoot the lights out to beat Bruen and did so, carding eight birdies. He went on to win the Irish Championship and in 1971 served as President of the Golfing Union of Ireland.

The Open at St Andrews

Although disappointed, naturally, not to have added another Irish title, he now focussed all of his efforts on the upcoming British Open at the home of golf. After his performances there the previous year, he was installed as third-favourite and justified that prediction in practice by shooting a 66, which included three-putting two of the par fives!

Bruen was peaking at the right time. On the 3rd of July, the teenager carded a 69 in the first qualifying round over the Old Course, to tie with the American Lawson Little and also Percy Alliss, father of Peter, who shot the same number around the New Course. The following day he shot another 69 over the New Course to lead the qualifiers for the Open and become joint course record holder at both courses.

The anticipation was immense. Was Jimmy the next Bobby Jones? Everything was certainly starting to

"In the hitting area Jimmy was spot-on. I have always worked from the ball backwards to the person in actual fact. I suppose I was rather different to the others; in other words, ball flight is everything to me. I look down the line and I can see the swing path and I can see where the ball goes, those two things put together tell me what the club face position is. He used to take it way outside his head, but then he got it back in the down swing and it was absolutely spot-on at impact. Jimmy was hugely long. At Birkdale, they still talk about the places that he drove the ball to, when winning the Boys and subsequently the Amateur Championships. He was a rare talent."
- Renowned teacher John Jacobs on the Bruen Loop.

point in that direction and he looked born to do it. He was entirely comfortable amongst his peers and genuinely seemed to enjoy the thrill of the crowds, who lined out in their thousands on the opening day to see 'the Hibernian Wonder Golfer'.

It all looked very good when he pitched to eight inches for an opening birdie and proceeded to record three more in his opening five holes. He was off and running, or so it seemed, after going out in 33, three under par. Poor form set in however and he came home in 39 for a 72, one under par and two shots back.

A frustrating seven shots were required on the Road Hole in round two, after his long-range birdie putt took an unfortunate turn into the infamous bunker, and an eventual second round of 75 saw him drop five shots behind the leaders. After his displays of sublime skill in the qualifying rounds, Bruen's magic was deserting him when he needed it most.
On the final day, Bruen shot closing rounds of 75 and 76, which gave him the Leading Amateur prize and he was only eight shots behind the eventual winner, 31 year-old Dick Burton of Lancashire. Curiously, if you add the two qualifying rounds to the total scores for the Championship proper, Bruen would have finished second overall, losing by one shot to the American Johnny Bulla, while the actual Open winner, Dick Burton would have been ninth!

Burton's prize money amounted to £100. Not exactly a windfall, but with victory in the Open came the opportunities for exhibitions and equipment endorsements. However, this avenue was immediately closed off because of the onset of war.

Within weeks of his victory, Burton was training to be a fighter pilot, while Henry Cotton had also joined up with the RAF. Jimmy himself had expressed a serious interest in joining either the British or Irish Armies, but because of strong pressure from his parents, he settled instead for a job under his father at Dwyer's, Sunbeam Wolsey in Cork.

He was entirely comfortable amongst his peers and genuinely seemed to enjoy the thrill of the crowds, who lined out in their thousands on the opening day to see 'the Hibernian Wonder Golfer'.

Talent on-hold

Life began to settle down for Bruen during the war years and he focussed more on developing a career. The National Championships were suspended and he chose not to play in bigger events like the South, East and West of Ireland Championships, all of which continued between 1940 and 1945. Although he was only in his early twenties during this period, he had been a public figure since his early teens and despite enjoying the challenges of playing top tier golf, he relished the opportunity to become more of a private person.

He was enjoying his golf, which consisted mainly of competitions in his clubs at Cork and Muskerry and his standard of play clearly didn't drop, when one considers that his strokeplay record in club competitions at Little Island saw him compile a cumulative record of 100 under par for forty seven rounds between 1937 and 1943!

It should also be pointed out that during this time, he suffered a severe bout of rheumatic fever, but recovered sufficiently after several months of rest to get back to work. The illness clearly had an affect on his general health and in some ways changed his outlook on life and his priorities. Bruen always looked older than his years, but this brush with ill-health certainly exaggerated his aged appearance.

In the autumn of 1943 there were happier times, as Jimmy married his beloved Nell, with whom he had played his first ever game of golf all those years ago in Rosapenna. As the war continued to rage, golf was decreasing as a priority. Domestic bliss and a quieter life began to appeal more and more.

While he continued to play golf in local events, the golfing public at large was denied the opportunity to see Jimmy Bruen in action. In many respects, it suited him. After some time working in the textile trade, he

Bruen always looked older than his years, but this brush with ill-health certainly exaggerated his aged appearance.

Jimmy thrills the spectators at Cork GC in 1945 during an exhibition match in aid of the Red Cross.

had itchy feet and again, on the advice of his father, it was decided that he set up his own insurance business. With a famous name and a wide variety of contacts built up, the Bruen Insurance business began to flourish.

Speaking to George Crosbie at his home in Summercove, Kinsale in June 2007, it would appear that Jimmy was somewhat reluctant to re-enter the fray of media attention when it was announced that major Championship golf would resume in the year after the war:
"Deep down, I felt that Jimmy was quite shy to be honest. He had so much attention throughout his teenage years and so much was expected of him that he wasn't convinced himself that he wanted to go through it all again. He was living comfortably and had a very happy life with Nell."

Crosbie, who was by this stage a regular playing partner of Bruen's, insisted that he contest the Amateur Championship, which was to be played over his beloved Birkdale, (home of his British Boy's victory ten years earlier) in May of that year. Jack Higgins, the pro at Cork also urged Jimmy to enter, telling him in no uncertain terms: 'I want the Amateur Champion in this club!'

Needless to say, when he did eventually enter, it was big news. As George Crosbie recalled: "he was playing fantastically well and we all knew that he had a great chance to win."

To do so, from an initial entry of 236 golfers, Jimmy needed to get through eight matches before he could finally lay claim to the one title that was missing from his impressive list of credits.

His play was superlative and he had lost none of his powers. He was regularly driving the ball huge distances, in the region of 300 yards, and given the equipment in use in 1946, it's no wonder that his

Jimmy with the highly respected Cork Golf Club professional Jack Higgins.

matches drew the biggest crowds. In his road to the final, Bruen was stretched in all but two of his matches. The standard of play, despite a seven-year gap since the Amateur was last played was exceptionally high and Bruen had to work really hard to stay alive. He managed to fend off all of his challengers and found himself just thirty-six holes away from his most prized jewel. The only man who could now stop him was the British-based American, Bobby Sweeny, a member of the R&A.

His play was superlative and he had lost none of his powers. He was regularly driving the ball huge distances, in the region of 300 yards

On the eighth hole, having again found heavy rough, Bruen broke his mashie niblick (9-iron) in an attempt to extricate himself from the hay.

Bruen's natural strength rescued him on many occasions during the 1946 Amateur at Birkdale, but it was his sublime short-game skills that saw him through to the final against American Bobby Sweeny.

Sweeny was the Oxford-educated son of a wealthy American financier. He had won this title in some style back in 1937 and had just returned from serving with the American Eagles Squadron as part of the Allied Forces in the second World War. Incidentally, he served under Brigadier General A.C. Critchley, father of golf commentator and 1969 Walker Cup player Bruce. Due to his family's vast wealth, Sweeny was a full-time golfer and spent his winters at Seminole Golf Club in Florida, where his regular playing partner was Ben Hogan!

According to the late Dave Marr, the 1965 PGA Champion and golf commentator par excellence, who was an assistant pro to Claude Harmon at Seminole, Sweeny's golf was of such a high standard that he had little difficulty in playing Hogan everyday for a $100 'Nassau'. That's $100 on the front, $100 on the back and $100 overall! Hogan was only warming up for the season ahead when he came to Seminole in January each year, whereas Sweeny was living there for the winter months and playing a minimum of five rounds a week. Consequently, after winning most of their early matches, Hogan was known to have asked Sweeny for a shot!

However, it was to be a level match when Sweeny teed it up against Bruen for the final of the British Amateur. The Corkman had not put in that much practise in the lead-up to the Championship, as he admitted to the Cork Examiner newspaper: *"if I had practised intensely in the weeks beforehand, I would only have gone stale. I decided to play myself into form during the Championship."*

It was both wet and windy as the pair set off in the final and because of the weather, only die-hard golf fans followed every shot, with the more casual attendee remaining sheltered near the clubhouse.

The standard of play in those early holes was far from vintage, with Bruen regularly missing fairways. On the eighth hole, having again found heavy rough, he broke his mashie niblick (9-iron) in an attempt to extricate himself from the hay. In actual fact, it was his Walker Cup colleague Gordon Peter's club that he

Jimmy accepts the British Amateur Championship Trophy at Royal Birkdale in the summer of 1946.

had broken, having severed his own club the previous day! Luckily, Henry Cotton was following the match and happened to be carrying his own version of the club, using it as a walking stick. Under the rules, Bruen was allowed replace his broken club during the match.

Sweeny was playing the tidier golf of the pair, but there was little between them due to Bruen's powers of recovery and sheer strength from some horrendous lies. After fifteen holes, the match was all square. A costly three-putt by the American followed by a sublime birdie two at the seventeenth saw Bruen move to two up before breaking for lunch.

The rain came down in torrents for the resumption of the final eighteen and despite a good win by Sweeny on the first hole, it was Bruen who enjoyed the greater share of good fortune, chipping in for wins on the fifth and eighth holes to get to three up. Sweeny did manage to get a hole back at the turn but it was Bruen's exceptional length that really turned the screw

Great friends. Sir Henry Cotton and Jimmy at Royal Mid Surrey GC near Richmond in London ahead of the Walker Cup matches in 1949 at Winged Foot, Mamaroneck, New York.

When he was presented with the famous trophy on the steps of Royal Birkdale, Bruen remarked to the assembled throng: "This is what I have always dreamed of, to take this back to Ireland. It has been my life's ambition."

on the long fourteenth. Getting home in two massive blows at the 520 yard par five, he calmly putted to within 'gimme' distance and as Sweeny attempted in vain to chip-in from long range for a half, Bruen huddled under the umbrella of Scottish journalist Sam McKinlay and whispered to him, *'this is the happiest moment of my life'.* He was dormie four and the long wait was almost over.

When the fifteenth was halved, Bruen was at last declared the British Amateur Champion. No longer was he the unlucky loser. He was proclaimed the best golfer in the field in the biggest Championship of them all and Jack Higgins finally had the Amateur Champion at his club!

When he was presented with the famous trophy on the steps of Royal Birkdale, Bruen remarked to the assembled throng: *"This is what I have always dreamed of, to take this back to Ireland. It has been my life's ambition."*

"the loss of Jimmy Bruen was a cruel blow for the British team, because he was the automatic number one of the side, and it is a great thing to have a player at the top of whom there is no doubt."

Jimmy suffers more wrist problems at the 1951 Walker Cup matches at Royal Birkdale. He managed to complete the 36-hole foursomes match on Day One but withdrew from his singles match on Day Two.

Jimmy Bruen played no other Championship golf that year. The game took a back seat as he concentrated on his work and family life. In early 1947, while playing a casual fourball alongside George Crosbie, he was hitting a nine-iron tee shot at the short par-3 ninth hole when, in taking a typically large divot, his club struck a stone. The club flew from his hand and he winced in pain as the impact jarred with his right wrist. There is a story which alleges that he initially injured his wrist when lifting paving stones at his Blackrock home. The bottom line is that Bruen was never the same again.

After several medical checks, it was decided to put his forearm in a cast for two months, effectively scuppering his whole season, including the chance of a second Walker Cup cap in 1947. As the famed Bernard Darwin, who was The Times of London's golf correspondent for many years and a Captain of the R&A in 1934 wrote: "the loss of Jimmy Bruen was a cruel blow for the British team, because he was the automatic number one of the side, and it is a great thing to have a player at the top of whom there is no doubt."

Although over time, he made a significant recovery, he never recovered his powers of old. He played on two more Walker Cup teams in 1949 and 1951, but in the latter, his wrist became so badly inflamed that he could not play at all on the final day.

From then on, his appearances in elite golf were sporadic at best. He played club golf and the odd Scratch Cup, but played in only a handful more Championships. He enjoyed more time at home and spent a great deal more time sailing and of course, growing his insurance business. He served as an Irish Selector for a time in the sixties, but his time in the spotlight was confined to the past.

In 1972, the 51 year-old Bruen and his wife Nell travelled to Penina to visit their good friends Henry and Toots Cotton. There was talk of making it more of

Jimmy pictured in 1960 when he became an Irish selector, alongside Cecil Ewing and Joe Carr. The Sutton star always acknowledged Bruen's greatness, labelling him the 'best Irish amateur I ever saw. From 1938 to 1942, he was among the best six players in the world, amateur or professional in my view.' – Praise indeed!

a permanent base, as he eased up on his work commitments. Jimmy's business was thriving but it was one that required a great deal of personal service and professionalism. He gave that and a great deal more. He had also taken on the responsibility of Presidency at Cork Golf Club, having twice served as Captain. All told, his life was extremely busy and the trip to Portugal had convinced him that it was time to take life at a gentler pace, if not then, at some stage in the near future.

Sadly, Jimmy suffered a massive heart attack in the days after returning home to Cork and after a spell in hospital, passed away, just five days before his 52nd birthday. A full life cut tragically short.

Sir Henry Cotton, in a special tribute a fortnight later for Golf Illustrated magazine articulated his sadness and cherished memories of the first superstar of Irish golf: "....I loved Jimmy from the very first days I met an enthusiastic boy wonder, then aged eighteen years, at the Walker Cup matches at St Andrew's in 1938. From that meeting on we were great friends. Just a bare month ago, he and Nell, his wife and mother of six children spent three weeks in my home at Penina, and to have anyone stay at one's home for three weeks is a test of friendship, but we were genuinely sorry when they left. I wish he had stayed, he might still be alive. I don't think I will ever forget him in action in his glorious youthful golfing days. His golf career at the top was short but it was exciting, very exciting."

Irish golf had lost one of its genuine legends.

Sadly, Jimmy suffered a massive heart attack in the days after returning home to Cork and after a spell in hospital, passed away, just five days before his 52nd birthday.

I Remember Jimmy Bruen

In 1959, writing in the Glasgow Herald, Sam McKinlay wrote of Bruen and Carr: "Bruen's record is not so good as that of his great fellow country-man, Joe Carr, partly because he did not have Carr's tremendous competitive compulsion. But when Bruen's imagination was alight and when his 'loop' was working and when he was not breaking steel shafts like matchsticks, he was the most thrilling accomplished golfer in the world."

PETER ALLISS:

"Jimmy had an aunt who lived in Bournemouth in an area called Talbot Woods, which was a rather smart area of town. He came to visit and he called me up to arrange a game at Parkstone, where I was the club pro. This was long after he had finished playing at the top level and I remember that his swing was not as quirky as I had been led to believe. Not as quirky as Jim Furyk for example, but what struck me that day was that he had the most beautiful short game, rather like John Daly, in that he had this wonderfully fluid action around the greens. When he stood over a putt, you felt that it was going in. He was like Tiger over a putt, everything looked so right.

I visited him in Cork a few times. Peter Townsend, Dave Thomas and I went down there to compete at Little Island and Jimmy had us around to his house in Blackrock; he and Nell were tremendous hosts. Jimmy Bruen was remarkable. To achieve what he did at such a young age was prodigious and to be installed as favourite for the Open Championship at St Andrews when he was only nineteen and an amateur. It was unheard of!"

To achieve what he did at such a young age was prodigious and to be installed as favourite for the Open Championship at St Andrews when he was only nineteen and an amateur. It was unheard of!"

TED HIGGINS

Professional at Faithlegg Golf Club and formerly at Ballybunion, he was the grand nephew of the club pro Jack Higgins and represented Ireland at amateur level in the early seventies:

"I was only about ten when I watched him at Little Island. It was an exhibition game featuring Jimmy, Henry Cotton, George Crosbie and Tom Egan. My job that day was to replace his divots. I'll never forget the excitement and on the second hole, the par 5, Jimmy hit the green in

Exhibition Fourball at Cork Golf Club, l-r: Henry Cotton, Jimmy Bruen, George Crosbie and Tom Egan

two and took a divot that must have been a foot long. I ran after the divot and had it back before he moved. He turned to me and said, 'sonny, take it home and practise on it!'

I became a long hitter of the ball and Liam (Higgins, Ted's brother) was long, but we never drove the first at Little Island as Jimmy used to do regularly. Jimmy could hit the ball as long as Tiger Woods does now and that's a fact. His driver was twice as heavy as everyone else's and the combination of his looping action and enormous strength meant that he was phenomenally long."

IAN BAMFORD

The Irish Open Amateur Champion in 1957 and President of the Golfing Union of Ireland in 1993 who witnessed Jimmy Bruen's last appearance in a British Amateur Championship:

"In the Amateur Championship at my home course of Royal Portrush, I happened to play my second round match immediately behind Jimmy Bruen, which of course, was a great thrill. Bruen was up against Billy Steele of Denham (a brother of golf writer and designer Donald Steele) and when we came up to Calamity (the 210 yard par 3 14th hole), I knew that I'd have a really good chance to see the great man close up. A local named Liken was his caddy and I knew him, so I sidled up to him to ask how the match was going and Liken informed me that Mr. Bruen was four up with five to play.

Bruen took this 5-iron from the bag and proceeded to play into a strong wind coming from the town of Portrush, slightly into him and across, left to right. I was quite amazed at his club selection because it would have been at least a low-cutting spoon (2-iron) and sometimes driver depending on the wind. As he swung, I distinctly heard this swish and the ball shot off like a bullet, eventually making the front of the green. Billy Steele had made it up to Bobby Locke's Hollow on the left and short. It was then that I saw Bruen fidgeting with his wrist on his way up to the green. It was one of his early comeback games and he hadn't been playing a great deal of competitive golf.

He was muttering something to Liken and then he proceeded to pick up his ball and walk over to Steele, shook his hand and gave him the match. We still had our match to play and it was only when we got back to the clubhouse that we found out that Bruen had tweaked his wrist with that tee shot at Calamity and knew that he would be unable to play his match in the afternoon and so, gentleman that he was, he conceded and the record books show W. Steele (Denham) WO (walkover)."

Ian Bamford had just seen what was Bruen's last ever shot in a British Amateur Championship.

He was muttering something to Liken and then he proceeded to pick up his ball and walk over to Steele, shook his hand and gave him the match.

DICK LORD

Irish Senior Amateur Champion (over-65) in 1982 and Cork Golf Club's longest-serving member, since 1935. Lord and Bruen played foursomes together in the Barton Shield for Cork GC:

"I remember playing with him in a meeting on St. Patrick's Day in Little Island; Jimmy was off plus four and I was playing off four. I was one over after the first nine holes, but I had lost all my shots. I went out in 38 and Jimmy went out in 30, and that included driving the 3rd green with a 2-wood and missing a short-ish putt for a 3. He had five 4's for starters and then he went 3-2-3-2, four birdies. Incredible!"

JOHN JACOBS

One of the world's greatest teachers, he is credited with founding the European Tour and is a former Ryder Cup player and Captain:

"I lost my father when I was very young; he had been badly gassed on the Somme, but my mother, who encouraged my love of golf greatly, took me to the Open Championship at Sandwich in 1938. I was then 14 and I wanted to see this guy Jimmy Bruen. He was playing a practise round and there was a massive crowd following him. He hit his ball down this fairway and I was standing only three yards from where it came to rest. He got to the ball and decided to play a long iron. I have to tell you, he hit the longest big double-hook you have ever seen in your life and let go with the longest string of Irish curses you ever heard. My mother said 'we are not watching him anymore,' so I never saw him play another shot!

Years later, we met again when I played with him in the An Tóstal at Killarney. He was a terrific fellow. I recall that Eric Brown won, Dai Rees was second and I was third. I remember it particularly well because we were all from different countries. Then Jimmy got in touch with me again some years later, when I was a pro at Sandy Lodge (North London). He wanted to come and have a week's golf lessons with me and he came during one of the very hard winters. We would get a whole patch of snow out of the way and he was the only one there and he whacked ball after ball and we had a guy picking them up.

That was when he was complaining a bit about that wrist problem. Anyhow, my mother ran my shop for me and when he walked in there one afternoon, I told him the story: 'now, you have met this lady before but only momentarily' and I told him exactly what happened, about him hitting this three iron and my mother never letting me see him hit another shot at the '38 Open! We had a great laugh about it!"

I have to tell you, he hit the longest big double-hook you have ever seen in your life and let go with the longest string of Irish curses you ever heard

NORMAN DREW

After Jimmy Bruen, Norman Drew was Ireland's next finalist in the British Boys Championship. Drew lost in the final in 1949 at St Andrews, but went on to become a dominant amateur on these islands before getting a Walker Cup cap in 1953 and then turning professional:

"Jimmy was a real gent. I used to marvel at the shots that I watched him hit. I remember one time at Knock Golf Club (Belfast); he drove the first green, a sharp dogleg left to right, all of 360 yards and uphill! There's also a bunker up the right with tall trees, so to get past the trees and to get up into the gap, most days you would hit a 3-wood - you wouldn't run out of ground with a 3-wood. Some days you would have to hit a driver to get up to the top of the hill. From there you played to a green that sloped very much from left to right. There were bunkers short of the green to pick up bad second shots and for him to carry the fairway bunker, keep it high enough to carry the trees and then to carry the greenside bunkers, hit the green, which sloped severely and stay on it, was unbelievable.

Jimmy was just colossal. He also had a beautiful touch around the greens. Strong hands for the rough, soft hands for around the greens. Jimmy Bruen had that."

NOEL FOGARTY

Former Irish international and acquaintance of Jimmy Bruen. (see page 87)

On a warm summer's evening in Killarney, the bar at the Lake Hotel was in full swing. Noel Fogarty sat deep in conversation with Jimmy Bruen after a day's action in the Foursomes Tournament that annually brought the best golfers in the country together, at one of the great picture-postcard locations.

Fogo was having what he likes to call 'a man-to-man talk' with Bruen. The pair had never played together by that time, which was surprising, but there was plenty of common ground and they were clearly enjoying the banter.

It was at this point that Fogo decided to enquire about his companion's famous length off the tee. "I said to him, 'give me a run through your golf in Portmarnock'."

And Bruen did:

"I drove the first, I drove the second, I drove the third, I got green-high at the fourth one day. The fifth, there were cross bunkers, I could always carry it over the bunkers. The sixth, I could reach in two, the seventh was a short hole, the old eighth I could drive. The ninth, just about 40 yards short of the green, there are little humps on the middle of the fairway. I drove it up to those humps one time!

I drove the old tenth, I drove it green high at the 11th and the 12th is a par three. The 13th, I could make in two. The 14th hole, I am sure I hit the ball far enough and hard enough, but I never got the luck of Joe Carr to run up between the two bunkers onto the green! Two blows were all that were required for the long par five sixteenth, I drove it about twenty yards short of the seventeenth one day and on another famous occasion, required only a chip for my second to the 18th!" recalled Fogarty.

These outrageous drives all took place during the thirties and forties. Given the equipment in those days, Bruen's driving feats are nothing short of spectacular.

MICHAEL FITZPATRICK
GUI President 1983:
"In 1937, Joe Carr and I were 15 years of age. I distinctly remember one time we were playing golf in Portmarnock on a Wednesday evening and Jimmy Bruen and Billy McMullen of Belfast, a younger brother of international golfer Clifford McMullen, also happened to be playing there. We were in having a cup of tea in the dining room afterwards and I mentioned to Joe that we had a semi-open fourball in Sutton the following Saturday, should we invite the boys? Joe thought it was a great idea and they accepted the invitation. I went on to partner Jimmy Bruen in the fourball and Joe partnered Billy. The handicaps were Jimmy Bruen plus four and I was four, Joe Carr was off two and Billy McMullen was four.

I remember the round well because it was rather funny at some of the holes. Sutton only had nine holes at that time and at the 5th hole, Jimmy cut his tee shot into a bunker beside the second green. He proceeded to take out a four iron and put the ball two feet from the pin, it was a par five and he knocked it in for a three and a win. Then we go to the 7th hole now and Jimmy played a four iron onto the green, it was a par four! Joe got on with a three iron and both Billy and I drove the green with drivers. The two top boys, Joe and Jimmy, holed their

"The photo here was taken by the Irish Press, but we were a little apprehensive about having it taken, because we were supposed to be in school on Saturday mornings. After all these years, I'm very glad it was taken!" Mick Fitzpatrick, June 2007.

These outrageous drives all took place during the thirties and forties. Given the equipment in those days, Bruen's driving feats are nothing short of spectacular.

putts for 2's and Billy and I both had two 3's. We were a total of 10 for the four of us playing a par four hole!

Jimmy and I did 12 up against par and Joe and Billy did 11 up! James A. Doyle, who subsequently became a member of Royal Dublin during the war years, was the Honorary Secretary of Sutton at the time. It took plenty of time to get Jimmy Bruen to give him his name and address so that he could post him on the winning voucher, but in fact we were beaten! Dan Cody and Dr. Harry Counihan, who was a medical student that year came in and the bastards had done 13 up. Jimmy got a guinea voucher in the post!

I got to know Jimmy well between 1940 and 1942, when I was apprenticed to the shoe trade in Cork. Every Wednesday we went out practising together. I enjoyed it immensely and learned a lot from him. For instance, I learned that a stiff wrist for short shots or short putts was essential and you just locked your wrists solid and you went back from the hole and straight through and you never missed. Now you see people today breaking their wrists on the way back. You have to break your wrist if you have a long putt, but it's only a slight break and then you come in straight. Of course he was a brilliant pitcher around the green too, absolutely brilliant and his driving? Well, I'll never forget the one that I saw in Portmarnock, when he was playing in the Home Internationals and he drove off the 18th tee and finished up where the water tank or tower was. Now, it would take most people a drive and a brassie to get there, but he got there with his drive!"

Of course he was a brilliant pitcher around the green too, absolutely brilliant and his driving? Well, I'll never forget the one that I saw in Portmarnock

JOHN BUTLER
Retired Bank of Ireland Manager and former Cork Golf Club Member, now resident in Galway:

"One of my earliest memories is of going over to the Walker Cup in Birkdale around 1951. Jimmy did his wrist in on the first day. He was playing in the foursomes with a Welsh chap called John Morgan. I had gone down early to get a close-up of the action. It was a par 3 and Jimmy hit off and he immediately gasped with the pain in his right wrist. It had been giving him trouble for a while.

The foursomes were 36-hole matches and in fairness to the Yanks, they wanted to allow a substitute after the first 18 and the British and Irish team captain felt that it was against the spirit of the competition and Jimmy played on. I remember well that he was putting Morgan into deep rough all over the place - he would hit it and he would take his right hand off the club as he was hitting it. At this stage, his wrist was like a balloon, it was massive. Essentially, that was the end of his Walker Cup and top class golf career.

It had a benefit for me in that the next day he met me and took me into the clubhouse, which was like getting into Fort Knox, so it was a great thrill for me as a young fellow getting in there and I sat with Jimmy and his great pal Henry Cotton!

When Jimmy was a very young fellow, Henry Cotton offered him £10,000, and that was an awful lot of money, to go on a tour in the States. Jimmy's father was well off and they were very comfortable financially, and he more or less knocked that on the head, so Jimmy didn't go. I can remember one day we were going on a trip to Ballybunion and I asked him did he ever regret that he didn't go on that trip, but no, he was quite happy.

Cotton came over to play two exhibition matches in The Island and he had just brought out a new set of irons at that stage; they had a very small head and he left his set with Jimmy. The first thing Jimmy did of course was file the back off all the more lofted clubs - he felt most clubs in those days were too heavy for pitching and for getting a feel. I can remember him well, destroying the back of the heads of Henry Cotton's new set of irons!

Jack Higgins was his coach at Little Island. I used to go to Jack Higgins now and again for a lesson, and he always maintained that why Bruen was so good around the greens was that he played everything with his right hand. Jimmy used to encourage me to hold the club only in my right hand and hit it - there was a totally different feel playing the ball with your right hand than trying to play it with your left, it was a much more natural feel.

While Bruen was long and strong off the tee and fairway, it was around the greens that he was incredible. He had this philosophy 'I can hole it as easy as miss it'. He had this incredible mental attitude.

I was in the National Bank on South Mall, where my dad was actually the manager, which was an unusual thing in those days. Jimmy was a customer there and came in and out regularly. We got on well and eventually he asked me one day would I like a game of golf that weekend and naturally I jumped at the opportunity.

At that stage I was a member in Little Island and Jimmy asked me to play with him on Sunday mornings which suited him because he wanted somebody to go out early - we would go down about 8:30, we would start at 9:00 and we were nearly always the first out. We'd be in at 12:30, come in, have one drink, a mineral, and off home. Jimmy never messed around, he got his 18 holes of golf and went back to the family. I suited him in that way - I was unattached so I was prepared to go out early in the morning and we played maybe every second or third weekend.

He was an exceptionally nice fellow to play with, very encouraging, no airs or graces. I would say that he was quite shy behind it all"

BRIAN HOEY

Former international and the oldest Irish Amateur Champion - at 50 years of age he won 'the Close' in 1984:

"Jimmy used to enjoy regular caravan holidays in Killarney. The 7th was then a short hole across the corner of the lake and there was a pathway that ran from the 4th green up to the 7th tee and half way down there, he parked his caravan. In 1963, I played in the Irish Close Championship and I was drawn against Jimmy in the first round. I was three up on him after thirteen holes and lost! I carelessly lost the 14th to a bogey and then Jimmy came alive, winning the 15th, 16th and 17th with birdies to leave me one down on the last. He was bunkered on the 18th in two and proceeded to putt out of the sand to within 'gimme' distance; I missed my long-range birdie and the match!

Jimmy went on to reach the semi-finals, even though he was only playing in the Championship for a bit of fun. He conceded the match on the eighteenth to Joe Carr, who went on to beat Eric O'Brien in the final. Jimmy invited me to join him for tea and cake one evening at his caravan and I remember him telling me that all these stories about him hitting long irons out of deep rough onto greens were all rubbish. He said that he only ever needed a wedge off most of his tee shots!"

While Bruen was long and strong off the tee and fairway, it was around the greens that he was incredible. He had this philosophy 'I can hole it as easy as miss it'.

CAREER HIGHLIGHTS

Full Name: James (Jimmy) Bruen Jnr.

Date of Birth: 8th May 1920-Died on the 3rd May 1972

Birthplace: Belfast (the family moved back home to Cork shortly afterwards).

Family: Wife Nell, 6 Children

Occupation: Insurance Company founder and Director

Club: Cork Golf Club & Muskerry Golf Club.

Lowest Handicap: + 6

CHAMPIONSHIP HIGHLIGHTS

British Open Championship

1938 at Royal St George's, Sandwich (Aged 18)
After first round of 70, Bruen became first amateur since Bobby Jones to lead the Open Championship. A second round 80 saw him miss the cut.

1939 at St Andrews (Aged 19)
Led qualifiers with two course record-equalling 69's and was installed as third favourite.
Eventually finished 8 shots behind winner in Championship proper. If one includes his qualifying rounds with his four Championship rounds, Bruen would have finished runner-up by 1 shot.

British Amateur Championship
Winner at Royal Birkdale 1946
Quarter-finalist in 1939

British Boys Championship
Winner at Royal Birkdale 1936

Irish Amateur Close Championship
Winner in 1937 & 1938
Semi-finalist in 1963 - Quarter-finalist in 1939

Irish Amateur Open Championship
Winner in 1938

Irish Open Championship (Professional)
Joint 6th overall & leading Irishman, pro or amateur in 1937 (aged 17)

6th overall & leading amateur in 1939 (aged 19) Bruen led after two rounds, having set new course record at Royal County Down with 66. The record still stands!

REPRESENTATIVE HONOURS:

GB & I *Walker Cup*: 3 caps in 1938, 1949 & 1951

International: 24 caps for Ireland 1937-1950

Interprovincial: 2 Caps for Munster 1938 & 1939 (no results available)

MISCELLANEOUS

Member of the R&A

Senior Cup winning team with Cork Golf Club in 1939

Barton Shield winning team with Cork Golf Club in 1937 & 1938

In 1944, Jimmy Bruen, playing off plus 5, won the Muskerry GC 36-hole Captain's Prize with stableford scores of 35 & 36 points. He won the overall nett prize by one shot.

Wife Nell was President of ILGU in 1985-1986 and the LGU in 1989-1991

Joe Carr

Inducted into the World Golf Hall of Fame in November 2007, Joe Carr was Ireland's most successful amateur ever, with an incredible 40 major Championship titles. He was on first name terms with Bobby Jones, led the Open Championship and made the cut in the Masters twice. The Dublin-born clothing merchant was a true legend of the game.

"The golf world lost a wonderful player in Joe Carr, but we all lost an even better man"

JACK NICKLAUS exclusively for *"Legends in Their Spare Time".*

"Joe Carr was a good friend of mine and a great guy, one that I was privileged to know and have as a friend. In addition to that, he was a great golfer. He left a legacy of golfing stories throughout the world. He was one of most highly regarded amateurs in the world. We played together and I enjoyed playing with Joe when I was in Europe and Ireland. He was a very great ambassador for the game of golf and for his country."
Arnold Palmer, exclusively for "Legends in their Spare Time", April 2007.

No regular Joe!

Joe Carr received three invitations to play in the US Masters as an amateur and made the cut twice!
His was indeed a special talent and he quite simply dominated amateur golf over forty years. He led the Centenary Open Championship at St Andrews in 1960. Upon closer examination, it would be fair to say that J.B. Carr's legend was borne out of four key elements. Firstly, there was his dominance of the Irish Championship circuit where he captured thirty-seven major titles. It is a superlative record that will never be broken. On the world stage, Joe enjoyed a record-breaking contribution to the Walker Cup over twenty unbroken years, with eleven appearances, ten of them as a player, which is quite staggering. There was his hat-trick of victories in the British Amateur Championship and fourthly, to bring the curtain down on his golfing career, he was accorded the Captaincy of the Royal and Ancient Golf Club of St. Andrews in 1991. His aforementioned induction to the World Golf Hall of Fame, awarded posthumously, speaks for itself.

"Joe Carr was a good friend of mine and a great guy, one that I was privileged to know ..."
- Arnold Palmer, April 2007

J.B. Carr's legend was well and truly earned and by way of tying all four distinctions together, it's interesting to note that he was born in 1922, the year of the first ever Walker Cup matches and died in 2004, during the week of the British Amateur Championship, as the R&A celebrated its 250th anniversary. As far as his supremacy on the domestic circuit was concerned, it was perhaps his destiny to be a golfing champion, given that his formative years were spent on arguably the nation's finest links, Portmarnock Golf Club, which hosted the Walker Cup matches in 1991 and famously, a British Amateur Championship in 1949 (won by Max McCready).

Joe Carr, a former member of Augusta National proudly wears his 'Green Jacket' in the trophy room at his Sutton home in the early seventies.
Carr was invited to become a member of Augusta National in the late sixties and retained his membership for five years.

Standing out from the crowd. JB in his distinctive white cap marches toward a first victory in the British Amateur Championship at Royal Liverpool, Hoylake in 1953.

Joseph Benedict Carr was unique. Not only did he have the talent, he also possessed a very special belief in himself which, when added to that impressive work ethic, meant he was destined for success on the biggest of stages. It helped enormously that he enjoyed being the centre of attention. JB relished the opportunity to execute his vast array of shots in front of a crowd.

How fortunate we were, to be represented by him on the fairways of the world, making friends, forging relationships and laying the foundations for what we now enjoy and almost take for granted: Ireland's place at the top table of world golf.

At the Open Championship at Carnoustie in 2007, the week had an Irish flavour from the start, when it was formally announced that Joe Carr was to become the first Irishman to be inducted into the World Golf Hall of Fame. It was richly deserved.

Timing is everything in golf and given Carr's relentless dedication to practice and achieving his goals, his timing could not have been better when it came

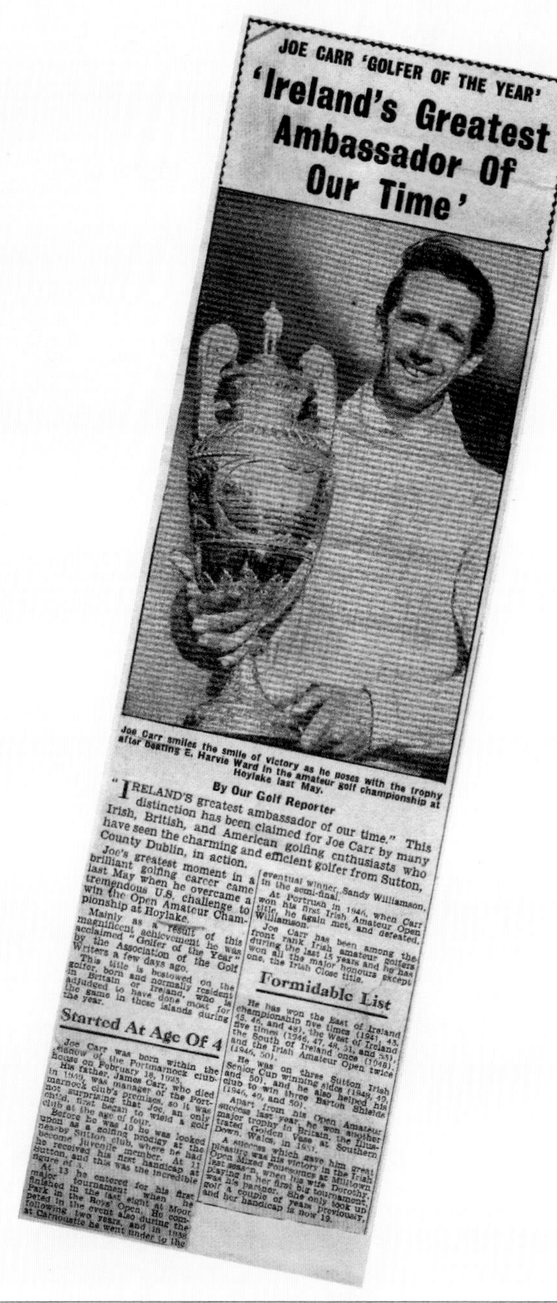

JOE CARR 'GOLFER OF THE YEAR'

'Ireland's Greatest Ambassador Of Our Time'

Joe Carr smiles the smile of victory as he poses with the trophy after beating E. Harvie Ward in the amateur golf championship at Hoylake last May.

By Our Golf Reporter

"IRELAND'S greatest ambassador of our time." This distinction has been claimed for Joe Carr by many Irish, British, and American golfing enthusiasts who have seen the charming and efficient golfer from Sutton, County Dublin, in action.

Joe's greatest moment in a brilliant golfing career came last May when he overcame a tremendous U.S. challenge to win the Open Amateur Championship at Hoylake.

Mainly as a result of this magnificent achievement he was acclaimed "Golfer of the Year" by the Association of the Golf Writers a few days ago.

This title is bestowed on the golfer, born and normally resident in Britain or Ireland, who is adjudged to have done most for the game in those islands during the year.

Started At Age Of 4

Joe Carr was born within the shadow of the Portmarnock clubhouse on February 18, 192[illegible].

His father, James Carr, who died in 19[illegible], was manager of the Portmarnock club's premises, so it was not surprising that Joe, an only child, first began to wield a golf club at the age of four.

Before he was 10 he was looked upon as a golfing prodigy at the nearby Sutton club, where he had become Juvenile member. At 11 he received his first handicap at Sutton, and this was the incredible figure of [illegible].

At 13 he entered for his first major tournament when he finished in the last eight at Moor Park in the Boys' Open. He competed in the event also during the following two years, and in 19[illegible] at Carnoustie he went under to the

eventual winner, Sandy Williamson, in the semi-final.

At Portrush in 1946, when Carr won his first Irish Amateur Open title, he again met, and defeated, Williamson.

Joe Carr has been among the front rank Irish amateur golfers during the last 15 years and he has won all the major honours except one, the Irish Close title.

Formidable List

He has won the East of Ireland championship five times (1941, 43, 45, 46, and 48), the West of Ireland five times (1946, 47, 48, 51, and 53), the South of Ireland once (1948), and the Irish Amateur Open twice (1946, 50).

He was on three Sutton Irish Senior Cup winning sides (1948, 49, and 50), and he also helped his club to win three Barton Shields (1946, 49, and 50).

Apart from his Open Amateur success last year, he won another major trophy in Britain, the Illustrated Golden Vase at Southern Down, Wales, in 1951.

A success which gave him great pleasure was his victory in the Irish Open Mixed Foursomes at Milltown last season, when his wife Dorothy, playing in her first big tournament, was his partner. She only took up golf a couple of years previously, and her handicap is now 19.

A newspaper clipping from 1954 celebrates the mastery of 33 year-old Carr's career thus far.

Joseph Benedict Carr was unique. Not only did he have the talent, he also possessed a very special belief in himself and when added to that impressive work ethic, he was destined for success on the biggest of stages.

Joe's boat comes in! Large crowds gathered in Dublin to greet the Amateur Champions arrival from Liverpool in June 1953 especially Dor and son Roddy, who would go on to enjoy Walker Cup glory himself 18 years later.

maximising his own potential. He was incredibly fortunate in one other respect: his late wife Dor (Dorothy) was his biggest supporter and managed his life with an amazing devotion and attention to detail. She contributed hugely to her husband's achievements as he became one of the biggest names in his chosen sport.

He was incredibly fortunate in one other respect: his late wife Dor (Dorothy) was his biggest supporter and managed his life with an amazing devotion and attention to detail.

Open Champions!
2007 British Open Champion Padraig Harrington alongside three-time British Open Amateur Champion Joe Carr at the 2003 Irish Open at Portmarnock.

She reared their family of six children and ran their home, which doubled as a hotel at times, with military precision. There is no doubt but that her husband would not have been able to become the golfing force that he did in those years without her ingenuity and love.

Joe and Dor Carr.

As the great Arnold Palmer alluded to, Joe Carr left a legacy of golfing stories and it is in that respect that an insight into the life and times of Ireland's greatest ever amateur golfer can be gauged. Success at his chosen sport was undoubtedly an all-consuming passion with him. That he achieved all that he did in the game ultimately points to a certain obsession, but in tandem with that drive and ambition, there was a keen awareness of the bigger picture; that top class golf was a form of entertainment and that it demanded of its greatest exponents that they give their fans what they came to see, and more often than not, that little bit more.

Entertaining the crowds. Large galleries were commonplace when it came to JB's participation in the biggest Championships of the forties, fifties and sixties.

So many words have been written about Joe Carr throughout his years of service to the game that it is impossible to do justice to his amazing career in one solitary chapter. What you will glean from the following pages however, is an insight into how Ireland's greatest ever amateur was perceived by his peers.

Some of the biggest names in the game have very kindly shared their fond memories of JB. Many of the leading lights of the Irish scene during his lengthy reign as the undisputed 'King of Amateur Golf' have also contributed many personal recollections, as have his family and close friends. Those who knew him best.

Early Days

Born in the Dublin suburb of Inchicore to George and Margaret Mary "Missie" Waters on the 18th of February 1922, Joe was the fifth of seven children. At 10 days old, he was adopted by Missie's sister, Kathleen, and her husband, James Carr, who were childless. They had recently returned home from India, where James had been posted as a warrant officer in the British Army. The couple had just been appointed steward and stewardess of the Portmarnock Golf Club, allowing young Joe to play golf from a very early age.

Being the steward's son, Carr was unable to become a juvenile member. However, he honed his interest over

A young Joe follows through.

The couple had just been appointed steward and stewardess of the Portmarnock Golf Club, allowing young Joe to play golf from a very early age.

"I was at school with Joe in the convent school in Santa Sabina (Sutton) and in 1933 we went to O'Connell's Christian Brothers School together. I suggested to Dad that he propose Joe for Sutton; he did and Joe was duly elected a juvenile member."
- Michael Fitzpatrick

JB the all-rounder in action for his secondary school in the early thirties as a sprinter!

the venerable links, picking up valuable tips from the club professional Willie Nolan and a variety of visiting luminaries from the world of golf. He eventually joined nearby Sutton, where he began to shine as a young golfer of immeasurable talent.

MICHAEL FITZPATRICK

School friend, Club-mate and team-mate. Mick Fitzpatrick played on the Sutton GC team with JB that enjoyed several successes in the Irish Senior Cup and Barton Shield. He was capped by Leinster in 1956/57 and was President of the GUI in 1983:

"I was 10 years of age when my father, who was a member of Sutton Golf Club, thought I might like to play golf so he put me forward and I was elected and accepted. The following year I was at school with Joe in the convent school in Santa Sabina (Sutton) and in 1933 we went to O'Connell's Christian Brothers School together. I suggested to Dad that he propose Joe for Sutton; he did and Joe was duly elected a juvenile member.

Our first competition was an Open Fourball competition up in nearby Howth Golf Club. We had no official handicaps at the time, it was 1934 and we were both twelve years of age.

Dick Quinn, who was subsequently a Captain of Sutton Golf Club, was organising this competition and he said 'what do you play off' so I said that I played off about 20 and Joe played to about 10. Off we went with two Howth members and we came in with a score of 8 up and it turned out that we won!

The following year my father went to Sutton Golf Club and made the point that 'these two lads needed competitive golf' and were not getting it as juvenile members of the club, - proposed that we become senior members and we were duly elected. We were given official handicaps then, I was given 10 and Joe was given 5. We played in the same competition up in Howth that following year with our new handicaps and we won again with 8 up!"

Father & Sons.
Joe alongside 3 of his five boys: John, Marty and Gerry at the opening ceremony of the new clubhouse and JB Carr Room at Sutton GC, September 24th, 2001. Behind them is a portrait of Joe in his R&A Captain's coat. The portrait was painted by Paul Dillon, a respected member of Winged Foot and father of actors Matt and Kevin Dillon. Also on the wall is a famous pair of photos showing Joe celebrating an eagle at the fifteenth at Augusta during the US Masters Tournament.

JB in action during his heyday of the forties and fifties.

Sutton was to become Carr's home club for the rest of his life and as a tribute to his golfing legacy, the club dedicated a room to his achievements, when the newly rebuilt clubhouse was opened in 2001. Donating all of his precious memorabilia from over sixty years in the sport, it has become a popular attraction and in many ways a place of pilgrimage, for die-hard golf fans to feast their eyes on Carr's connection with the sport at the highest level.

KITTY MacCANN

British Amateur Champion in 1951.

"Myself and Harry Bradshaw played Philomena Garvey and Joe Carr in several exhibition matches at Elm Park and Clontarf Golf Clubs in the fifties. The crowds that turned out were always big as it was always for charity. Harry and I always won! I don't think Joe minded too much, he always enjoyed entertaining the crowds and talking to them. I remember watching him play an exhibition match at Rosses Point one time alongside Frank Stranahan, Henry Cotton and Cecil Ewing. Joe was a great golfer and was very exciting to watch."

FRANK STRANAHAN

Frank Stranahan was, in many ways, Joe's opposite number in America. Twice a winner of the British Amateur in 1948 and 1950, he had the distinction of finishing runner-up in the British Open (to Ben Hogan in 1953) and the US Masters (to Jimmy Demaret in 1947). He eventually turned professional in 1954 after losing to Arnold Palmer at the US Amateur Championship. Stranahan was the heir to the Champion Spark Plug fortune.

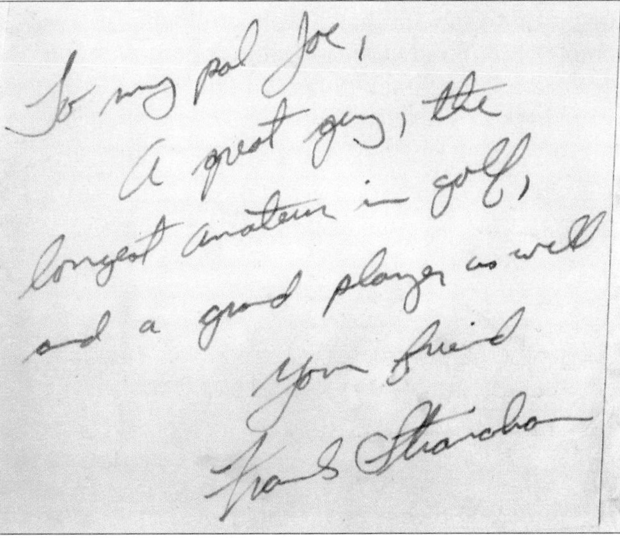

To my pal Joe,
A great guy, the
longest amateur in golf,
and a good player as well
Your friend
Frank Stranahan

A note from Frank Stranahan to JB.

Sutton was to become Carr's home club for the rest of his life and as a tribute to his golfing legacy, the club dedicated a room to his achievements

PETER ALLISS

BBC Commentator. 9-time Ryder Cup player, twice winner of Vardon Trophy and twenty one Tour titles.

Peter Alliss,
a great friend of Joe Carr and indeed Irish golf

"When I was a young man, one of my few heroes was Joe Carr. Why? I thought he had the most wonderful lifestyle. Joe was gallant and dashing, he was handsome enough and he played golf in a cavalier fashion. He used to play with all the big boys, Nicklaus and Palmer and he'd play them for fifty pounds, which was an inordinate sum of money back then.

Joe was gallant and dashing, he was handsome enough and he played golf in a cavalier fashion. He used to play with all the big boys, Nicklaus and Palmer and he'd play them for fifty pounds, which was an inordinate sum of money back then.
- Peter Alliss

It was a lifestyle that I absolutely envied. He lived in this magnificent, big house overlooking the course at Sutton Golf Club and had a wonderful wife Dor, who completely supported his ambitions as a golfer and they had a large family to boot. There were floodlights at the back of the house onto the 2nd green, allowing him to work on his short game in the evenings and in his living room he had the biggest television that I'd ever seen at that time.

Joe putts out at Portmarnock. Watching is playing partner Cecil Ewing, while their guest Danny Kaye the Hollywood entertainer looks on.

Famous enough to become a caricature!
The 'turkey' cartoon relates to JB's prowess one winter at winning the weekly turkey competitions at Sutton GC. Eventually, the club forced him to play off a handicap of plus 13, to give other members a chance of bagging a yuletide bird!

He had a successful business in his heyday selling ladies fashions and material and he had a wonderful business partner (Freddie McDonnell). They gelled together just great, establishing one of the biggest fashion houses in Ireland (The House of Carr).

His was a splendid house to visit and two things stick out in my memory of my trips there; one was of the two crates of fresh milk bottles outside the back door! Such was the openness of their attitude and welcoming nature that Joe and Dor Carr had, what was effectively, an open-door policy in their home. You never knew who you'd find there and with so many children and a constant stream of visitors, the milkman was kept very busy! It says a great deal about their personalities that they were always that welcoming. Dor was such a lovely lady. The other thing that remains a vivid memory is the wonderful trophy cabinet that Joe had built to house his innumerable awards and prized cups. I'm delighted that these can now be seen by visitors in a special "Joe Carr Room" at Sutton Golf Club.

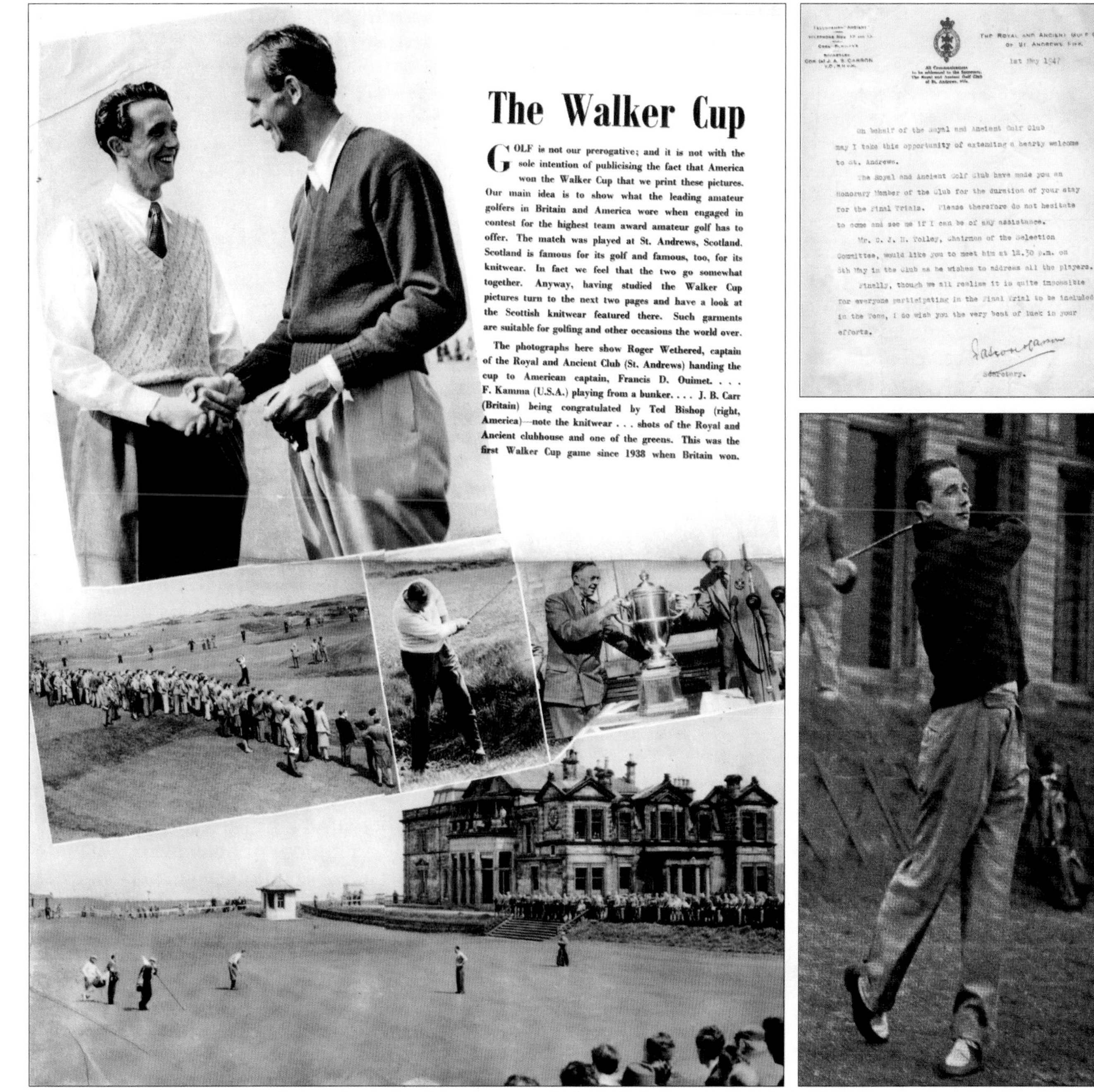

The Walker Cup

GOLF is not our prerogative; and it is not with the sole intention of publicising the fact that America won the Walker Cup that we print these pictures. Our main idea is to show what the leading amateur golfers in Britain and America wore when engaged in contest for the highest team award amateur golf has to offer. The match was played at St. Andrews, Scotland. Scotland is famous for its golf and famous, too, for its knitwear. In fact we feel that the two go somewhat together. Anyway, having studied the Walker Cup pictures turn to the next two pages and have a look at the Scottish knitwear featured there. Such garments are suitable for golfing and other occasions the world over.

The photographs here show Roger Wethered, captain of the Royal and Ancient Club (St. Andrews) handing the cup to American captain, Francis D. Ouimet. . . . F. Kamma (U.S.A.) playing from a bunker. . . . J. B. Carr (Britain) being congratulated by Ted Bishop (right, America)—note the knitwear . . . shots of the Royal and Ancient clubhouse and one of the greens. This was the first Walker Cup game since 1938 when Britain won.

THE ROYAL AND ANCIENT GOLF CLUB OF ST. ANDREWS, FIFE.

All Communications to be addressed to the Secretary, The Royal and Ancient Golf Club of St. Andrews, Fife.

1st May 1947

On behalf of the Royal and Ancient Golf Club may I take this opportunity of extending a hearty welcome to St. Andrews.

The Royal and Ancient Golf Club have made you an Honorary Member of the Club for the duration of your stay for the Final Trials. Please therefore do not hesitate to come and see me if I can be of any assistance.

Mr. C. J. H. Tolley, Chairman of the Selection Committee, would like you to meet him at 12.30 p.m. on 8th May in the Club as he wishes to address all the players.

Finally, though we all realise it is quite impossible for everyone participating in the Final Trial to be included in the Team, I do wish you the very best of luck in your efforts.

Secretary.

JB Carr makes the first of his 10 appearances in the Walker Cup as a player at St Andrews in 1947.

On behalf of the Royal and Ancient Golf Club may I take this opportunity of extending a hearty welcome to St. Andrews ....

Joe was such an outstanding golfer and competitor that his record and reputation, especially in America, will never be seen again. He epitomised the true amateur. I played against Joe quite a few times in the amateurs versus 'pros' matches that preceded many Ryder and Walker Cup matches. I remember playing alongside Dai Rees against Joe and Philip Scrutton one time (over 36 holes) and as 'pros', we always gave our amateur opponents a four-up start. They beat us easily by 8 & 7! Joe played one of the most incredible shots that I have ever seen, until Tiger Woods came along. At the 14th hole at Hoylake, he was buried in the rough. I was sure he'd just hack it out, but he took a five-iron and carved it out of the thick stuff a distance of about 190 yards onto the green. That's when I came to the conclusion that he must have had clubs made by Gillette! I loved being in Joe's company and I am very proud to have known him and to remember him as a dear friend."

"Joe played one of the most incredible shots that I have ever seen, until Tiger Woods came along."
- Peter Allis

One of JB's hallmarks was his ability to get out of trouble. It added to his entertainment value!

NOEL FOGARTY

Fogo's admiration and respect for his departed friend remains undiminished and with all of Carr's amazing successes, many of which he witnessed first hand, he regularly cites Carr's performance in the Dundalk Scratch Cup one year as his perfect display of superiority. The two men were playing partners, there was a big field and Carr had spent the whole winter practising a draw off the tee. With the honour, he stood up on the first tee and blocked it out of bounds: "He hit it out of bounds on the 36th hole as well so he gave me a four shot start, but he still won the scratch cup!

"I have great memories of Suncroft (the Carr family house, which some mistook for the Sutton GC Clubhouse!). It was an open house and I don't think the hall door was ever locked. It was used by the good, the bad and the ugly, it was a hotel, it was a running home and everybody was welcome in it. Dor Carr, Lord have mercy on her, was a wonderful lady."

Joe with Tip Anderson at St Andrews.

Anderson, one of the iconic caddies at St Andrews famously caddied for Arnold Palmer in countless British Open Championships. In addition, he was Joe's bagman during his memorable second victory in the British Amateur Championship in 1958 at the Home of Golf. The link continued when Tip caddied for Roddy Carr at the Walker Cup at St Andrews in 1971 and again a decade later when another of Joe's sons, John, availed of Anderson's expertise in making it to the semi-finals of the British Amateur Championship over the hallowed links in 1981.

JOHN JACOBS OBE

One of the most respected teachers in the game, Jacobs was founder of the European Tour. A former Ryder Cup Player, he was also twice Captain of the Ryder Cup side. Jacobs was Walker Cup coach during Joe Carr's years as a top player. Such was their mutual respect, Jacobs insisted to JB after his first win in the British Amateur in 1953 that he needed to change his swing radically. JB always credited 'Jake' with giving him a new swing that allowed him to stay at the top of his game for many more years than his old 'wide-stanced handsy' action would have allowed.

"I played with Joe on and off for a little bit when he was competing in some of our professional events, but when we built the Jacob's Golf Centre in the middle of Leopardstown Race Course, that's when I really got to know him and his family because I used to stay with Joe and his first wife Dor, a lovely lady. I used to give all the children lessons before I went across Dublin to the golf centre. He did all his practise at Sutton Golf Club, which was, obviously, just behind his back wall and in the mornings, there were always golf balls teed up and ready for him and Joe would go out, never mind about starting with a short iron, he just took a driver and wiped these balls all across Sutton golf course into the sea.

I taught Joe quite a bit and got him to hit it from the inside as he always came over the top. By doing that, the ball starts left but it comes back, so in actual fact he was a fairly accurate driver. His swing was not unlike Sandy Lyle in that Sandy's bad shot was a good one, so essentially, Joe's bad shot was a good one. It always interested me because in practice I could get him to hit it 100% right in the back of the ball when there was nothing in the way and no pressure. Then when we brought players to Portmarnock for a game, the two of us, he would go straight back to whacking it down the left and bringing it back and took my money every time I played him - he was too good for me. He could talk you out of it! We always had a lovely time. To be with Joe was always something very special."

John Jacobs was the Walker Cup coach during the sixties and on one occasion before sending the team

"His swing was not unlike Sandy Lyle in that Sandy's bad shot was a good one, so essentially, Joe's bad shot was a good one."
- John Jacobs

into the matches, he distributed notes to each member, giving them some key thoughts on their swing that they should focus on when practising. JB was a little miffed that he hadn't received a note from Jacobs and told him so, leading 'Doctor Golf' to scribble on the back of JB's hand in ink, 'turn you bastard!'

SIR MICHAEL BONALLACK

Writing exclusively for *"Legends in their Spare Time".*
Former Secretary of the R&A. A five-time British Amateur Champion, five-time English Amateur Champion and Walker Cup player on 9 occasions.

"Some of my most enjoyable times on a golf course were spent in the company of Joe Carr, who I first came across in 1956, when I played in my first Amateur Championship. Little did I think that we would subsequently become firm friends and that we would not only play in various golf teams together, but that eventually, I would become Secretary of the Royal and Ancient Golf Club and Joe would be Captain.

The best of friends. Bonallack and Carr at St Andrews.

"In matchplay he was fearless and was a very intimidating opponent, hence his winning of three Amateurs."
- Sir Michael Bonallack

In matchplay he was fearless and was a very intimidating opponent, hence his winning of three Amateurs. I played him on three occasions, the first time being at St. Andrews in the semi-final in 1958, which was played over 36 holes. I was very much in awe of him but went out in 33 to be 2-up, and was still the same on the twelfth tee.

Just as we arrived on the tee Joe said to his trusted caddy Andy Doherty, in a loud enough voice for me to hear, 'we've got him now, he can't play in a left to right wind', and of course he proved to be correct and I eventually lost by 4/3 and Joe went on to win his second title.

Two years later, he beat me in the last eight at Royal Portrush on his way to his third victory.

Our last meeting was in 1968 at Troon, as it was then, when Joe was past his best and I had learned to play in a left to right wind. Being such good friends we were both looking forward to it. To introduce a little of his own style of gamesmanship I announced on the first tee that I was playing a Dunlop 65 number 6, which was the same number I knew he always used.

'You can't use that' Joe said, 'Why not' I replied, to which he responded 'because I always use that number and I have been playing the game a lot longer than you.' 'Sorry', I said, 'but I haven't got another number'. 'Well I hope you lose the f....ing thing!' came back the reply. At this stage the referee wondered what on earth was going on, but the crowd loved it and realised it was all in good fun.

We turned for home at the end of the course and standing on the 10th tee with a left-to- right wind, I picked up a piece of grass and threw it in the air. I said to my caddie 'Good, the wind's left to right.' Joe remembered exactly what he had said to me years earlier and was now himself having trouble with that particular wind direction. Hence his remark 'You bastard!'

Anyway, he tired on the way home and I went on to win comfortably. At the thirteenth hole he cut his drive and hit the President of The English Golf Union in the middle of the back and went over to apologise. I could not hear what was said, but Joe came back to me looking very cross and told me that the President had said 'don't worry, it wasn't going hard enough to hurt'. 'What bloody sauce' said Joe, 'I wish I'd hit him with a drive three years ago!' What a great sportsman and what a wonderful player he was.

The GB & I Eisenhower Trophy team at Merion GC, Ardmore, Pennsylvania in 1960. L-R: Michael Bonallack, Joe Carr, Philip Scrutton, Guy Wolstenholme and team captain Charles Lawrie.

He played in more Walker Cups than anyone before or after him, although his singles record did not do him justice - he was always playing either first or second in both the foursomes and singles and hence was up against some of the finest US amateurs that have played in the matches.

Getting tired of this at Seattle in 1961, he suggested to Charles Lawrie, the Captain of the team that he should be dropped down the order to say number 5, so that he might get an easier match. Charles duly agreed, only to find that number 5 for the US team was one Jack Nicklaus!

However, the following week Joe played superb golf to reach the semi-final of the US Amateur Championship at Pebble Beach, his best performance in that event. Putting was not the strongest part of his game, but he used a very old and rusty hickory shafted blade putter that looked as if it belonged in a museum. Sometimes he discarded a putter altogether and putted with a three iron. To tell the truth, he was better with this than with a putter, but would not admit it!

During the Walker Cup foursomes in 1959, he and his partner Guy Wolstenholme were involved in a tight match against Bill Hyndman and Tommy Aaron. Whilst the players were walking from a green to a tee, a schoolboy running to get a good view, trod on Joe's beloved old putter and broke it. Joe was distraught and told Guy what had happened, to which Guy remarked 'Thank heavens for that, I wish he had done it before.' As it turned out he was right, for although they only lost their foursome (36 holes) on the last green, in his singles match Joe putted with a three iron and beat Charlie Coe, one of the great American players. He was also an inspirational Captain and

'What bloody sauce' said Joe, 'I wish I'd hit him with a drive three years ago!' What a great sportsman and what a wonderful player he was.

under his captaincy in 1965, the GB and I team halved the match on American soil, which was the best result ever achieved in America at that time.

It was a great and popular choice when Joe was appointed Captain of the R and A in 1991. He was a wonderful ambassador for not only the Club, but also for golf and I was delighted that he and I were able to spend so much time together during his year of office. Mind you, I think it's fair to say he was not the easiest of Captains to organise! However, between the R&A's Pat Ciesla, the Captain's secretary and Lorraine in Dublin, they managed to get him to most places on time and once he arrived he was an enormous success! After he finished as Captain, he was often on the phone to me asking if I could get starting times for friends of his on the Old Course, although the friends were more often than not business acquaintances. As the R&A do not own or run the Old Course, it is almost impossible to meet such requests, but it did not stop Joe trying. One day he rang me up in my office and told me that he realised that it was impossible for me to always help him, but this time it was a very special occasion for four of his very best friends and he really would like me to help them. As he sounded so concerned, I thought I would try and do something and said I would see what I could do. 'That's great' said Joe, 'they are such good friends.' I then said I would put them in for a time but I would of course need to know their names. There was a very long pause at his end of the line, so I repeated that I would need their names to complete the request. 'I'll have to phone you back,' he finally said, at which point we both started roaring with laughter!

What a man, what a player and what laughter he brought to so many people."

"I think it's fair to say he was not the easiest of Captains to organise! However, between the R and A's Pat Ciesla, the Captain's secretary and Lorraine in Dublin, they managed to get him to most places on time."
- Sir Michael Bonallack

J.B.Carr, Captain of the Royal and Ancient, 1991-1992.

DEANE BEMAN
Former PGA Tour Commissioner. Winner of the British Amateur in 1959, US Amateur Champion in 1960 & 1963. Walker Cup 1959, 1961, 1963 & 1965

"I first met Joe when I travelled to Scotland to play in the Walker Cup in 1959. All of the team members were known by their first names. So those of us who were on the US team were naturally anxious to meet the guy known only as 'The Great Joe Carr'.

Joe more than lived up to his title. Every guy on our side fell in love with the magical Irishman. Just imagine my delight when I followed in Joe's giant footsteps and succeeded him as British Amateur Champion. Years later, in the late 1980's, I travelled to Ireland several times to play. My wife Judy and I fell in love with Dublin and Ireland, through the eyes of Joe and his wonderful family. Joe was very special to us."

DAVID SHEAHAN
Walker Cup colleague 1963 and Ireland team-mate, 1961-1968.

As highlighted in his own chapter in this book, David Sheahan was a huge fan of Joe Carr's and it was a huge thrill for him to line up alongside his idol when he won his Walker Cup cap in 1963. The debutant, in the company of his vastly experienced compatriot, shared one memorable practice round ahead of the matches proper.

The Irish pair and two other team-mates joined up for a fourball, with a singles match on the side. In the singles, with several pounds riding on the outcome, Sheahan took on his great mentor and rival.

"I found myself three up with three to play, and to demonstrate JB's prowess at matchplay, I finished par-birdie-par and still lost all three holes! Carr contrived to finish birdie-eagle-eagle to level the match. He hit two onto the seventeenth and holed the putt, to leave me one up. On the eighteenth, I hit what I considered to be an excellent shot, a six iron to the green, about fifteen feet away from the cup and was full sure that I had him; and Joe proceeded to hole out his second shot for an eagle. We were really getting involved in the match, which I loved, despite it only being a practice round. Joe really wanted to take it up the nineteenth and so did I, but Charles Lawrie the captain intervened, in an effort to preserve the team spirit!"

Sheahan played alongside Joe Carr in a practice round for the Amateur Championship at Troon in 1968. They joined up with a pair of American golfers on the first tee and Carr wasted no time in negotiating terms with the pair.

"It was huge money that was being wagered and I decided to have a word with Joe going down the first fairway, because I thought that the sum involved, roughly one hundred pounds, was excessive and he completely admonished me: 'what are you on about Sheahan? I never lost my confidence!'

Carr went on to make the final, one last time, at the age of 46, losing 7 & 6 to Britain's greatest-ever amateur, Michael Bonallack.

"I found myself three up with three to play, and to demonstrate JB's prowess at matchplay, I finished par-birdie-par and lost all three holes!"
- David Sheahan

WARREN HUMPHREYS
Golf Channel commentator. Former European Tour Player and winner. He played on the victorious Walker Cup team at St Andrews in 1971, alongside Roddy Carr.

"The first time I met Joe was when I went across for Surrey to play Leinster in a county match - we were going to play at Portmarnock. Everyone knew Joe and I knew prior to going over that I would be playing his son Roddy for, as I thought it then, a Walker Cup spot. I thought whoever wins they might just pick one of us. So there was a bit of an edge.

Joe insisted on entertaining both teams, 24 people, at his house! They laid out a big table in the upstairs

"He had a great personality, was very charismatic, but yet in many respects I think he was also shy. He dipped out of the limelight, he didn't really want it, in my opinion."
- Warren Humphreys

room, fed everyone, lots of wine flowing and everyone was enjoying themselves. Joe was a great host, except he wasn't there, he kind of disappeared!

I think that kind of typified what Joe was about. He had a great personality, was very charismatic, but yet in many respects I think he was also shy. He dipped out of the limelight, he didn't really want it, in my opinion.

That's why when we played the Carroll's Irish Open at Portmarnock and Royal Dublin, so many golf pros' stayed at Suncroft. In all probability, just about every top golfer stayed there at some stage; Sandy Lyle, the lot, they had all been there, but you never saw Joe!

Joe was a friend to everyone and yet he was the most difficult man to talk to because he had this great charm and character, but he never really wanted to talk about himself. You would be there and he would say to you 'how did you get on today, what did you score?' and you would say '74'. If you didn't drive very well, he'd say, 'go out on the range and hit 10,000 balls, that will sort your driving out' and he was gone. He never heard the rest of the story. He wasn't kind of interested in that and he never wanted to hear anything negative.

He was a very positive character, an enigma in many ways, I think he was charismatic but shy, a great host, but he was never there either. He set it up for everybody else: 'this is my house and away you go, enjoy yourselves'. He was a strange man in some ways, but a likable and lovely man also."

JB at the Majors

British Open
Joe Carr very nearly emulated Bobby Jones by winning the Open Championship as an amateur. The Championship at St. Andrews in 1960 goes down in history as the Centenary Open.

"I finished 8th overall. I was in the lead at one stage with about 16 holes to go and then the rains came down and the day got quashed (abandoned). *Anyway, it was a good thing to finish 8th. Christy O'Connor and I played with Kel Nagle and Peter Thompson the week beforehand in practise, playing for serious money and Kel maintains that we got more money out of him during that week than he got winning the Championship!"* - Joe Carr speaking to the author in October, 2002.

Joe Carr competed in the Open most years during the 'fifties and 'sixties. He won the Silver Medal awarded to the leading amateur on two occasions, in 1954 and 1958. Interestingly, despite 'leading' in the abandoned round in 1960, he didn't win the leading amateur award, despite finishing eighth overall. That honour went to Guy Wolstenholme, who finished tied for 6th overall.

CHRISTY O'CONNOR
"I played a lot of golf with Joe Carr. We had a good innings together. Joe and I used to play against one another a great deal and we used to have the few bob on the outcome, it was great fun! I played together with him a lot and we never lost a game as partners against other professionals before tournaments. I had a lot of respect for Carr.

He practised when others didn't back in those days. His talent was fantastic, just look at his record, it speaks for itself really. I've seen hundreds of players with great swings that haven't done anything in the game, but it's the guy who has the concentration, the tummy for it, the will to win and that wants to win, which is far more important to me. That was Joe Carr. I think he could have been a great professional golfer."

On the occasion of the launch of his authorised biography in 2002, "Breaking 80, the Life and Times of Joe Carr written by Dermot Gilleece, Joe signed a copy for O'Connor, in which he wrote, 'you were always better than me!'

JB at the MASTERS

"In 1958 at the inaugural Eisenhower Trophy (World Amateur Team Championship) matches at St Andrews, Bobby Jones was the captain of the American team and I was on the Great Britain and Ireland four-man team. I was Amateur champion that year so it was a great occasion for all of us to meet Bobby. He was in good shape at that time and his record, obviously, was unsurpassable. I didn't get to know him properly until 1967, when I got a letter from Bobby inviting me to play in the US Masters. I got to know him by his Christian name then, he and Mary, his wife. I stayed in the clubhouse in 1967 in the 'Crow's Nest', Bobby was staying in the Eisenhower house at that time, by the 18th green. I used to go in to him every afternoon for a cup of tea and a chat. At that stage he was a few years away from dying and had very bad arthritis of the hand. I'll always remember him sitting there, with a cigarette in a long holder and a bucket of sand which he would drop the cigarette into because he couldn't do very much with it. He and I had many great chats about the game. I remember in 1969 Mary asked me how I did that day when I arrived into the house and Bobby said 'Mary, if Joe had done well, he'd have already told us!' Bobby was a legend of the game and that's a certainty." - Joe Carr speaking to the author in October 2002.

In the late 1960's, Carr accepted invitations from Jones to play in the Masters Tournament, which he duly accepted. He played in the US Masters on three occasions. He made the cut twice. On his debut in 1967, he was paired alongside Jack Nicklaus, the defending champion. Joe made the cut, Jack didn't. The following year, he was put out alongside Arnold Palmer. Once again Carr made the cut, while Palmer failed to qualify! On his last occasion to play in the Tournament, Carr played alongside Sam Snead. Both men missed the cut.

Joe Carr was also the recipient of the prestigious Bob Jones Award in 1960. According to his son Roddy, it was his father's most prized accolade. He was presented with the award by the world's greatest-ever amateur himself, at a ceremony in New York.

"That was in 1961 and I travelled to New York to collect the award. It was a huge thing in those days and I'm not sure that they gave it out every year, but they gave it out where they felt it was deserved and I think I was the first Irishman to get it and certainly the first non-American." - Joe Carr speaking to the author in October 2002.

IRISH CAPTAIN

Joe Carr was Captain of the Irish Men's Team from 1979 to 1981. Many of those who played, and prospered under his captaincy, share their memories:

Joe and Mary Carr pictured with Sam Snead at the 2000 British Open at St Andrews.

" Mary, if Joe had done well, he'd have already told us."
- Bobby Jones

“Joe had tremendous charisma. He could be a hard taskmaster and at the same time he was very kind with his time. What he did for Irish golf!”
- Arthur Pierse

ARTHUR PIERSE

Pierse played No.1 for Ireland for much of Joe Carr's captaincy. He played on the Eisenhower Trophy Team in 1982 and on the Walker Cup team in 1983. Pierse teamed up with JB's son John in July of 1983 for what proved to be an unbeaten foursomes partnership as Ireland claimed their first European Team Championship in 16 years at Chantilly, France.

“Joe had tremendous charisma. He could be a hard taskmaster and at the same time he was very kind with his time. What he did for Irish golf! He received all the accolades as an amateur golfer in winning the biggest Championships, but I think his legacy goes beyond that. What I admire most about Joe was the amount he actually gave back afterwards; what he gave back to the Irish team and to the Irish set-up as a whole.

I think that without him you wouldn't have the Clarke's, McGinley's or Harrington's. In the eighties, the money started to come into golf, the affiliation levies went up at golf clubs and our international players benefited from that. The Irish team and Irish players could train properly, travel to a greater extent and were treated appropriately.

The Golfing Union moved forward, away from the old days of a player being told ‘you have played well in the Interpro's, now pack your bags, you are going to the Home Internationals’. Irish teams went to the Home Internationals, only to be beaten time and time again. Joe's attitude was ‘you get the players, treat them right, get them the best gear, make them feel good, make them feel important, encourage them to practise, train, in course management’. He did that and he made the Irish team think professionally and the results came flying from every quarter after that. Garth McGimpsey won the British Amateur Championship (and subsequently Michael Hoey and Brian McElhinney), so many players performed better on the international stage from 1979 on and they can all thank Joe for it.

Wherever we went, there was always a letter from Joe to our hosts. He thanked them on behalf of the Irish team for looking after us so well. He was a tremendous communicator and well loved by everybody, not just in Ireland. Joe, I think, was better loved abroad than he was in Ireland and garnered tremendous respect. No matter who you would meet and you would talk to, from Nicklaus to Player, they all respected Joe. He had a charisma about him. Whatever ‘it’ is, Joe had it in spades!”

PHILIP WALTON

The 1995 Ryder Cup hero was one of Ireland's greatest amateurs of the modern era. He played for GB & I in the Walker Cup in 1981 & 1983, winning 3 points out of 4 on each occasion. A full Irish International between 1979 and 1983, he was Irish Amateur Champion in 1982.

“Joe Carr was the first guy that really got the Golfing Union of Ireland to spend some money. I remember he brought 22 of us down to Spain for 10 days on a training session at Sotogrande in 1979. He was the captain of the senior team. He was very professional in actual fact. In my opinion, he was way ahead of his time really and his whole attitude was very positive.

I got on great with Joe, but he was a tough nut at

the same time. You'd know all about it if you didn't play ball with him and didn't toe the line, which Ronan Rafferty discovered to his cost at St Andrews in 1981 at the European Team Championship! (See Arthur Pierse chapter about 'the small ball - big ball row').

Joe was very strong with the R&A and had a lot of power. He was always pushing me and Ronan Rafferty during that time. The Walker Cup team was tough to make, I was only 19 but I had to go and prove it to myself. He advised me to go and play in a couple of tournaments and said if I did well that he'd support me in whatever way he could. I'm grateful that he took me under his wing. He was pushing all the time and I went over to the Scottish Strokeplay on his advice and actually won it that year, which helped my selection no end. Joe Carr helped me a lot!"

McGimpsey wins the British Long Drive Championship in 1980 and is presented with his prize by Henry Cotton.

GARTH McGIMPSEY

1985 British Amateur Champion, three-time Walker Cup player and Walker Cup Captain 2003-2005. Winner of 14 major Amateur titles.

Ireland's first winner of the British Amateur Championship since Joe Carr.

"The Golfing Union of Ireland sent their first group of players to contest the Lytham Trophy in 1979. This was a new departure, to give Irish players a greater chance to gain Walker Cup status by playing in bigger English events. This was instigated by Joe and after we came back, Joe wrote a personal letter to us all. The advice that he gave to me was that I had been blessed with natural length off the tee and that I should use it!

He had seen me plotting my way around Lytham, using irons off a lot of the tees and he advised that I get my game in good enough shape, so that I'd have the confidence to use my driver everywhere. It was a ploy that he used himself and he was telling me that in future, I should take lines off the tees that I'd never even seen!

I remember thinking that Joe was taking amateur golf to a new level and it was great to think that a golfer of his calibre was taking such an interest in my game. It was just unbelievable to be getting letters from Joe Carr. I was only playing for Ireland a year when Joe came on board and he really raised the bar. We started to get treated in a whole new way. It was a bit like when Tony Jacklin took over the Ryder Cup captaincy. It was all about the players and giving them the best, so that we'd feel better about ourselves and play with greater pride and with greater confidence. Joe Carr was certainly instrumental in me taking my game to the next level, that's for sure!"

"I remember thinking that Joe was taking amateur golf to a new level and it was great to think that a golfer of his calibre was taking such an interest in my game."
- Garth McGimpsey

MARK GANNON

Irish Amateur Champion in 1977, Winner of: 'The West 1974; 'The East' 1977; 'The South' 1973 & 1988. Irish Youths Champion in 1971 & 1972. GB & I team at St Andrews Trophy 1978. GB & I Walker Cup selector 2007.

"I was only in my late teens when I played Joe for the one and only time at 'the West'. Even though Joe was coming to the end of his career, he was still very competitive and wanted to win all of his matches. It was the time of the old clubhouse at Rosses Point and they had a microphone and speakers announcing the players onto the tee. So we were announced on this occasion, 'next on tee, Mark Gannon, County Louth versus J.B. Carr, Sutton.'

As I made my way up to the tee, I noticed a big crowd gathering. It was an Easter Sunday, so it was busy. The announcement came again and I was ready to go, but Joe hadn't appeared and the crowd was getting bigger, which made it difficult for me. Joe then arrived, in a flourish with his caddy, resplendent, dressed very colourfully; you'd have seen him from a mile away! Joe was very tall, about six foot two and I'm about five foot six. He says 'ah Mark Gannon, how are you and how are your Mum and Dad!' Un-nerving.

"Mark, just one thing, I hope you took it the right way earlier, but there's more to this game than hitting golf balls!"
- Joe advises Mark Gannon

L-R: Frank Gannon, Padraig Harrington & Mark Gannon after the US Masters in 2006

I had the honour and was just about to get ready to hit when he says out loud, 'Mark, what number ball are you using?' We were all using Dunlops at that time and I said it was a number one and he came over to me and said, 'Mark, I always play a Dunlop 1'. I knew that with the honour I was perfectly within my rights to play whichever ball I chose, but the circumstances were a little different on this occasion, with about four hundred people gathered around the tee and there was a bit of a whisper from the crowd. I went over to my bag and found another ball, a Dunlop 2 and got ready again and proceeded to half-top it off the tee, in an effort to get off the tee as quickly as I could. In a few minutes, I was three down after four!

To cut a long story short, we had a very good match and Joe beat me on the eighteenth. He came up to me and put his arm around my shoulder and congratulated me and told me that I was a great player with a bright future and he asked me to join him for a drink in the bar, which I agreed to. He came over a bit later in the bar and gave me great encouragement and then said, 'Mark, just one thing, I hope you took it the right way earlier, but there's more to this game than hitting golf balls! It's something that I wanted to show you there today, there are things that are going to happen in matches, and you're just going to have to get hardened to these matters.' There were no hard feelings, but I learned a lot about matchplay that day!

It actually helped me a great deal to be honest and in future years, when I played for Ireland in the various Home Internationals, I used to love coming up against these tall blonde English guys with fantastic swings and beating them! I learned how to play my own game and get tough. Joe was fantastic. When he was our Captain for that period in the late seventies and early eighties, he was terrific and you always felt one up on the first tee, because he'd stand up there alongside you and everybody knew who he was. He had massive presence."

Mark Gannon was one of the greatest short game exponents that this country has ever produced. When Peter Alliss presented a programme in the seventies, highlighting the best players 'through the bag', from driving to putting, it was Gannon that he chose as supreme with a wedge.

DECLAN BRANIGAN

Five-time Major amateur Champion in Ireland. He won three of the five Championships in 1981, including the Irish Close, 'The West' and 'The East'. Irish Close and 'West' Champion in 1976. Irish Youths Champion in 1969.

"When I was in short pants, I used to watch Joe Carr play in 'the East'. He stood out a mile. Obviously, he wore all these bright colours, but on the old first hole (now the fourth), I used to stand on the hill with my father and watch the drives land about 90 yards short of the green. Then this ball would appear and it was fifty or sixty yards past the others, it was nearly on the green. Everybody knew that it was Joe's ball. He hit it so far and all the biggest crowds used to follow him.

What I'll always remember about him were the size of his hands. It was like a bunch of bananas being wrapped around the grip and he always had the index finger of his right hand going down the shaft, it was almost divorced from the rest of his grip! He was very long off the tee, but he wasn't straight and he'd often find himself knee deep in the rough, surrounded by ferns, which were widespread at Baltray back then. Most people would have to hit a sand wedge to get out sideways, but Joe, he just whipped everything out of there and by a fair distance, more often than not. He was never inhibited by the rough or any sort of trouble that he'd find his ball in, he was incredible. With those big hands, he could do anything with a club.

I played under Joe for Leinster and Ireland and he was tough to play for. If you didn't perform, he wouldn't be long telling you about it. Even though we were amateurs, we took that responsibility on and knew that we had to perform. It was quite an experience playing under him.

I remember one time the Leinster Branch of the GUI, in their wisdom, decided that they weren't going to pay for our caddies, when we played in the Interprovincials for Leinster in Carlow. It was tough enough in the seventies trying to work for a living and fund your amateur career, without having to fork out for a caddy when playing representative golf, but Joe, who was captain, told us to get a caddy if we wished, he'd pay for it personally! Joe was a leader, an amazing character and sadly now, the characters have all but disappeared from the game. He was one of a kind."

MATCHPLAY GLADIATOR

"I think that you can get a reputation for being a fighter or not according to how the first couple of games (in a Championship) go. If you happen to get beaten in the first couple of games from being up, then you are a quitter. I was lucky enough to come from behind a few times early on and it gave me great courage and it gave me a reputation.

I went down the 19th three times in the amateur at Hoylake (1953) and I was lucky enough to win on each of those occasions. I think I have a good record in ties, but most of them didn't get that far!" - Joe Carr speaking to the author in October 2002

"I played under Joe for Leinster and Ireland and he was tough to play for. If you didn't perform, he wouldn't be long telling you about it."
- Declan Branigan

RODDY CARR

Joe's second eldest son established himself as a top amateur when he succeeded his father by winning 'the East' in 1970 and later that summer finishing runner-up in 'the North'. After winning 'the West' in 1971, Carr was selected to play for the winning GB & I team in the Walker Cup where he was undefeated at St Andrews before turning professional.

Roddy on JB's matchplay prowess:
"One of the most fascinating things about JB was the way he approached matchplay. It was always mano á mano, man to man combat. I would say he probably won 70% of the matches he ever played. His psychology was purely natural, never pre-meditated. It would start on the first tee. Everything he did before the first tee was done to present himself on that tee looking superior, where the opponent felt he was two down.

"One of the most fascinating things about JB was the way he approached matchplay. It was always mano á mano, man to man combat. I would say he would probably have had a 70% win rate in every match he ever played."
- Roddy Carr

JB's psychology was always to put as much effort as possible into the first three holes because, in his view, the opponent was expecting to be two down!
I remember at the West of Ireland his goal was always to start 4-4-4-3, one under par minimum. He knew that he'd always be two up.

At the Championships, 36 hole days were the norm and in the morning match my mother would be walking along quietly, and whenever he got 3 up, she would head in to make the sandwiches for the afternoon match because in JB's mind, whenever he got to 3 up there was no man on this earth that could ever take four holes off him so it was an automatic win. He had incredible self-confidence.

Rarely, did anyone ever get JB after being three down, it was just a mental thing with him, he would dismiss them, most of them were wheeled in at 7 & 6 or 8 & 7, whatever it was. In1969 I went down to 'the South' at Lahinch. JB had sent me off to America to 'learn how to play' as he said and I came back for the summer season. I was beaten early and JB, who was about 48 at that stage said to me that it was ridiculous that I wasn't contending, that I was a far better player, so he decided to show me 'how easy it is to win one of these things!'

I caddied for him and had all these yardage books and notebooks prepared for myself, so I used them for him instead and he made it all the way to the final, without any great difficulty."

JB's great friend Noel Fogarty was his opponent in that famous final and in those days there were crowds of about 2,000 people following the bigger matches. Fogo got off to a flier and in no time at all, JB found himself three down, after just five holes. His eldest son and caddy was scratching his head thinking that if JB was three down then there'd be no way out, given his father's famous philosophy, as mentioned earlier.

Joe's son Roddy pictured in the JB Carr room at Sutton GC in 2007. Roddy is wearing his father's Walker Cup jacket. "I can no longer fit into my own one!"

Upon enquiring about his golden rule, Roddy was quickly admonished by JB with a terse 'what are you talking about?' Roddy replied 'you know, three down - when you are three up mother goes in' and he said to me 'no, no, if I don't lose another hole I will win by 2 & 1', which was stunning because that was the instinct of the man. In other words, JB had his own rules when it came to combat, a reverse psychology if you will."

Roddy went on:
"Although three down, he wasn't going to try and get them all back immediately because 'if you do, you'll make a mistake.' His natural instincts were to hang around, just keep chipping away. So sure enough three holes go by, one hole comes back, another three holes go by, another one comes back and now one down, everything is going according to plan. Back to square but then he hits two drivers onto the long 13th, three putts it and goes back to one down. We end up getting to the 16th hole, a par 3, and I get up on the tee, we are one down, it is still very tight for him. He is not a bit worried. He gets up and it's 174 yards with an elevated tee. I have the book out and I am measuring, '184, height one tee, wind half a club' and he says '8 iron'. I said 'pop, there is a breeze into you' and he said '8 iron'. He just wanted to hit this raking hook with a divot a foot long. Anyway, he hooks it in to the top of the bunker, plugs under the soft 'linksy' base of this trap. Fogo hits a scrappy, as he would, low raking hook that somehow scrambles its way on to the front of the green. Now, one down, not funny, I go down to the ball, I could be in there for a week and I wouldn't get it out. JB had this old wedge called 'The Monster' so he looks at this thing, the green is about 15 yards away from this bunker and I could not get it out and there is no man I know that could get it out. He gets into the trap, he lifted the face of the bunker, the whole face of the bunker came out, debris, sod, grass, weeds, daisies, everything just landed on the green and it was like a cartoon. The ball just appeared out of the debris that landed on the green, he had lifted the bunker face onto the green and rolls about an inch inside of Fogo. So I am thinking still not funny, 40 foot, one down, there for two. Fogo hits a kind of defensive putt up to about five feet short and I am thinking we're still in trouble here. JB goes down to putt and all of a sudden, freeze, the Angelus bells ring out, and I am thinking this is crazy, but everything stops. 2,000 people around the green and they all take their hats off and I am watching this scene play out in front of me. I am not saying the Angelus because we are one down. JB looks over at me and he winks and I am thinking to myself what are you winking at Pop, you are one down, two to play, your man is five feet short, you are there for two. The Angelus finishes up and he gets down, blesses himself, gets back up, addresses the putt and bang, he breaks the back of the hole with this putt, in she pops for a par! Fogo, obviously shaken, pulls it left. On the next hole, Fogo hooks it out of bounds, Pop wins one up!

So a couple of hours later, we're heading home, and I will never forget it, JB was driving, doing the usual, flying over some country roads in the Merc and I am in the back, looking at his face in the mirror and I said 'how did you know, Pop?' I'll never forget this, but he looked at me in the rear view mirror and said, 'sure he left the door open, didn't he?' Of course I remind him that he was three down, how in heaven's name did he leave the door open? He said that by not putting his first putt up dead on the 16th, Fogo handed an immediate advantage to him. It was this instinctive feeling that he possessed, knowing that if he holed that putt, Fogo would snap, and he did. It was frightening. This is a 40-footer. He knew he was going to hole it, which he knew would snap Fogo's back, brain, everything! Which was exactly what happened. He actually winked at me, knowing what was coming. That's the way his mind went. He was ahead of his time when it came to golf psychology. If anybody ever showed weakness or he sensed any weakness like with Fogo on that occasion, who had a chance to put him

"JB looks over at me and he winks and I am thinking to myself what are you winking at Pop, you are one down, two to play, your man is five feet short, you are there for two."
- Roddy Carr

away but didn't do it." The gladiator in JB Carr came out in no uncertain terms. Like all gladiators, JB had the instinctive ability to deliver the killer blow at the most unsuspecting times. A trait that he displayed time and time again throughout his illustrious career. Incidentally, JB's win in that 1969 'South' final was his 40th and last Championship victory.

Superior

Such was his incredible self-belief and trust in his own game, there were few on the domestic circuit that JB Carr feared. He was also well aware that, given the work that he put into the game, he always believed wholeheartedly that it gave him an edge. Having said that, there were some on the domestic circuit whose game he respected.

Vincent Nevin was one such player. The Ennis native was feared by his peers due to a deadly short game, which broke the hearts of many in the Championships of the sixties and seventies. As Roddy Carr put it, the diminutive Nevin never looked to be a serious threat because of his short stature, but JB Carr knew only too well how tough he could be. Roddy played Nevin in the West of Ireland one year and JB warned his son that it would be his toughest match and to 'not let up on him until he is in the grave!'

"In other words, watch him all the way home, he will be like a dog holding on to your foot, he won't let go, so don't ease up when you have him two or three down and you think it is all over, put him away! JB knew instinctively who he had to be up on. He knew when he was down what he had to do. All those things he knew as a combat fighter, he was an amateur combat fighter, not a machine that rolled out numbers. That's why they enjoyed the Championship so much in those days, it's such a great pity that the characters are no longer part of top-class amateur golf," recalled Roddy in 2007.

"In other words, watch him all the way home, he will be like a dog holding on to your foot, he won't let go, so don't ease up when you have him two or three down and you think it is all over, put him away!"
- The Carr's respect for Vincent Nevin

VINCENT NEVIN
Irish Amateur Champion 1969. 'West' Champion in 1972, 'South' Champion in 1976 & 1978. Member of winning Irish Team alongside Joe Carr in the European Amateur Team Championships in 1965 & 1967.

Vincent Nevin in 2007

Now in his seventies and beating his age regularly around his home course, Limerick Golf Club, Nevin has fond memories of JB and acknowledges the Sutton legend's great presence in amateur golf.

"Joe was very superior, he was very, very superior. He gave you the impression that he was far better than you, which is an ideal thing for matchplay. We would go out to play in the ordinary shirts that we arrived in, just take off the tie and what have you, but Joe would more or less be dressed to the nines with the shoes shining, pants creased, the latest in pullovers and beautiful caps.

He had an enormous presence and was absolutely and utterly adored. However, my own opinion at that time in life was that Tom Craddock was as good as him, but didn't exude the confidence that Joe did. Nobody did. Joe, you see, had international fame. He had such a reputation that you were just frightened to play him. He totally and utterly commanded the stage. He was a performer. A born actor in every sense. I liked him a great deal, despite us being total opposites in many ways."

Look good, feel good, play good!

NORMAN DREW

The first Irishman to play Walker Cup, Ryder Cup and Canada Cup (now World Cup). He was a hugely talented amateur and was riding the crest of a wave in the early fifties, especially in 1952 when he won the Irish Amateur Open, 'the West' and 'the East' titles in addition to finishing runner-up in 'the North' and 'the South' Championships. Drew played foursomes for Ireland with Joe Carr in the Home Internationals at Killarney and retained the Irish Amateur Open title the following week at the same venue, assuring him of a place on the Walker Cup team.

"Joe was different to most amateurs at the time in that he probably had a bit of dough, but there were a lot of guys who played amateur golf who actually couldn't afford it really. It was lovely to play in the North of Ireland every year, and then if you got time off, you played in the South of Ireland and that was your golf for the season, but the way Joe played, it was every day of the week! As an apprentice coach builder, I couldn't get off to play any more than Saturdays in those days.

Joe and I were great pals. We spent a lot of time together travelling to matches and in those days, at the Walker Cup in Massachusetts for example, you all stayed in the one house, so you'd get to know each other pretty well. Joe loved the Americans. I remember when we met Charlie Coe one time, he was on the US team that played against us at Kittansett in 1953. We went to his house one evening on the trip and Joe says to him 'Charlie, how do you make your money,

"Joe was different to most amateurs at the time in that he probably had a bit of dough, but there were a lot of guys who played amateur golf who actually couldn't afford it really."
- N. V. Drew

what do you do in life to make money and make your living?' Charlie brought us down to the bottom of his garden where we could see this giant rig arm going up and down. Charlie turns to us and says 'every time it goes up and down, that's a barrel of oil!'

I had a bit of trouble with Joe when we were foursomes partners for Ireland in 1953. He kept driving the ball into the rough. It was long and thick stuff at Killarney and I couldn't get it out of there, but Joe kept saying to me that I could get it onto the green! After a few holes of this I turned to Joe and told him that from now on every time he put me in the rough, I was going to chip it back out onto the fairway for him, that I can't play golf out of heavy rough, it's not my game! That's what we did and we went on to win our foursomes games against England and Wales.

In our final game together against Scotland, we took on Major David Blair (future Captain of the R&A) and Sir Robin Carter (future Chairman of Distillers). We were one up playing the downhill sixteenth on the old course and the Scottish pair put their approach shot into the drain, short right. I tell Joe to take a 9 iron and leave it short, that I'd knock it on and we'd win with a five, but he wasn't having any of it. He went for the pin with a five iron and ended up following the Scots into the drain! They got up and down for a win to bring the match back to all square and that's how it finished. I ended up with five and a half points out of six that year.

Joe played most of his golf at Portmarnock, but he practised at Sutton where he lived beside the second green. What he used to do is come out of the house in the morning and he would hit balls up towards the clubhouse and do you know who picked them up? Nicky Lynch the pro!

Joe would hit them up and Nicky got a nice few quid out of picking balls up that Joe would practise with in the morning. Joe would hit them up towards the clubhouse and head off to his office and then Nicky would come into work and gather them up. He missed Joe when Joe stopped practising!"

BRUCE CRITCHLEY.

Sky Sports Golf Commentator. Critchley was a Walker Cup player in 1969. His father, Brigadier General AC Critchley was a former English Amateur Champion, while his mother Diana Critchley, both played and Captained the Curtis Cup.

"Joe achieved such a great deal on the back of a phenomenal belief in an ability that was great, but flawed. So much of amateur golf was matchplay and he was imperious. The only one who ever bested him was Michael Bonallack.

The only time I ever played with Joe was in the Brabazon Trophy at Little Aston in the late sixties. He had a very strong presence. As we were setting off in the third round, he said 'I don't want to be taking too long about this, I've got a plane to catch' and within five minutes I am rushing and am ashamed to say, it took me 90 to go round that morning. Joe knew the laws of gamesmanship and won quite a few on the back of that.

Joe was a 'Pied Piper' sort of a character. When we would come over for the Mullingar Scratch Trophy, the whole crowd would turn out to see Joe. He was some way past his peak in the late sixties and had developed the yips and couldn't putt. There was no cack-handed putting in those days or long putters, so Joe resorted to using a three-iron and he got the ball in the hole. He had this phenomenal belief. It was 'Seve-like' in that one day, he believed that it would all come back to him.

Joe would take on any match. His character demanded that this was the way he went through life. He

"Joe was a 'Pied Piper' sort of a character."
- Bruce Critchley

The Pied Piper!

genuinely believed that he could beat anybody! At the Eisenhower Trophy in 1960 he lost a huge amount of money to Jack Nicklaus, who went on to win the individual title that year, by beating Ben Hogan's record at Merion by about 18 shots. Joe started the bet before the Championship began, so you can imagine how out of control it got. Naturally, he won all his money back on the poker table!

He used to play all these great players off the level, even when they had turned pro. There was never any question of claiming shots. There were times when he got hammered by Arthur Lees, who was a serious gambling pro and very good at it, yet it never bothered Joe, he wasn't fazed by it at all. My abiding memory of Joe is of this man whose belief went on long after the ability would have told him otherwise. Joe did it all on personality. If you dissected his swing, you would spot innumerable flaws in it. In a sense he was like Padraig Harrington, in that the more trouble he got into, the more fun he had getting out of it and entertaining the crowds along the way. He was very difficult to play against, either in matchplay or medal golf. Like Seve at his best, it was almost like an act of levitation, the way he could get the ball around. Joe was larger than life."

GARY PLAYER

(Exclusively for "Legends in their Spare Time")

A winner of 9 professional majors, Gary Player was only the third professional, after Gene Sarazen and Ben Hogan, to achieve the career slam of all four majors, when he added the US Open title to his illustrious resume in 1965.

"The more trouble he got into, the more fun he had getting out of it."
- Bruce Critchley

Gary Player

"I remember that although he did not have the best-looking swing, he could really play. And I mean he could really play. He was also the first man I saw using a long-iron to putt – and that was through his own choice!"
- Gary Player

"I knew Joe Carr very well and actually played quite a lot of golf with him, despite the fact that he was an amateur and I was a professional. I remember we even played together at The Masters in Augusta one year, as well as at The Open Championship.

I remember that although he did not have the best-looking swing, he could really play. And I mean he could really play. He was also the first man I saw using a long-iron to putt – and that was through his own choice! I tell you, if he could have putted better, there would not have been another amateur in the game that would have come close to him.

I remember him being a big man, perhaps made larger through his demeanour, which was always so cheerful and friendly. And how proud he was of being Irish! He was a terrific man with a terrific family and a man that I admired greatly; he served the game he loved so well and golf is certainly better off for his presence."

PETER THOMSON
The Australian who won the British Open five times.

"Joe Carr was a rare talent as a golfer. Very Irish in that he had his own special style of swinging and hitting. Other Irish players of the time were also unique in that regard, Bradshaw, Kinsella, Bruen, Daly and the mighty O'Connor himself.

Joe was gregarious and everybody's friend. But being an amateur golfer he spent his life in that field. So although I played the last two rounds with him in the 1951 Open at Portrush (which Thompson won), I did not get nearer than that.

His golf was capable of great heights but he never climbed. Perhaps had he set his mind to the professional side, he might have done it. Eire's greatest golfer? I wonder. 'Himself' would win that contest I think. Best personality? Certainly Carr."

NOEL FOX
Ireland's most successful amateur over a seven-year period from 1996 to 2003 winning 'The West, three 'East's' and two Irish Amateur Opens. In addition to 64 caps for Ireland, he played for Britain and Ireland in the St Andrews Links Trophy in 1999 and in the winning Walker Cup team in 2003.

"In his latter days, Joe used to appear at the driving range at Portmarnock Golf Club with his wife Mary and he'd rarely get out of his buggy, but he was giving Mary pointers on her swing. On several occasions, I would be beckoned over from my practice spot to demonstrate what Joe was teaching Mary. No matter what I did, be it a bunker shot or a mid-iron, he'd always say 'that's it!'

He gave me great encouragement, and knowing the amateur golfing calendar as he did, he'd always know where I'd be headed next and was always full of encouragement. In actual fact, some of the things he'd say to me are exactly what you'll hear from all these sports psychologists today. So, he was really way ahead of his time on the mental game and his record and skill at matchplay proves it. He always told me not to mind the begrudgers and to go out and beat the heads off my opponents! I loved talking to him, but to be honest, I was just thrilled that he knew my name!"

JOHN O'LEARY

A Ryder Cup player and European Tour professional, O'Leary was a rising star of Irish amateur golf in the late sixties and early seventies. He won 'the South' in 1970 having finished runner-up in 'the West' that Easter. He was runner-up in the Irish Close in 1969, losing to Vincent Nevin. A hugely talented Boy golfer, he was runner-up in the Munster Boys' in 1965 and lost the in the final of the Connacht Boys' in both 1966 & 1967. The Carr influence on O'Leary's progression was significant as he went on to be coached by John Jacobs, who also became his first manager.

"When I was in my early teens and starting out in golf, I played in the Joe Carr Trophy for Under-15's at Laytown and Bettystown one year and finished last! My game had improved a great deal by the following year and I managed to win it and one of the special bonuses, apart from Joe presenting me with the trophy was that he invited me to Sutton to play a game with him, which was unbelievable. I played with him and enjoyed all of the amazing hospitality in Suncroft and ended up staying for the entire school holidays! It was an amazing place and my parents, who were wonderful people, were just as happy seeing me with such an interest in a sport and fully supported the extended visit to the Carr's!

Joe was incredible, obviously, and really impressed upon me the importance of work, work and more work. I really enjoyed it, even when Joe would wake us all at 7 in the morning, getting us up and out of the house for a two mile jog followed by some short game practise on the second green at Sutton. After that, Joe would head into work in the city and we'd while away the day playing golf and having so much fun. It was an incredible summer.

The house was amazing. Dor would never seem rushed or under pressure, yet it was like a busy hotel that she was running and beneath the calm, was this military precision, with which she ran the home. There could be twenty people sitting down for a meal in the kitchen at any one time. The world of golf passed through that room at some stage."

"Joe was incredible, obviously, and really impressed upon me the importance of work, work and more work. I really enjoyed it, even when Joe would wake us all at 7 in the morning, getting us up and out of the house for a two-mile jog."
- John O'Leary

BILL THOMPSON

JB's great friend from Portmarnock and Sutton Golf Clubs fondly recalls one particular incident when the pair were returning home from a fund-raising function in Milltown Golf Club for The Leitrim Gaelic Football Association. It was about 2am and they took the option of travelling northwards to Howth via the East Link toll bridge over the River Liffey. JB of course, was in his R&A Captain's suit of Red tails and black tie. As they pulled up to the toll booth, the attendant, spotting JB in the passenger seat, all decked out, couldn't resist passing comment, in a classic Dublin accent, *"you'll find no fuckin' foxes where you boys are goin'!"* he said.

ALEX HAY
BBC Commentator from 1977-2004. Retired Director of Golf at Woburn Golf & Country Club.

"Just shortly after the end of World War II when I took up golf, around about 1947/48, a very kind neighbour of mine offered to take me in his car – not many people had cars in those days – all the way to Gleneagles to see Henry Cotton play golf in the Gleneagles Foursomes. Off we went for a great adventure, I was just a learner golfer and the great Cotton was playing in this famous event and he was playing with an amateur partner who happened to be Joe Carr. Here was this lanky, skinny Irishman, but my goodness, it was a gale force day and he played shots in under the wind, he punched long irons, he did all sorts of things and I was so impressed with him.

Over the years I met him now and again with Peter Alliss who was a great friend of his. The last time I saw Joe was when he invited me to Howth for his birthday party. A magnificent book had been published ('Breaking 80, The Life & Times of Joe Carr' - Dermot Gilleece) about him and we had this most magical evening in a glorious sunset overlooking the harbour. We sat and we all drank probably too much and we talked and we laughed. He got his book out and he wrote a full page of nice things to me and I treasure it to this day. And I recall that inspirational moment way back in 1947 where I saw and learned a little bit about how to handle oneself in wind, well Joe was the master of that."

"We stayed with the Carr family which was an experience I shall never forget. The bench of children lined up either side and the way they fed all those children!"
- Lady Angela Bonallack

ANGELA BONALLACK.
6-time Curtis Cup player. Twice winner of English Amateur Championship, twice runner-up in British Open Amateur Championship and wife of Michael Bonallack.

"Dor Carr was a wonderful lady, a lovely, lovely person. She was so devoted to her family. Joe never packed a little case for a day's golf, she did everything. She ran the house so that he could do what needed to be done work-wise and then practise as much as he possibly wanted to, she was just tremendous.

We stayed with the Carr family which was an experience I shall never forget. The bench of children lined up either side and the way they fed all of them! People used to call in and Joe would be behind the newspaper and wouldn't even know that somebody had walked in and nobody took any notice! They were a most incredible family. It was like a hotel there.

I love the story about when one of the children had measles just before the Amateur. Joe's mother came to visit and Dor was having to put a tray of food outside Joe's room because he wasn't going to mix with the children because they had measles and he was getting ready for a Championship. His mother arrived and said 'where is Joe?' Dor said 'oh, the children have got measles and he doesn't want to get near them in case he catches it and his Mother assures Dor that there isn't much danger of that considering that he had that when he was young!' They were a fantastic family.

Joe was such a character, such a wonderful person. He used to have the crowd in the palm of his hand. I can remember at Royal St. Georges when he was playing Michael in the late sixties in the European Championship and there were lots of other countries playing, but everybody went to watch Michael playing Joe. They were the star attractions.

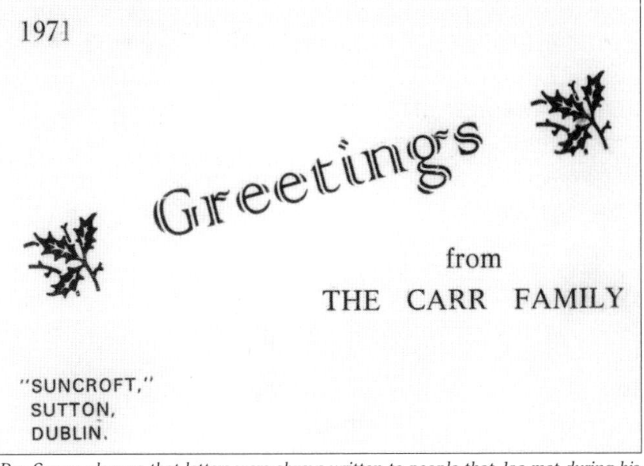

Dor Carr made sure that letters were always written to people that Joe met during his golfing travels. Christmas cards like the one above were also sent each year to many hundreds of personal, golfing and business acquaintances, keeping their friends and associates up-to-date with their growing family.

The camaraderie that they had was infectious. When one went in a bunker, the side quips that went on were tremendous, the people were absolutely adoring it. That is how I remember Joe. He was larger than life, a real character."

IAN BAMFORD

Golfing Union of Ireland President in 1994. British and Irish Universities Champion in 1956, Irish Amateur Open Champion in 1957 and North of Ireland Amateur Champion in 1954 & 1972. He was an Irish International team-mate of Joe Carr's from 1954-56.

"It was the 1956 Irish Open Amateur Championship at Portmarnock. I got into the semi-final and low and behold I was drawn against the great J.B. Carr and was I scared? I was petrified! I was playing well because I had won the British Open University Championship at St Andrews, the 'Boyd Quaich' with a very good score and I was very confident, but very, very nervous. I went onto the tee, there was a huge crowd and Joe always arrived on the first tee two to three minutes before his tee off time, he never had to be called from the putting green. He was always there with his caddy and always looked supremely confident. He would be very polite, he'd look you straight in the eye and just say 'have a good game' and he would look at you and you knew you were in for a game. I got my game going and I think I got two up on him after the turn. That even made me more nervous because I knew his reputation of coming back. To beat Joe Carr in the semi-final and get into the final would have been an unbelievable thing for me really because Joe was such an icon. People just held him in complete awe.

"I got into the semi-final and low and behold I was drawn against the great J.B. Carr and was I scared? I was petrified!"
- J. L. Bamford

"I always remember at Troon, I said to him 'Jack, be very careful of that 11th hole, it will catch you out if you don't watch it'. He said 'no problem, and took 11 at it. From there on he did all right!"
- Joe on Jack

Anyway, as things happened, I three putted the 15th and he hit the (par 5)16th in two at Portmarnock, so we were level playing the 17th. He did not like the left to right wind, he could not handle a left to right wind, but it was his honour and he hit this ball really high in the air. It was probably about 280 yards in the rough on the right on an upslope and I was probably 40 yards shorter, but in the middle of the fairway.
I actually went over to look at his lie because I was going to play reasonably safe if I knew he couldn't make the green in two. I made a decision and my judgment was Joe could not make that green in two. He was about 175 yards away.

So I played a spoon (3/4 wood) just onto the front of the green at the 17th which I felt comfortable enough with. There was such a crowd around Joe I couldn't really get over to see his shot, I didn't really want to see it, but I was confident he wouldn't try to make the green. Ijust heard a swish, I heard a gasp from the crowd and I saw this white object going into the sky and Isaid he is in the bunker. It didn't come down. He carried the bunker, carried the rough on the other side of the bunker, got a bit of a kick on the down slope and was ten feet past the pin. I came up for a four and he holed his putt and we halved the 18th, so he beat me one up.

The next morning I was actually so intrigued that I went out and paced where he had hit the shot from. Apparently he had hit an 8 iron! Now, it was a left to right wind fair enough so Joe would have slashed it high and used the wind a little bit, but that is the gospel truth. That was the sort of thing that Joe could do!"

THE GOLDEN BEAR

"Pros like Arnie and Jack were so used to playing their strokeplay tournaments that when they came over to the Open, they were all of a sudden playing this flamboyant young amateur who was looking for their money in matchplay! It didn't exist in the States and was a sort of flashback to their amateur days and they were having a bit of fun. That's why they loved him."
- **Roddy Carr speaking to the author in April 2007**

Joe on Jack:
"I first met Jack in 1959 at a Walker Cup match in Muirfield. I played with him every time he came to the Open, we played practice rounds together. I went over to Seattle to play in the Walker Cup match and I said to Charles Lawrie, who was our captain, 'Charles, I have been playing top of this team for a long time, put me down a bit and I will teach some of these young fellas a lesson' and then I got Nicklaus...and the lesson was taught to me in actual fact!

I came back and wrote to the Irish Independent at the time and said that I had seen the best golfer the world would ever see, which was true until Tiger came along. I don't know what set him apart, but he was actually the best player in the world in all departments. He had one bad department, in my opinion, that I used to give out to him about and that was his bunker play, it wasn't up to scratch!

I played a lot with him prior to all the Open Championships. We played maybe three or four rounds together in practice each time. I suppose I had a great knowledge of link's play that he hadn't got. I always remember at Troon, I said to him 'Jack, be very careful of that 11th hole, it will catch you out if you don't watch it'. He said 'no problem, and took 11 at it! From there on he did all right."

Both Carr and Nicklaus shared an undying affection for St Andrews. The Golden Bear won two of his three Open Championships there (1970 and 1978). Carr meanwhile, was victorious in the Amateur Championship there in 1958. Carr always insisted that the long and straight hitter always had the best chance of victory at the Home of Golf.

"You haven't got to be that great a putter, the driving was the whole thing. I met Tiger Woods when he practised one day at Portmarnock ahead of the 2000 Open at St Andrews. I said to him (one gladiator to another) at a barbeque in Dermot Desmond's house later that evening: 'Tiger, nobody will beat you at St Andrews, but those fairway bunkers will beat you', and he said 'I won't be in a fairway bunker' and he wasn't! Jack's course management was beyond compare and now Tiger's is even better, I think. I mean to say that Tiger in St Andrews used a 4 iron off the 16th tee, you couldn't believe that. The green is virtually drivable, but there is too much trouble. As I say he won the thing. I thought that he would win, I thought that Daly would win in St Andrews, I thought that I would win in St Andrews!" - **Joe Carr speaking with the author in October, 2002.**

Jack Nicklaus with Joe Carr at Sutton Golf Club in 1990 to mark the club's centenary.

"Jack's course management was beyond compare and now Tiger's is even better, I think. I mean to say that Tiger in St Andrews used a 4 iron off the 16th tee, you couldn't believe that."
- Joe on his fellow gladiator

JACK NICKLAUS
For "Legends in their Spare Time"

The world's most successful professional golfer ever, with 18 professional majors (including three career slams). Two victories in the US Amateur Championship in 1959 and 1961. Walker Cup 1959 & 1961. Eisenhower Trophy 1960 (leading individual).

"Joe Carr was a great friend. I played a lot of golf with Joe, probably 50 rounds or more over the years. We played against each other in 1961 at the Walker Cup. Then, at the '61 US Amateur at Pebble Beach, Joe lost in the semi-finals. Had he won, we would have faced each other in the finals. We always had a great time together, on or off the golf course.

As a player, he had massive hands and an unbelievable touch around the greens. When I played my first two British Opens (1962-63), I played practice rounds with Joe. I loved to kid Joe. See, I could always count on Joe for 50 or 60 pounds, so I could get Barbara to the (cashmere) sweater tent. He was always my ticket to get Barbara sweaters. That's what I always kidded him about.

Joe was one of golf's great characters. In fact, I was over in Ireland the December before he passed away in 2004, and we had dinner with him at his club, Sutton Golf Club. He was in great form then. Joe got up there and entertained everyone with his quick wit. He was 82 years old and I kidded him, 'Joe you are amazing! You look absolutely great for a guy who's 95!

The golf world lost a wonderful player in Joe Carr, but we all lost an even better man."

"The golf world lost a wonderful player in Joe Carr, but we all lost an even better man."
- Jack Nicklaus

The Great Joe Carr at eighty years of age reflects on a life of golfing excellence

CAREER HIGHLIGHTS

Full name: Joseph Benedict Carr

Born: 18th of February 1922, died on 3rd of June 2004.

Family: Pre-deceased by first wife Dorothy (Dor), survived by wife Mary & children, Jody, Roddy, John, Sibéal, Gerry and Marty.

Occupation: Clothing Merchant.

Home Club: Sutton Golf Club.

Lowest Handicap: + 6

CHAMPIONSHIP HIGHLIGHTS:

British Open Championship (Professional)
Leading Amateur in 1954 & 1958. (He led in final round at St Andrews in 1960, before heavy rain led to the round being abandoned, he eventually finished 8th overall.)

British Amateur Open Championship
Winner 3 times in 1953, 1958 & 1960.
Runner-up in 1968.
Semi-finalist in 1951, 1952 & 1954.

US Amateur Open Championship
Semi-finalist in 1961, losing to Dudley Wysong on the 18th, thus denying him a chance to play Jack Nicklaus in the final.

Irish Amateur Close Championship
Winner 6 times in 1954, 1957, 1963, 1964, 1965 & 1967.
Runner-up in 1951 & 1959.

Irish Seniors Amateur Open Championship
Winner of over-65 title in 1987.

Irish Open (Professional)
Leading Amateur 4 times in 1946, 1948, 1950 & 1953.

Dunlop Masters (Professional)
Tied second (alongside Norman Drew) in 1959. Christy O'Connor shot 66 on the final day to overtake Joe who was the third round leader. Joe fired rounds of 69, 68 & 69 in the opening 3 rounds against a par of 74 to lead by four shots.

West of Ireland Amateur Open Championship
Winner 12 times in 1946, 1947, 1948, 1951, 1953, 1954, 1956, 1958, 1960, 1961, 1962 &1966.

East of Ireland Amateur Open Championship,
Winner 12 times in 1941, 1943, 1945, 1946, 1948, 1956, 1957, 1958, 1960, 1961, 1964 & 1969.
Runner-up twice in 1944 & 1946.

South of Ireland Amateur Open Championship
Winner 3 times in 1948, 1966 & 1969 (JB's final Championship title).
Runner-up in 1946.

Irish Senior Cup
On winning Sutton GC team 6 times in 1948, 1949, 1950, 1956, 1958 & 1963.

Barton Shield
On winning Sutton GC team 3 times in 1946, 1949 & 1950.

REPRESENTATIVE HONOURS

Great Britain & Ireland ***Walker Cup***: 11 caps in succession from 1947-1967. Played 10 matches after electing to be a non-playing captain in 1965, having been selected to play and captain. He was the playing-captain for his final appearance in 1967.

Great Britain & Ireland ***Eisenhower Trophy***: 1958 & 1960. Non-playing captain in 1964 & 1966.

Great Britain & Ireland ***St. Andrews Trophy:*** 1954, 1956, 1964 (playing captain), 1966 (non-playing captain) & 1968.

International: 157 Caps for Ireland in the Home Internationals, European

Amateur team Championships and in the Quadrangular Internationals.

On winning team at European Championships in 1965 & 1967.

Interprovincial:
44 caps for Leinster between 1938 & 1970.

MISCELLANEOUS

ADMINISTRATION

Captain of the Royal and Ancient 1991/1992.

Captain of Sutton Golf Club in 1948, 1949 & 1990 (Centenary Year).

President of Sutton GC in 1985 & 1986.

President of Mount Juliet from 1993-2004.

Life-Vice-President of Association of Golf Writers (AGW).

Trustee of Golfing Union of Ireland.

Trustee of Darren Clarke Foundation.

AWARDS

AGW in 1953, Bob Jones in 1960, Walter Hagen in 1967. Honorary PhD from Dublin University (Trinity College) in 1993.

Inducted to World Golf Hall of Fame in 2007.

Tiger Woods and John Harris observe Fanagan in full flow.

Jody Fanagan

The Dublin undertaker who not only defeated Tiger Woods but formed an impressive foursomes partnership with the 2007 British Open Champion.

"Jody Fanagan was the ideal partner to play with, especially when it came to foursomes. He was as steady as can be, very dependable, very reliable, no ego about him at all, so when you were playing foursomes there was no captain or vice captain in the team. We both played together and it was very much a partnership.

It was easy going, dependable, very assured; you knew he was giving it 100%. He would never look at you after you hit a bad shot as if it was your fault or anything like that. I have got to say, definitely, that he was a superb partner to have."

PADRAIG HARRINGTON, January, 2006

"My team-mates had warned me that he was a particularly tough competitor ... it was well known that Jody and Padraig Harrington had taken Woods and John Harris on in the Walker Cup and beaten them convincingly".
- Luke Donald

Jody Fanagan gets ready to caddy in the Par 3 Tournament, the traditional curtain-raiser to the Masters Tournament

Magnolia Lane

Underneath the old oak tree at Augusta National, the world of golf gathers annually to press the flesh. It is the place to be in early April for throwing shapes, networking and being seen. For golfers taking part in the year's first Major, the lawn area by that famous tree is merely a junction, a thoroughfare if you will, on the way to more important destinations like the practice green, or the crucible that is the first tee.

On a sunny Wednesday afternoon in 2005, the day before the 70th US Masters Tournament began, two men stood no further than twenty yards from each other. In truth, they could have been a million miles apart. Back in late September 1997, their paths had collided, quickly diverging, until intersecting here once again, on the verdant pastures of Bobby Jones' masterpiece at the end of Magnolia Lane, some eight years later.

One of the men was Luke Donald, about to make his competitive Masters debut. The other man was Jody Fanagan, who was there at the invitation of his friend Padraig Harrington, for whom he was caddying in the Par 3 tournament.

Luke Donald remembers his singles match against Jody Fanagan, on the final day of the 1997 Home Internationals at Burnham and Berrow:
"My team-mates had warned me that he was a particularly tough competitor. I was aware of his great record and in 1997 when Tiger Woods had burst onto the professional scene with his amazing win at the Masters, it was well known that Jody and Padraig Harrington had taken Woods and John Harris on in the Walker Cup and beaten them convincingly only a couple of years before, so Jody was a player to be respected!"

England were going for their fifth Raymond Trophy in a row and for Donald, it was his final match in what had been a terrific debut as a full international. He was also about to start a golf scholarship in Chicago and was determined to end on a victorious note.

England were clearly the favourites, with youngsters like Donald, Justin Rose, Paul Casey and stalwart Gary Wolstenholme in their line-up. Fanagan however, knew in his heart of hearts that whatever the overall result, he would likely retire from the international scene following that singles match, so he too was resolute about finishing on a high.

After eight long years of wonderful service in the green sweater, his game was in good shape and so it proved, when after a titanic tussle that went the distance, the result went the way of the Irishman. *"If I hit a great shot during the match, Luke would follow up with an even better one. Thankfully though, I holed everything and eventually beat him on the 18th green by one hole,"* Fanagan recalled.

Donald concurred: "My memories of the match are that it was tight all the way. Jody played superb golf; it was a great game and I'm happy that Jody won, given that it was his finale for Ireland. It could have gone either way, but he holed a great putt on 18 to claim the point and finish a great career."

What a career indeed! It's probably fair to say that Jody Fanagan was destined for success at golf, and yet in hindsight, there was never a grand plan. There was certainly no over-zealous parent pushing from the wings, and there was no ambitious coach charting a course for him.

Undoubtedly he had a natural gift for the game, but in the truest sense of what this book is about, it was a sport which Jody pursued and enjoyed in his spare time. This was often in the summer months, on the links at Laytown & Bettystown, the course that produced such stars as Des Smyth and Declan Branigan.

Donald concurred: *"My memories of the match are that it was a tight match all the way. Jody played superb golf; it was a great game and I'm happy that Jody won, given that it was his finale for Ireland. It could have gone either way, but he holed a great putt on 18 to claim the point and finish a great career."*

Luke Donald follows through at Augusta National

The fact that his mother Rhona always played to a single figure handicap during his formative years had a lot to do with his appreciation of the game. (She is still playing off low single figures and has been an Irish Seniors panellist). Added to that, his maternal grandparents had serious sporting credentials that would in turn, influence his sporting aims.

Jody's maternal grandmother, Rachel Murray, played golf for Ireland. Her husband, Paul was a three handicapper from Milltown Golf Club, who claimed the South of Ireland title at Lahinch in 1940 but made his name on the rugby pitch, playing for Ireland and most notably, the British and Irish Lions. Their son Paul (Jody's uncle) was also capped for the Irish rugby team.

As Jody himself puts it, "*There was a lot of sport on my mum's side of the family, but I had no ambitions in golf. Rugby was my game. I loved the team spirit and the camaraderie and it's something that stood to me when I started to achieve at golf. To be honest, I played my best golf when I was a member of a team, especially when I played for Ireland and on the Walker Cup side, but rugby was my passion. Golfing success just sort of happened.*"

The Fanagans spent fourteen consecutive summer holidays in Bettystown, the coastal town in Meath, not far from Drogheda and learned from one of the best teachers in the game. Club pro Bobby Browne took the Fanagan children and a host of youngsters under his wing for weekly lessons every Saturday morning on the 18th hole and the basic fundamentals of the game were honed under his watchful eye.

Jody, a shy but clearly talented young ball player enjoyed those formative days, but golf was never a

As Jody himself puts it, *"To be honest, I played my best golf when I was a member of a team, especially when I played for Ireland and on the Walker Cup side, but rugby was my passion. Golfing success just sort of happened".*

Jody, back row, 2nd from left gets his first Irish Cap, Irish Universities 1985.

priority. *"Bobby taught us all, but for me it was just a summer pursuit. We've always played golf, I probably picked a club up at three years of age, but even as I'd improve, year on year, all my competitive juices were focussed on rugby. I joined Milltown Golf Club, in Dublin, when I was twelve and have been there ever since. I never played serious competitive golf as a junior or youth, which is probably surprising - rugby was number one".*

Fanagan clearly had great skill with the oval ball, but a lack of serious speed hindered his progress to the level enjoyed by his uncle and famous grandfather. Regardless, he played the game seriously all through secondary school, while boarding for six year's at Dublin's Castleknock College.

Whilst in school he played a key role on the side that reached the final of the Leinster Senior Cup in 1983 and then for three years he lined out with his College side while studying politics and history at University College Dublin. Upon graduating, he followed his father Joe's footsteps and played his club rugby with St Mary's College.

Operating at full back and out half, Fanagan was capped for Leinster at under-19 and under-20 level and subsequently played on the Irish Universities side.

Jody is uncertain as to how his golf handicap was faring during that time, but it's fair to say that his late teens saw him reduce it enough to contest a few golf championships, but never with any great intent. *"I never really played in a serious way at junior level, I think I played in one Irish Youths Championship, maybe the Leinster Youths once or twice and perhaps once, I contested the Leinster Boys Championship."* Rhona, Jody's mother and 'archivist', certainly wasn't busy cutting newspaper clippings regarding her son's golf during that time.

His standard of golf was high enough however, to

Milltown's Barton Shield team in 1988, after losing the All-Ireland final at Cork GC. l-r: Andy Butler, Des Fitzgerald Team Captain, Padraig McInerney, Joe Fanagan, Club Captain, Jody, John Gleeson.

attract the attention of the UCD golf team, who enlisted his services for three Colours matches against arch-rivals Trinity College. In three annual contests, Jody who was playing off a handicap of four, then three, featured on two winning sides.

The real golfing pedigree first came to light however, in 1988, when Fanagan was part of Milltown GC's Barton Shield team that contested the National Cups and Shields finals in Cork.

His high standard of play and obvious talent led to his inclusion in the Leinster senior squad that winter. After a flawless performance in the Interprovincials at Rosses Point in June of 1989, where he achieved the maximum six points out of six, there was to be a distinct change of focus when it came to his potential with the small dimpled ball.

I think I played in one Irish Youths Championship, maybe the Leinster Youths once or twice and perhaps once, I contested the Leinster Boys Championship." Rhona, Jody's mother and "archivist", certainly wasn't busy cutting newspaper clippings regarding her son's golf at that time!

The winning Leinster team at the 1989 Interprovincial Championship at Rosses Point.
Back Row, l-r: John Hutchinson, Noel McGrane, Declan Branigan, Adrian Morrow, Jody, Leslie Walker, David Errity, Paul Rayfus, Padraig Hogan
Front Row: Heineken Sponsor, Liam Reidy GUI Leinster Chairman, Mick Mandeville Team Captain, Heineken Sponsor, Mark Gannon.

"At Lahinch, I was just hoping to do well, but it was an amazing week. I beat Paul McGinley in the last 16 and Darren Clarke by 2 & 1 in the quarterfinals. These guys were very seasoned at this stage and I was just on a quick learning curve."

In July that year, Fanagan made it all the way to the final of one of the most prestigious amateur Championships in the country. The South of Ireland Championship, played over the famed Alister MacKenzie-designed links at Lahinch was always one of the most sought-after prizes in domestic amateur golf. It was also one of the most popular tournaments in the season, due to its position in the golfing calendar.

In the heart of the Irish summer, the holiday town of Lahinch always embraced the arrival of the country's best golfers and Fanagan, like so many at the time, revelled in the atmosphere that this seaside town generated. Not only was it a time for serious golf, Lahinch was a town favoured by many Dubliners as a bolthole during the summer months, so the craic was always good.

With generous beaches, a lively nightlife and a championship golf course on its doorstep, Lahinch was the quintessential Irish holiday destination. Families would rent or even purchase houses for their seasonal getaway. Others would avail of mobile homes, enjoying the relaxed atmosphere and the special ambience that both the golf links and town had to offer.

Fanagan's ties with the County Clare town had special significance of course, due to his grandfather Paul Murray's great victory in 'the South' 49 years earlier. Although Jody had no clear ambition to match that

significant achievement, he had new-found confidence in his own game:
"Despite playing 'the South' a few times previously and with very little success, 1989 was different. Golf had started to interest me a lot more and a lot of things just came together very quickly for me. At Lahinch, I was just hoping to do well, but it was an amazing week. I beat Paul McGinley in the last 16 and Darren Clarke by 2 & 1 in the quarterfinals. These guys were very seasoned at this stage and I was just on a quick learning curve."

Giant killer. Fanagan beats Paul McGinley before accounting for Darren Clarke that afternoon.

"I've known Jody for a long time, since the mid-eighties, when we were on the Grange and Milltown teams that were involved in Senior Cup and Barton Shield. There was always a great rivalry. Jody was always known as a good rugby player at that stage and obviously as a good golfer. He swung the club great, very athletic. He had this rugby build with very strong legs, but he was a really stylish player." **Paul McGinley, March 2007**

Fanagan didn't finish there either, beating another dominant player of the era, Liam MacNamara, in the last four to reach his first major final, where he took on another rookie in Galway's Stephen Keenan.

The fact that he lost was admittedly, disappointing but there was now a firm belief that he could really play with the big boys. *"It was a great final and not many finals go all the way to the 22nd hole. Maybe if I had won, it would have given me greater confidence to go and win many other Championships, but little did I know that it would take six years to win my first major. Then again, that's golf!"*

Reaching the final of 'the South' brought an about-turn to Jody's sporting life in the space of ten months. From club golfer one year, he went on to make his debut in a 'green blazer' at the Home Internationals held at Ganton in September of 1989!

It was the beginning of an exciting eight-year period, where golf became the greater priority. However, he continued playing rugby for St Mary's for a further two years, before making the decision to step down from senior level.

That international debut at Ganton saw his inclusion amongst a team of Ireland's most experienced and youthful talent. He roomed with Dungannon's Darren Clarke, who was being touted as the country's next big star and Fanagan had no doubt about it: *"Darren was fantastic. He was unique really. I was delighted to be there and thrilled to be getting the Irish jumper, the blazer, the shirts and a brand new pair of Footjoy shoes... and there was Darren, with 8 different pairs of shoes in eight different colours! He was born to be a pro and really had it all. He was a great guy to be around, telling me some great stories and really putting me at ease. He was far and away the best player that I had seen at that point."*

Others on the team included fellow Dubliner Paul McGinley, who was the reigning Irish champion, Garth

" He swung the club great, very athletic. He had this rugby build with very strong legs, but he was a really stylish player."
- Paul McGinley, March 2007

Room-mates and team-mates.
Darren Clarke & Jody at the Home Internationals, Ganton, September 1989.

McGimpsey who was approaching legendary status and other luminaries including Mark Gannon, Liam McNamara, Dr. Neil Anderson and Ken Kearney. *"I won three out of six there and never looked back,"* recalls Fanagan.

He is bashful in admitting to beating England's Gary Wolstenholme by one hole in their singles match on the final day. Wolstenholme, now acclaimed for having played on four Walker Cup winning sides, was, and still remains, well known for his self-belief and self-promotion. Victory over Fanagan would have given him six wins out of six in those Home Internationals but the Milltown rookie had other ideas and managed to win on the final green.

"The entire English team each bought me a drink later that evening for beating him. They had won the overall series, but they applauded my victory over Gary!" Curiously, the English team reacted similarly the previous year, when Mark Gannon beat Wolstenholme.

"The entire English team each bought me a drink later that evening for beating him. They had won the overall series, but they applauded my victory over Gary!"

Despite his recent elevation in standard, at no point did he even consider the professional ranks:

"I wasn't good enough at all. I was twenty-three, but I wasn't good enough then. Nobody was saying that I should go pro or that I was good enough and to be honest, it didn't even cross my mind. Sometimes you need a mentor who says that they're taking you under their wing, but most Irish sportspeople, I think, have to do it their own way. They have to have the hunger within themselves and do it themselves and, for me, it was never a burning ambition. Darren Clarke, Paul McGinley, Padraig Harrington and Graeme McDowell all had that goal and went after it very successfully."

In latter years, Peter Lawrie and Gary Murphy have sought success as professionals and Fanagan is delighted that his former team-mates have turned the corner. *"When they decided to turn pro, I felt that there was work to be done with their games, but the pro game is where they wanted to be. They were prepared to travel the mini tours and learn the craft and through massive perseverance and dedication, they've started to reap rewards. It's brilliant to see.*

Darren, Paul and then Padraig and Graeme all turned at the right time for them and didn't have a shaky start. For me though, I never seriously considered the pro game and I never even enquired about Q school. I felt that I didn't have what it took to be amongst the top fifty in Europe, which is where you need to be in order to make a good living. By the time I was at Walker Cup level, I was married, there was a mortgage and I had a career in the family business (Fanagan Funeral Directors)*".*

Around the same time as Jody's international debut, Harrington was emerging as a quality player and the pair went on to share many glorious moments together as they formed a wonderful foursomes partnership at provincial and international level. Harrington's international record as an amateur is revered to this day, but some credit should also go to the undertaker who contributed in no small way to his impressive win ratio.

The victorious Irish Team, after winning the Home Internationals at Conwy, Wales in 1990.
Back row l-r: Howard Bennett, National Coach; Paul McGinley; Ken Kearney; Gary McNeill; Gerard Golden, GUI President; Padraig Harrington; David Errity; Niall Goulding; Jody
Front row l-r: Liam McNamara; Neil Anderson; George Crosbie, Captain; Garth McGimpsey & Mark Gannon.

Fanagan himself certainly didn't look back after that international debut in 1989, but individual victories at Championship level proved hard to find. Harrington, who remains a close friend, has this theory as to why Fanagan wasn't an individual 'major' winner more often:

"Jody was always a very solid player. He would produce 72 on the roughest day on the toughest golf course every time. He was just very dependable, a good ball striker, with a very tidy short game. He was also a good short putter so he revelled in the tougher conditions. Windy, tough weather conditions were commonplace in our Championships and Major tournaments and Jody was an expert at shooting the solid score, therefore, he was very dependable in team formats.

A lot of times in matchplay you can come up against a guy who is hot, who is going to shoot five or six under par on the day and it could be nice weather, so Jody's consistency wouldn't get its just reward over six rounds. He would have been better off if he was erratic and got lucky in one or two rounds and then played erratic golf to win towards the end, but he was probably too solid a player, too steady to win more Championships. However, his game was of the highest order and was particularly suited for high pressure, big occasions because you could depend on him. You nearly didn't have to send Jody out, as you knew what he was going to come up with!"

With a new decade dawning, the consistency that Harrington referred to reaped reward for Fanagan and he became a key member of the first Irish team to win

"However, his game was of the highest order and was particularly suited for high pressure, big occasions because you could depend on him. You nearly didn't have to send Jody out, as you knew what he was going to come up with!"
- Padraig Harrington

Garth McGimpsey and Padraig Harrington 2nd & 3rd from left, Raymie Burns 5th from right, Jody 2nd from right on St Andrews Trophy Team 1992.

"On reflection I was probably a bit star struck during the week and practised too much on the range, got tired and it showed as I progressed in the tournament. I loved the week but at the end of the day I never felt good enough to turn pro."

the Home International Championship on foreign soil as Ireland triumphed at Conwy in Wales in September, 1990.

Further appearances for Ireland followed in 1991 despite his lack of individual 'Championship' success. Once again Ireland were victorious in the Home Internationals, retaining the Raymond Trophy at County Sligo.

In 1992 after finishing joint second at the prestigious Lytham Trophy, Fanagan received an invitation to play in his first European Tour event, the Carroll's Irish Open, which was to be played at the scenic Killarney Golf and Fishing Club, by the banks of Lough Leane. He was determined to enjoy the experience and try his best to play his own game and it all came together beautifully. Carding rounds of 71 and 74, he made the cut comfortably despite the obvious pressure. He had guaranteed himself the low amateur prize and after closing with a pair of 75's for a 7 over par total of 295, Fanagan found himself tied with one other player, a certain rising young star from South Africa called Ernie Els. It mattered little to him that they were both twenty-one shots behind the tournament winner Nick Faldo.

"On reflection I was probably a bit star struck during the week and practised too much on the range, got tired and it showed as I progressed in the tournament. I loved the week but at the end of the day I never felt good enough to turn pro."

Fanagan was by then well ensconced in the family business and upon reflection, a full-time career was very beneficial when it came to those concentrated periods when he was at a major amateur tournament.

"For me, I loved the fact that it was a great release from the golf when I'd come back to work. I certainly

wasn't getting bored with the game by hitting golf balls all day everyday.

It created less pressure on me when I would arrive at a golf tournament. If I had spent two weeks practising ahead of a tournament and set off expecting to win then I would have been hugely disappointed if I didn't play well. Tournament golf was always a release from work for me. I was so happy to be there and I was relaxed and as a consequence I often played well. I never really expected too much."

Fanagan's growing reputation saw him included alongside fellow countrymen Garth McGimpsey, Padraig Harrington and Raymie Burns in the Britain and Ireland team that won the St Andrew's Trophy that summer against the Continent of Europe at Royal Cinque Ports.

By the time he got to Portstewart in County Antrim in mid-August for the big one, the Irish Close Championship, he was clearly one of the favourites.

Cruising through the two rounds of qualifying, the Milltown player won his opening matches in some style, especially when carding five birdies and an eagle over the tricky new layout when dispatching Portrush's David Cameron 7 & 6 in the second round. The following morning's third round encounter against the dogged veteran Barry Reddan nearly proved his undoing however. The Baltray golfer manufactured an outrageous five at the last, holing from 45 feet, to force Fanagan into holing a six-footer for a one hole victory.

Michael Sinclair of Knock was the next to fall at the quarter final stage, as Fanagan's quest for a first Championship victory continued in earnest. Awaiting him in the semi-final however was the renowned giant-killer JP Fitzgerald. The Dubliner who played out of Co. Louth had stunned Darren Clarke five years previously by holing an audacious eagle putt on the eighteenth hole of their semi final match at the Irish Close in Tramore. Fitzgerald went on to beat the Dungannon superstar on the 19th, only to lose in the final against local favourite Eddie Power. But Fanagan was upbeat about his chances: *"I suppose I was the favourite, but it didn't bother me too much. I was playing well, but not over-confident. How could I be? I had yet to win a major!"*

Fitzgerald was accustomed to the big stage but yet again he was the underdog which probably suited him. The other side of the draw saw 1983 champion Tom Corridan of Ballybunion face an emerging Kilkenny teenager by the name of Gary Murphy.

Fanagan knew that it would be a grind against Fitzgerald (who went on to caddy for the likes of Darren Clarke, Paul McGinley and Ernie Els on tour): *"JP's a great character. He had a very unusual swing like so many Irish players, due to the nature of our weather in my opinion. He was a very methodical player, with a very solid routine. Once he got the bit between his teeth and putted well, he was a match for anyone."*

It was a tense battle and Fanagan was in the driving seat as they neared the clubhouse. Despite putting poorly, he still found himself one up with three to play. Fitzgerald however won the 16th and 17th with fine pars and Fanagan's poor efforts with the blade cost him dear as another par from Fitzgerald gave him victory by that narrowest of margins, one hole. (Fitzgerald went on to lose his second Irish Close Final in five years to Gary Murphy later that afternoon).

That September, Fanagan once again played a pivotal role in the Irish team that claimed an historic three-in-a-row in the Home International Championship over the ancient links at Prestwick. Unquestionably, he was by now a wonderful team player, but his inability to win a Championship, given his obvious ability, proved very frustrating.

"I suppose I was the favourite, but it didn't bother me too much. I was playing well, but not over-confident. How could I be? I had yet to win a major!"

"You begin to doubt yourself. Yet, when I was playing on teams, I had no trouble closing out matches, but it wasn't happening for me in Championships and that was beginning to affect me."

"Maybe my golf wasn't improving enough year on year. Perhaps because I was working full-time, I didn't give myself enough opportunities to work more on my game, but I say that only in hindsight. It was frustrating though, especially with so many people close to me wishing for a victory."

Fanagan admits to winning nothing at this stage, not even a club medal. With a plus one handicap, that was never really on the cards anyway, but his career put paid to any forays on the Sunday Scratch Cup circuit - he limited himself to the major Championships only to find himself near, but yet so far.

After leading the qualifiers at the West of Ireland Championship in 1993, he once again reached the semi-finals of a major, only to lose out to the most successful amateur of the era, his Irish team-mate and 1985 British Amateur Champion, Garth McGimpsey. It was a high class match; there was very little between them.

All square after 16 holes, Fanagan struck a poor drive that ended up in a gully and needed four shots to make the green, eventually conceding. The last hole was halved and victory went to the Bangor legend, who went on to secure his third and last 'West' title, with victory over Arthur Pierse of Tipperary.

There was some consolation for Fanagan in that he did get a much-coveted selection for the six-man Irish side that contested the European Team Championship that year. Poor form there, however, had the inevitable effect of denying him his ultimate goal for the season: *"I had a poor European Championships and that put paid to any chances of Walker Cup selection."*

Harrington and Burns were chosen for the ten-man Great Britain & Ireland team which lost 19-5 to the Americans at Interlachen in Minnesota. It was satisfying to a point for Fanagan to be included in that year's squad, but the need for bigger performances and especially wins at Championship level began to take on greater significance.

Work was taking up a great deal more of his time during this period and there was also the not inconsiderable task of planning his upcoming nuptials to Alison, his girlfriend of three years. Nonetheless, he remained determined to win some big titles and entered the 1994 season with renewed vigour. By now Fanagan was very familiar with the courses used for the four provincial Championships and the prospect of the national title being played over Portmarnock's classic links was also whetting his appetite - he was a five-day member there and knew the vagaries of the course intimately.

The West of Ireland in 1994 once again beckoned as the season began in earnest. Having previously featured in a quarter-final and a semi-final, he was a player to be accorded respect at the County Sligo venue. Sailing through qualifying and early rounds, he claimed notable scalps like the talented Newlands youngster Peter Lawrie in the last sixteen.

He saved his best form however, for the quarter final, where he once again came up against the undisputed king of Rosses Point during that period, defending champion Garth McGimpsey. Regrettably, the jubilation at defeating the dominant player of that era was to be short-lived, as he went out in the last four yet again, losing to Ken Kearney who ultimately lost the final to Padraig Harrington in what was the future British Open Champion's first major amateur victory.

If Fanagan was concerned about his apparent inability to win Championships, then his failure to bring home the trophy at that summer's North of Ireland Championship was a real worry.

"I played super golf to reach the final. Nobody knew much about Nick Ludwell other than that he had once been a pro. He had beaten Padraig (Harrington) in the semis', so he was to be respected. Losing the match having been one up after eleven and in control of the game was, on reflection, another great opportunity missed. You begin to doubt yourself. When I was playing on teams, I had no trouble closing out matches, but it wasn't happening for me in Championships and that was beginning to affect me."

If it was bad enough to come up short again, it wouldn't come close to the pain that Fanagan felt a month later when the Irish Close was played at Portmarnock.

The world-class links on Dublin's northside was in magnificent shape, there was plenty of run on the ball and the greens were difficult to hold. Fanagan knew full well that his form was good, but in matchplay, you didn't have to tell him that anything could happen.

"Portmarnock was big for me because of my membership there. I did an awful lot of my practise there and while not being the favourite necessarily, I knew that I was playing really well and that this could be the one for me! I felt great about my chances and I would have had plenty of support through my membership."

For the third time that year, the Milltown player made it to the final day of a Championship, this time he faced Waterville's hot prospect David Higgins in the morning semi-final. Higgins himself had lost in the final of the Irish Amateur to Irish international Eddie Power (the Waterford native's second title) only two years previously. Crucially though, the Kerryman was on a high after beating Padraig Harrington a fortnight earlier in 'the South' at Lahinch.

Higgins had been 1 up with 3 to go, but had bunkered his second shot at the long par-five sixteenth. Fanagan, who was in the rough off the tee, decided to take advantage with a four wood second shot and proceeded to do something completely out of character. *"Inexplicably, and never before in my life had it happened, nor since for that matter, I topped it along the ground and followed him into the bunker! I don't know where it came from or why it happened, but it was a disaster!"*

Higgins won the hole with a bogey six and then closed out the match on the penultimate hole. *"The weather was really difficult, it was extremely windy, but to lose the match in the way that I did was a crushing blow. I was distraught at the time. It was all over. I was so fed up and it was probably the worst that I ever felt on a golf course. What's worse is that I didn't have the answer as to why I couldn't close these games out."*

Higgins went on to match Darren Clarke's notable double of 1990, by capturing both 'the South' and Irish Close titles (Clarke also managed victories in 'the North' and in the Spanish Amateur Championship that year), by beating Jody's foursomes partner on the 20th hole in a tense final later that afternoon. Although Harrington had one victory that year, there can be no doubt that it was a very disappointing season for the foursomes partners. The following month's Home Internationals at Ashburnham in England saw Fanagan achieve 3½ points out of six for Ireland and his season was over.

"Inexplicably, and never before in my life had it happened, nor since for that matter, I topped it along the ground and followed him into the bunker! I don't know where it came from or why it happened, but it was a disaster!"

Two partnerships, made in heaven!

It may have been another bridesmaid year on the golf front, but he did manage to emerge victorious and in a much more important way that September when Alison Farrell walked down the aisle at the Cathedral in Waterford City to become his bride. "*We met at a dinner party hosted by a mutual friend and hit it off*

immediately. We've never looked back!"
It may have been a huge disappointment for the Milltown golfer not to have bagged a major title by this stage, but his record, especially with Harrington in foursomes golf at representative level was gaining a great deal of notoriety.

Harrington smiles when he remembers their on-course magic and readily confesses to doing most of the talking:
"Yes. I am a chatter box without a doubt on the golf course and Jody and myself, through years of experience would know how to respond to each other when things were good or bad, knew how to settle things down or how to knuckle down when things were struggling a bit. I think that was the key thing to our partnership, that we were very assured of what the other person was doing, that the other person was 100% committed. We obviously knew each other's strengths and weaknesses, so we played for those.

I think the key thing is we didn't judge each other. If one of us hit a bad shot we never looked at each other in disgust or anything like that. We accepted everything and looked forward to recovering it. The great thing about me and Jody is that if one of us missed a green, we knew it was important to give each other a chance with the next shot; so get it into ten feet, eight feet, six feet or whatever and the other guy would do his best.

It was always a great partnership in the sense that we could rely on each other and when it was all said and done in the bar afterwards, nobody would ever be going to somebody else and saying 'my partner didn't play very well'. I think that was very important to both of us. We both had the confidence in each other that we weren't going to talk out of school that if one guy played bad that day it was the partnership played bad, it wasn't the individual."

By the time 1995 rolled around, Fanagan's reputation as a top-flight golfer was well-established but the mantelpiece was seriously lacking in silverware. How much more could a player of his calibre take? For how long more could he continue to devote the precious extra hours to the game, given that he was now married and working full-time, often at weekends?

The fact that it was a Walker Cup year gave him cause to look forward, instead of dwelling on previous near-misses. Once again he was named on the GB & I panel of players and by this stage, he was very familiar with all of his peers on the team. *"I reckoned that I was of a similar standard to all of them and if I could play well in the important events, then I could sneak a place on the final ten-man Walker Cup side, but I knew full well that a victory was required to force my way on!"*

"I reckoned that I was of a similar standard to all of them and if I could play well in the important events, then I could sneak a place on the final ten-man Walker Cup side, but I knew full well that a victory was required to force my way on!"

He played some casual rugby in the winter to keep fit, but it was work and not golf that took precedence. He did however, make one change to his usual hibernation in the off-season, insofar as he decided to make some swing changes under the watchful eye of long-time family friend Paul Cuddy, who was the pro at the Portmarnock Driving Range. *"He was certainly more radical than anyone who had given me swing advice in the past. He wasn't afraid to tell it as it was and having trained for a time under David Leadbetter in Florida, I followed his recommendations and began to see more consistency in my game."*

He was starting to feel very upbeat about this hugely important season. In the past, Fanagan never saw the sense in working too much on his game over the winter, leaving it all until the Irish squad's annual trip to Spain in March, where he felt that he could catch up on his latent game by playing and practising every day with the squad. The upcoming season clearly changed that mindset.

A key move towards Walker Cup selection took place when he enjoyed an especially good week at the

European Team Championships that June in Antwerp. Winning five points out of six was a positive step towards impressing the selectors and going undefeated in the foursomes alongside Harrington, who was a certainty for selection also did him the power of good.

What was even more spectacular however, was his progress through the field at the British Amateur Championship a few weeks later at Hoylake. Having played every year since 1990 and qualified for the matchplay stages on each occasion, he relished the opportunity to head to Liverpool in search of the Holy Grail. It proved to be a worthwhile investment.

"I actually managed to scrape through in the first couple of matches by winning on the 19th hole, so it could have gone either way. As you start to progress in a Championship, you can't help but start thinking ahead to what may happen. All of a sudden there's a bit of interest amongst the Irish press and you start getting calls!"

The calls continued, as Fanagan made it all the way to the second last day, easing past the pre-tournament favourite Marcus Wheelhouse of New Zealand by 2 & 1, and in so doing, setting up a semi-final meeting with former pro Michael Reynard of England. Two up with four to play, the Irishman was on the verge of a place in the final. The overall winner would get an invitation to both St Andrews for that year's Open and to the 1996 US Masters. Could he finally get the job done?
Regrettably not.
"I didn't really feel that I had done anything terribly wrong, I mean he birdied two of the last four holes and I bogeyed two of them. I really lost it on 17 though. Reynard missed the green with his second and was staring at a five, minimum. I was in the fairway with a five-iron approach. All I had to do was hit the green and it was all over. I pulled it left and got a terrible lie, made double bogey. All square up 18 and he birdies and here I am again, stunned. My chance to win the ultimate prize as an amateur was over, but having said that it was no certainty that I would have won the final, because Gordon Sherry (who went on the beat Reynard 7 & 6 in the 36-hole final) was the dominant player at that time."

The accolade of Amateur Champion is one of the greatest in the game and he had come so close. The memories remain bittersweet: "*It was very disappointing. My family and friends had all booked to fly over the following morning for the 36-hole final and that was all swiftly cancelled.*" Fanagan and his clubmate and good pal Dave Coolican, who had caddied for him throughout, made the lonely journey home together. Would the Milltown man ever get across the line first? The answer, thankfully, wasn't too far away.

Cometh the Hour

Talk to Jody Fanagan now about 1995 and he readily admits that it was the time of his life, sports-wise. Everything was falling nicely into place. He and Alison were now happily married, work was also very important to him as it gave great balance to his life, and there was a sporting passion that was taking him on a unique journey. His goal of representing the elite of Great Britain and Ireland was also within touching distance, if he could keep this impressive run of performances going.

He knew that without a victory to his name, he would be far too reliant on the selectors' largesse. A 'Major' could force the issue, now that there were just two spots remaining on the team of ten:
"I was playing as good as I ever had. In a lot of tournaments over the years, I'd arrive after a few weeks working and I'd be hoping to win, if I played well. Now I was turning up playing well and knowing that I was playing well. So it was nice to feel that. I was a good driver, which always helped me in

"It was very disappointing. My family and friends had all booked to fly over the following morning for the 36-hole final and that was all swiftly cancelled."

"We'd played together so much, so I didn't really know what to expect. I was looking forward to the challenge, but it was windy and I was struggling to put some good golf together. In the conditions, it was never going to be a classic!", Jody admitted.

Jody Fanagan lines up a crucial putt against Padraig Harrington in the final of the South of Ireland Championship, Lahinch, 1995.

matchplay. Hitting a lot of fairways means that you're always in contention in every hole, you're not giving much away. I had a good short game and wouldn't make that many mistakes and was difficult to beat."

In July he travelled to Lahinch in County Clare for 'the South' feeling like he had never felt before. Call it karma, call it what you like, he was in such a positive mood about his game; he adored the golf course and almost felt that he could play it blindfold. It was a case of now or never.

Belief and determination were as one, as he marched towards the final day, brushing aside some of his opponents by massive margins, with few taking him beyond the thirteenth green. His date with destiny however, almost crumbled when he was taken to the 20th by John Langan of Castlebar (Langan would go on to train as a pro at Milltown soon afterwards), but he came through to book a berth in the last four on the final day.

Tipperary's Pat Murray was his semi-final opponent and he looked to have the match sewn up when he went to the eighteenth one up and made a par. Fanagan however, proceeded to square the match, by holing a ten-footer for a winning birdie.

Murray overshot the green at the first tie hole and Fanagan's comfortable par was enough to claim a place in that afternoon's final. His opponent was none other than his good friend and foursomes partner, P.P. Harrington!

The Stackstown player had finally claimed a National title earlier in the summer with victory in the revived Irish Open Amateur Strokeplay Championship, but his inability to close out matchplay finals was itself becoming a concern. Since winning 'the West' the previous year, Harrington was on a losing run of three championship finals. He, too, was in determined mood to shed his bridesmaid tag.

"We'd played together so much, so I didn't really know what to expect. I was looking forward to the challenge, but it was windy and I was struggling to put some good golf together. In the conditions, it was never going to be a classic!" Jody admitted.

It didn't look good either when Fanagan found himself three down after 11 holes. Going up the 12th, he received words of encouragement from his clubmate Padraig McInerney, who was himself a Lahinch native. Suitably re-focussed, he promptly holed a 40-footer for a birdie three and a win. Halving the 13th, he managed to get up and down for a great birdie and another win on the 14th to be one down. Game on.

Missing from five feet for a par at the next, Fanagan was stunned to see Harrington miss from inside him and after the Stackstown player pulled his tee shot to the left of the green at the par-three sixteenth, Fanagan capitalised and brought the match back to all square. *"I was now feeling good about myself, Padraig was on the back foot and I had the momentum."*

Both players played superb approach shots to the penultimate green, Harrington missed his fifteen-footer and Fanagan, in a moment of inspiration, holed his putt from a similar distance to a tumultuous roar from the crowd. *"The hairs were standing on the back of my neck, it was an incredible feeling. I was now in the same position as I was in my first South final six years earlier, but this time I made myself wait for a about 15 seconds before heading towards the tee. Don't rush I kept telling myself, calm yourself down and get the job done."*

The Fanagan family at Ganton in 2000, celebrating a unique Irish golfing record as Suzanne makes her Curtis Cup debut.
L-R: Denise Fanagan, Andre O'Brien (Suzanne's husband), Rhona and Joe Fanagan, Suzie and Jody.

Finding rough off the tee, Fanagan watched as Harrington, from the middle of the fairway nailed a tremendous three wood to the heart of the green. Opting for a lay up, Fanagan pitched on in three to about five feet. This was turning out to be a classic after all!

Harrington's eagle attempt nearly succeeded and conceding the birdie, Fanagan managed to hole out in four for his maiden Major victory. The famine was over and he became the first Milltown player to achieve a championship victory since his grandfather's great moment in the sun all those years ago. *"A great feeling, arguably the best feeling ever, to finally do it after a long journey!"*

There's a fascinating footnote to this achievement in that while Jody was celebrating his great win in Lahinch, his sister Suzanne was giving the family even more good news. She had just been selected to represent Ireland in the Ladies Home Internationals that September. Having won the Finnish Ladies title the previous month, her elevation to international status gave the siblings a unique place in Irish golfing history. (Suzanne herself went on to achieve Curtis Cup status in 2000 to create a unique record in Irish golf, as Jody and Suzanne became the first Irish siblings to win Walker and Curtis Cup caps.)

In Jody's case, Walker Cup honours had to be on the cards now. After all, he had proven his worth as a match player with that victory in 'the South' and reaching the semis at the British Amateur added a new dimension to his standing in the game. His ability to cope with pressure-cooker situations in team events was well established and there was no denying his hugely successful partnership with Harrington in foursomes. *"Beating Padraig to win the South of Ireland at Lahinch was probably the key, as Padraig was already a lock on the team, so to beat him made a huge difference."*

"Beating Padraig to win the South of Ireland at Lahinch was probably the key, as Padraig was already a lock on the team, so to beat him made a huge difference."

"Padraig and I were named as a foursomes pairing and we took on Kris Cox and Trip Kuehne. The first tee is always the hardest. I had to hit the tee shot. The beach is on the left of the first at Porthcawl and I nearly hit the opening drive onto it! "

Jody raises Irish flag at 1995 Walker Cup matches.

The following week, he was back in Lahinch, this time to compete in the Irish Amateur Close Championship. The Walker Cup selectors had already named eight players, including Harrington, for the biennial clash against the Americans. Jody could still not afford to rest on his laurels, even as a recent Major winner. Those same selectors would not name their two remaining players until the National Championships of the four 'home countries' had been completed.

"I played great that week again, but in fairness to Richie Coughlan who beat me in the semi final, he deserved to win **(by 3&2)*****. Still, I felt that the message I was giving the selectors was that I was playing well and that it wouldn't be a risk picking me for the Walker Cup"***

Two days later, when he heard the voice of Rupert De Lacy Staunton on the other end of the line, he knew that his dream had come true. *"If you weren't on the team, they wouldn't be calling you!"* The final two spots went to Gary Wolstenholme and a thirty-year-old undertaker from Dublin by the name of Joseph Michael Fanagan!

In many ways, it was no more than he deserved. Fanagan had all the attributes necessary to become a key player for Great Britain and Ireland, as they attempted to beat the Americans for the first time on home soil since 1971. The excitement caused by his selection resulted in huge numbers from Milltown and many of his UCD Rugby Club pals travelling to Wales three weeks later to support their golden boy.

Jody focuses in on the task in hand on the first tee in his opening foursomes match against the USA at Royal Porthcawl.

The usual pomp and ceremony applied when it came to the opening ceremony and as is expected from Irish supporters these days, great cheers erupted when the two Dubliners were officially announced to the assembled onlookers.

Jody remembers the occasion vividly: *"the pressure of playing against the Americans was immense. We had a very strong team and I was playing well in practice, which gives you great confidence."* He was far from calm on that first morning:
"Padraig and I were named as a foursomes pairing and we took on Kris Cox and Trip Kuehne. The first tee is always the hardest. I had to hit the tee shot. The beach is on the left of the first at Porthcawl and I nearly hit the opening drive onto it!"

Harrington could clearly appreciate what his partner was going through:

"I had accumulated enough experience to realise that you shouldn't be the one to hit the tee shot off the first, so I gave that job to Jody! I did it on my debut in the 1991 Walker Cup at Portmarnock and by the time I got over the ball, I couldn't see it! Jody was there thinking maybe he didn't hit the best drive in the world, but my memory of hitting the first tee shot in a Walker Cup or a Ryder Cup, for that matter, is that anything airborne, that is in play, anywhere in play, is a good tee shot! I would have been very happy with Jody's drive there. I would have understood exactly what he was going through, but that was always a thing with Jody, we understood exactly what each other was thinking."

Once they got away down the fairway, the hype was behind them and it was a relief to Fanagan to be finally able to concentrate on the job in hand. With Harrington playing his third consecutive Walker Cup, it was reassuring to him that his partner could bring that extra dimension to what was a nerve-wrecking few hours: *"He was very calming that day, he was always*

Ireland's finest get ready for battle against Tiger Woods and John Harris on the final morning of the Walker Cup matches in 1995.

very composed and pitched out of the rough to about four feet, I knocked it in and we're one up. We'd played together about forty times at provincial and national level by that time, so it was easier to knuckle down and play my game. I'd been playing well so it went better after that, we won the second and were never behind". The pair ended up winning five and three.

Fanagan wasn't named in the singles that afternoon, which he had known about the previous evening, but after that opening foursomes performance he was certain that captain Clive Brown would name him for both matches the following day.

Brown duly delivered, and to the delight of the Irish fans Jody teamed up with Harrington for a memorable foursomes match against an American pairing that included the man who is now undeniably the best in the world and arguably, the greatest player ever!

Eldrick 'Tiger' Woods, then a 19-year-old with the world at his feet alongside the vastly experienced John Harris went head-to-head against the Irish boys in the

"It was an awful day, really brutal for playing golf and Woods was under massive pressure," recalls Fanagan. *"He was the US Amateur champion for two years running, the boy who would be King. There was this huge expectancy about him and they did not get off to a good start."*

Fanagan drills a tee shot down the middle in singles match against Jerry Courville.

morning's top match. Harrington was the new Irish Amateur and Irish Strokeplay Champion. Woods was the three-time US Junior Amateur champion and by that stage, the two-time US Amateur champion.

"That was probably the peak of our foursomes partnership," says Harrington. "We were put out there against the most experienced amateur in the game (Harris) and probably the most talented amateur in the game (Tiger). But Jody and I knew what we could do and sure enough after five or six holes the match was really swinging in our direction and the other two were struggling as a partnership to get on together while myself and Jody were going from strength to strength."

"It was an awful day, really brutal for playing golf and Woods was under massive pressure," recalls Fanagan. *"He was the US Amateur champion for two years running, the boy who would be King. There was this huge expectancy about him but they did not get off to a good start. John Harris had a ten out of ten record in the Walker Cup up until that point, including two wins the previous day, but on the Sunday, he had an awful time. He topped two shots and he and Woods didn't get on well at all. We were sheltering under brollies the whole time and there was very little said between us and them. Tiger was clearly unhappy with the playing conditions, clearly upset with his playing partner and probably trying a little too hard in pretty alien conditions. We felt we had the upper hand and went on to win 2 & 1".*

Fanagan then dispatched Jerry Courville in the singles on that memorable, but soggy afternoon by three and two. It was a wholly miserable day for golf with heavy rain and wind pelting the Welsh coast, but the overall result was in favour of the home side, with Fanagan emerging undefeated. There was some uncertainty as to who holed the cup-winning putt as David Howell (now a leading European Tour player and a Ryder Cup star) and Jody both clinched points at around the same time, but the Dubliner remains unconcerned, having taken great satisfaction from his valuable contribution to the team effort.

Fanagan was the only member of the team to achieve maximum points with three points from three

The scoreboard tells the story. A great day for Irish golf and the Fanagan household.

Tiger was clearly unhappy with the playing conditions, clearly upset with his playing partner and probably trying a little too hard in pretty alien conditions. We felt we had the upper hand and went on to win two and one".

The victorious GB & I Walker Cup team at Royal Porthcawl, 1995.

matches. No Irish player had previously completed a Walker Cup with a one hundred per cent record. Sutton's Roddy Carr had come closest with three wins and a half in 1971 and Killarney's Eoghan O'Connell had won two and halved two of his four matches in the famous victory at Peach Tree in 1989.

At the celebration dinner later that evening, Fanagan and Harrington sat beside Notah Begay and an empty chair reserved for the future world number one who stayed in his room, suffering from 'flu'!

Harrington and Fanagan concluded their tremendous partnership in September of 1995 at the Home Internationals in Royal Portrush. They both achieved five points out of six, losing just one foursomes match, against the Amateur Champion Gordon Sherry and Graham Rankin of Scotland. In all they won 22 out of their 30 matches as a foursomes pairing. Quite an achievement.

Fanagan nearly defended his title in the final of 'the South' the following year, only to lose to some superb play from the evergreen Adrian Morrow, but other than that it was a fallow year. Although he contended for a place on the 1997 Walker Cup side, he didn't display the required form in the run up to selection, despite finally winning the West of Ireland for his second Major championship.

His failure to make the 1997 side once again came down to a below-average performance, by his standards, at the European Championships that year in Portmarnock. Despite a notable foursomes scalp alongside Noel Fox against Sergio Garcia and Jose Manuel Lara, Fanagan had to content himself with watching the Walker Cup matches on television while playing in the Irish Close in Westport, where defending champion Peter Lawrie lost out to Ken Kearney in the final.

Subconsciously, he knew that 1997 would be his last year of serious commitment at the top level of competition and signed off in style with that terrific win against Luke Donald.

Jody and Padraig with the Walker Cup on a rain-soaked but glorious September Sunday, Royal Porthcawl, 1995.

Despite a notable foursomes scalp alongside Noel Fox against Sergio Garcia and Jose Manuel Lara, Fanagan had to content himself with watching the Walker Cup matches on television

Justin Rose, fellow Walker Cup panellist in 1997

"Jody was a terrific player and a great guy too. A wonderful match player, he was as tough as nails in competition and a hard man to beat." - Justin Rose, fellow Walker Cup panellist in 1997 and European No. 1 in 2007.

After that singles win, Fanagan made his way to the locker room alone and quietly shed a tear, as he prepared to call it a day as an international golfer.

These days, Jody Fanagan continues to play off a handicap of plus one. While he continues to play representative golf for Milltown, he admits that he'd like to move up to scratch "*to give me more of a chance in medal competitions!*"

On the 7th of January 2007, Jody Fanagan drove in as captain of Milltown Golf Club. It was a fitting recognition for all the honour that he brought one of Dublin's most established clubs, and made all the more special given that it was their Centenary Year. To add to his legendary status, Fanagan also claimed the Golfer of the Year accolade.

CAREER HIGHLIGHTS

Full Name: Joseph (Jody) Michael Fanagan

Date of Birth: 24th June 1965

Birthplace: Dublin

Family: Wife Alison, 3 sons Hugo, Harry and Stephen

Occupation: Funeral Director

Lowest Handicap: + 2

CHAMPIONSHIP HIGHLIGHTS

British Amateur Championship
Semi-finalist at Royal Liverpool (Hoylake) 1995

Irish Amateur Close Championship
Semi-finalist 1992, 1994 & 1995

Irish Open Amateur Championship
Runner-up 1999

West of Ireland Amateur Open Championship
Winner in 1997
Semi-finalist in 1993, 1994 & 1998

East of Ireland Championship
Runner-up in 1992 & 1993

South of Ireland Championship
Winner in 1995
Runner-up in 1989 and 1996

North of Ireland Championship
Runner-up in 1994
Lytham Trophy
Joint 2nd in 1992

Carrolls Irish Open (Professional)
Leading amateur in 1992

REPRESENTATIVE HONOURS:

GB & I *Walker Cup*: 1 cap in 1995. Played three matches, won all three.

GB & I *St Andrews Trophy*: 1992,1994 & 1996

International: 77 caps for Ireland 1989-1997

Interprovincial: 54 caps for Leinster 1989-1997

MISCELLANEOUS

Centenary Captain of Milltown Golf Club 2007

Member of the R&A

Barton Shield Winner (Leinster) with Milltown 1988

Leinster Club Youths winner with Milltown 1984

Golfer of the Year at Milltown 2007

Noel Fogarty

The Dublin bookie who took the 'Golden Bear' Jack Nicklaus into extra time at the British Amateur Championship.

"Noel was one of the great characters amongst the bookmakers in the betting ring and a very honourable guy." - **JP McMANUS, August 2007.**

Noel Fogarty, sporting his international golfing blazer, turning on the style in the mid '80's at the Curragh Racecourse.

Noel Fogarty and his wife Bella pictured with the Golden Ball trophy, an event that he dominated at the Curragh Golf Club in the early sixties.

Fogarty, with his outgoing and friendly nature, not to mention a quality golf game, was no slouch when it came to standing up and being counted.

A Moment in Time

In the company of his great friends JB Carr and Michael Fitzpatrick, Noel Fogarty travelled to Sandwich in Kent to compete in the British Amateur Championship. It was June, 1959 and the trio were perfect travelling companions: they had all grown up together, each was in a successful business so money was never any object, and they could socialise with the best of them!

Fogarty, with his outgoing and friendly nature, not to mention a quality golf game, was no slouch when it came to standing up and being counted. He was keen to take on whomever he was drawn against in the Championship and when it came to any post-round activity, be it a poker game or dinner, he had no trouble when it came to paying his own way. There were certain advantages to being in a cash business, such as bookmaking!

Arguably, Fogo's largesse was one of the main reasons why he could fit in with Joe Carr's lifestyle in those halcyon days of the fifties and sixties. As Fogarty himself puts it: *"I had been an international golfer at this stage for three years. If I was good enough to win big Scratch cups or whatever was going on at home, I just felt, well, let's go and see how the rest of the world lives!"*

The triumvirate stayed at the White Sands Hotel in Sandwich and set about learning the course over three or four practice rounds. Big and all as the Championship was, it was still a great social event. The Americans were there in force, having played in the Walker Cup matches the previous week at Muirfield, defeating Great Britain and Ireland by 9-3 and they really added to the significance of the Championship that year. The field was littered with big names like Frank Stranahan, Deane Beman, the eventual winner (who went on to become the Commissioner of the PGA Tour) and a certain 19 year-old from Columbus, Ohio.

Carr and Fogarty were on opposite ends of the draw and on the evening that it went up, Carr, the defending champion said to his old friend, 'Fogo you're in the thick of the fray', noting that if he did well in the opening rounds, he'd surely come undone against America's rising teen sensation Jack Nicklaus. Fogarty, of course, loved a challenge and rose to the occasion by getting through his first three rounds to tee up a meeting with the man who would change the face of world golf forever.

Fogo gets ready for battle

He can recall many special moments of their fourth round encounter: *"I played in six British Amateurs and three British Opens. The best I did was in that year when I played Jack Nicklaus, and in Jack I made a friend for life...there is a lot to be achieved by just playing golf and meeting people.*

I was two down early on, in the first five or six holes. I remember one incident at a short hole, I forget the number, where Jack was nicely on the green and I was in a bunker at the front. I must have been 35 yards short of the pin - bad clubbing naturally. Anyway, I barely got it out of the bunker and it was still my putt from about 40 feet or so and I managed to hole it for three! It left Jack with two putts for a half, which he duly got. So I was still two down but it gave me a bit of momentum and I managed to get it back to all square by the ninth.

There was another incident on the 12th hole, which is the dog-leg. I cut my tee shot and it faded away right. I was in rather thick rough. There were a good few following the match, but they were there to see the kid Nicklaus!

Jack was up the fairway and we were looking for my ball. A spectator said: 'this is the ball here that came up'. Now, it did happen to be the same golf ball that I was playing, a Dunlop, whatever the number was I don't remember. I said 'I thought mine was a little more right of the line'.

Jack was 50 yards up the fairway, so I called him back. I said, 'Jack, we have a little difference here'. I explained what had happened. The very words Jack used were: 'Noel, if that man says that's your ball, that's your ball, so play it'. It was the same make, number and all. I wasn't 100% happy it was mine, but Jack took the spectator's word and I could have lost that hole very easily. I remember I chopped it out up near the green, pitched and one-putted for a half, which was kind of a miracle!

It wasn't long before I was two down again but on the tricky 14th hole with out of bounds all the way down the right, I managed to hit two good shots up beside the green. I chipped and one-putted for a birdie four and a win. At the par-four 15th, I chipped and one-putted again, this time for a half. So Jack Nicklaus, who at 19 was considered to be the best amateur in the world, was now just one up on me with three holes to go!

At the short 16th (where Denmark's Thomas Bjorn blew his chance of the Open some 44 years later) *we both hit the green. I putted up first to about a foot and a 'gimme'. Jack was at the back of the green and he putted down to five or six feet past the hole. He missed the putt and our match was now all square!"*

The best I did was in that year when I played Jack Nicklaus, and in Jack I made a friend for life... there is a lot to be achieved by just playing golf and meeting people.

By this stage, the crowd numbered over a thousand.

The man who became known the world over as the Golden Bear was up against it, playing a 34 year-old gentle giant of a Dubliner who had hands like shovels and a thick red Barnet to boot. All square and just two holes to go. Could there possibly be a fairytale ending?

"We headed to the 17th, a dodgy little hole in those days. We both hit our tee shots up the fairway. I was to play first so I had a seven or eight iron and I hit a deplorable hook off to the left of the green. Jack played a great shot into about twelve or fourteen feet, while I chipped to about eight feet, didn't hole the putt and Jack won the hole with a par four. That left me dormie one down."

Reality was striking hard for "Fogo". The 18th at Royal St George's is a tough finishing hole with a long carry to the fairway. To go this far against such an outright favourite, he was well aware that he was defying the odds, and given his profession, Noel Fogarty knew a thing or two about beating them!

To go this far against such an outright favourite, Fogarty knew that he had defied the odds, and given his profession, he knew a thing or two about beating them!

"It wasn't the right time to go one down, that's for sure but to be honest, I was delighted to have gone so far. There were cross-bunkers on the 18th and we both hit good tee shots up the fairway, short of the bunkers. We had a look, Jack says 'who's shot is it, Noel?' We're looking at it and I said 'Jack, I think it's you'. He says 'I agree with that, it's my shot'.

I apologise for what I am going to say, but I think if Jack remembers it, it is the truth. Jack got the "unmentionable" (a socket) with his second shot. To such an extent that he had to play his third shot before I even played my second!

He got it up somewhere round about the green and I was just up off the green and ended up winning the hole in five! Sorry about that Jack, but if it's the truth, then it must be told!

Off we go down 19, two good tee shots. I played first and caught the top of a bunker, on the right-hand side. If I had carried the bunker I would only have been ten or twelve feet away, but I just caught the top of the trap and fell back into it. Jack had hit a poor second shot and he was in the left-side bunker. I played out to about 8 or 10 feet and Jack actually hit the hole with his bunker shot and it spun out to about a foot, which I duly conceded.

I had the putt for a half. I only had to hole it and I was still in the game. I struck it and unfortunately, it lipped out and Jack won the match, on the 19th. Jack's father Charlie, Lord have mercy on him, was with him. Jack brought him over and 'Geez', said the old man, 'you are a tough cookie'. Jack and I are friends ever since. I love the guy.

'Noel was a wonderful player' - Jack Nicklaus

In my opinion Jack and Arnie are the two men who made golf what it is today. When all is said and done, I don't know who was the better player but I was certainly proud to have shared a precious moment of Jack Nicklaus' golfing life. It's a day that I'll never forget."

"I played Noel Fogarty in the British Amateur in 1959. Noel was a big, strapping Irishman. I remember him being a long hitter of the golf ball. In some ways, he was more brawn than finesse, but nonetheless, he was a wonderful player. Noel was also one heck of a nice guy and I enjoyed his company." - **Jack Nicklaus, April, 2007**

'Larger than Life'

'Larger than life' is an expression that goes a long way towards describing Gerard Noel Fogarty, who was a permanent fixture in Ireland's golfing and racing life for nearly fifty years. In his pomp, Fogo could really lay claim to walking with Kings, while never losing that common touch.

In the fifties and sixties, especially in Ireland, very few people had money. Numbered amongst the few was Fogo. He was in a business that dealt strictly in cash and he happened to be very good at his job. He also took the broader view on life and reasoned that it was one to be *"enjoyed, explored and lived to the full. The greatest memories I have are of the people that you meet along the way"*, and what a way he's come.

Working hard and playing even harder

To illustrate Fogarty's unique lifestyle, it's worthwhile recounting one memorable (but typical) weekend in 1961. The sobriquet 'legends in their spare time' could not be more apt as Noel and his lifelong friend and golfing rival J.B. Carr concluded a busy working week with both a social and sporting pilgrimage to the southern capital, Cork.

On the Saturday, Fogo had put in a good day's work at the Phoenix Park races. A good bookmaker, he had enjoyed a more than satisfactory return, despite the 'great uncertainty of the turf.' Making the odds and making cash were his stock in trade. After the last race he drove down to Kingsbridge, (Heuston Station). Having parked his car, he met J.B. (the reigning British Amateur Champion) as arranged, and with clubs and overnight bags, they climbed aboard the Cork-bound train.

On board, the pair ventured to the dining car where Fogo was introduced to a man who would become a life-long friend, Mr. Ben Dunne Senior. Dunne, a Northerner, would become the leading retailer in Ireland and he was also a keen student of form. *"Ben and I became very friendly through the racing. He used to do his bit of business with me, quite a bit, and we became good friends."*

Arriving in Cork, they were met from the train by another prominent local businessman, Frank Bennett, who brought the pair up to his house in Montenotte. *"We had a bit of grub, a bit of banter and settled into a game of cards. On leaving the racecourse earlier, I had put £100 in my pocket for the weekend. You could have bought some of Cork city for £100 at that time. Well that night my £100 was gone in the space of an hour or whatever. I asked Joe if he had any cash. He said, 'You know me, Fogo, I never carry money!' In any case, Joe said to the lady of the house, Mrs. Delia Bennett, a lovely lady, 'Would you get us some money?' Delia went somewhere, I don't know where, but she came back and if I tell you there was enough money to lodge in the bank that'd be the least of it. She pushed it over and she said 'take what you want out of that.'*

I said, 'No way, I only met you about two hours ago. Give it to Joe.' I said to Joe, 'take some money out of that and give some to me.' I think I got £200 off Joe. We proceeded to play the cards and we finished up at 3:30 in the morning.

'Larger than life' is an expression that goes a long way towards describing Gerard Noel Fogarty, who was a permanent fixture in Ireland's golfing and racing life for nearly fifty years.

Joe was staying in Bennett's house, I was actually staying with George Crosbie of the Cork Examiner Newspaper Group (now the Irish Examiner). *George was waiting on me to go back. The night finished up and I had won £360. I gave Joe back the money I had borrowed, went home with George, had about three hours sleep, got up and had breakfast, went to Mass and out to Douglas Golf Club.*

I had never seen the course before and I went out and shot 73 or 74, which was one or two over par. We went in and had a bite of lunch and in the afternoon I think I shot 66 or 67! I started out with five straight birdies and I won the Scratch Cup!

Noel Fogarty receives the Douglas Senior Scratch Cup in 1961.
Also pictured are Joe Carr, Frank Bennett (back left) and Zelie Fallon (back right).

I had never seen the course before and I went out and shot 73 or 74, which was one or two over par.

Frank Bennett was actually the Captain of the Golf Club that year. One of their most famous golfers, a wonderful lady golfer called Zelie Fallon (an Irish international for 15 years and a GB & I cap for the 1964 Espirito Santo Trophy) *was there for the presentation.*

We were done at about eight or eight-thirty. Frank thought we'd never get back to his house! We weren't even allowed to go and eat. We got maybe one or two drinks in the clubhouse, then into his car and back to his place, where we had been the night before.

At about 10pm we started playing cards and to make a long story short, at seven in the morning (Monday) the game of cards stopped because Joe and I had to catch the 8:45 train to Dublin because I had to play Senior Cup golf in Royal Dublin that afternoon! I gave all of my winnings from the previous night back to the pot and had broken dead even. I still had my original £100 in my back pocket at the end of the weekend!

Frank's son Martin drove us to the station. We got on the train, up to the dining room, had a bit of breakfast and all the rest, got into Kingsbridge and my car had a puncture so I had to change the wheel. I got home around about one o'clock or something and said to Bella (Noel's very patient wife!) *that I was going to bed, as I had to play golf at four. I got about an hour's sleep, got up, had a bowl of soup and a sandwich and left the house for Royal Dublin. I was playing a great friend of mine, long since dead, Dr. Jim Mahon* (originally a Sligo man, but he played out of Portmarnock and won the Irish Amateur Close in 1955).

It was always a big game against Portmarnock in the Senior Cup, so it was quite a deal. A clash of the ash or whatever you want to call it. Anyway, off I went out and not having seen the bed for more than two or three hours for two days, I beat Dr. Jim 6 & 4 around my home course!

I started the golf at about four, allow three hours for the round so we were finished at about seven and my work at the greyhound racing at Shelbourne Park started at eight. That finished up as it always did, at about ten-thirty!"

A typical 48 hours in the life of one of Dublin's true golfing legends!

Fair City Beginnings

Noel Fogarty, was born in a nursing home on the fifth of December, 1924, near Church Street, in the heart of Dublin's city centre. Growing up in the city as a youngster, Fogarty was completely unaware that the game of golf and its charms were ever likely to form such a massive part of his life.

During those early years, his father Jeremiah (Jerry) Fogarty was carving out a career as a jarvey (a jaunting car driver). In those days, the only mode of transport was by horse and cart, or horse-drawn carriage. In actual fact, the Fogarty's would go on to run one of the earliest taxi services in the city, not to mention the country, when the era of the jarvey came to an end and the motor car took over.

In the years before and after the 1916 rebellion, the Fogarty family were busy around Dublin city with their carriages and sidecars. Jerry also had a great head for figures and put it to good use making the odds at greyhound and horse racing meetings. Not long after, he carved out a second career as an on-course bookmaker.

In 1924, after a few solid years of industrious endeavour, Jerry and Katie Fogarty (nee Wall) moved their young family out to Portmarnock village on the northside of Dublin. Jerry by this time had moved full-time into bookmaking and in time, young Noel, one of seven children, followed in his footsteps.

In those early days, Portmarnock was nothing more than a small village and didn't even have its own church until 1933. Although sport played a major part in his development, the world-famous Portmarnock golf links, which were a mere two miles away, did not feature in Noel's life for several more years.

With the beach nearby and hundreds of undeveloped acres on their doorstep, the youngsters of the area had a massive playground. Then, in 1934, at the tender age of ten, Noel was presented with a mashie niblick (a wooden-shafted 7 iron) by one of the green-keepers at Portmarnock, who knew the Fogarty family.

At such a young age, the implement aroused no more than idle curiosity, but it would give the youngster an entrée into a new 'club' that was enjoyed by many of his peers at the time.

In nearby land, adjacent to Portmarnock Golf Club, a three-hole facility developed by locals became a magnet for youngsters during the summer months of the thirties and forties. It was famously known in those days as "The Hollow".

The land eventually became part of what is now 'the third nine' at Portmarnock, but in his youth, Fogo and his peers would while away the days amongst the sand dunes, competing for bragging rights in those regular one-club challenges.

"*We'd spend our whole summer holidays down there. Every kid in the village including Joe Carr and myself started our golf there. Tom Craddock* (Walker Cup 1967 and 1969) *used to cycle over from Malahide, and every kid from anywhere nearby had one golf club."* The seeds were being sown, but the harvest was some way off.

His formal education began in the National School in Portmarnock village, with brief periods in Killinure in Laois and the nearby national school in Baldoyle, Co.

At such a young age, the implement aroused no more than idle curiosity, but it would give the youngster an entrée into a new 'club' that was enjoyed by many of his peers at the time.

Dublin. Fogo finished up in O'Connell's School in North Richmond Street where his sporting prowess gained full flight. Two years ahead of him at O'Connell's was his friend, Joseph Benedict Carr.

At about the same time, horse racing also became a major part of his life. His earliest memories are of days off school for the Punchestown Festival in late April. Noel and his brothers would watch the racing while their father would go to work. A 'good grafter', he was doing well enough to build a row of houses, which included two cottages, two shops and the bungalow in which Noel has lived for the best part of fifty years.

Not the greatest academic at his various schools, he gained huge satisfaction from his love of sport and, such was his ability at rugby and Gaelic football that he found favourable support from the Christian Brothers when it came to swapping the classroom for the Gaelic pitch or handball alley. Fogo's ambidextrous ability at handball is one of the reasons, he claims, that his famous hands are so big!

If there was money to be made, then Fogo made it his business to be there come rain or shine and for two or three years, he even cycled to the Galway races.

Having witnessed the torrid time that Ireland suffered during the national uprising and First World War, Jerry Fogarty was shrewd enough to prepare for the rationing that would follow during the Second World War. He set about purchasing 30 tonnes of coal, which they stored in a back shed. Fogarty senior also purchased two chests of tea, weighing half a hundred weight between them and one hundred weight of tobacco for his smoking. Not knowing how long the war would last, 'but having lived through one war, he knew what was going to be short during the next one!' Forewarned is forearmed.

"We used to have a couple of cattle, so we had our own milk and butter. Every year my father would rear a pig and when the summer was over, the pig was killed and we had our own bacon right through the whole winter. It was only experience. He had seen it the other way in the First World War and he said he wasn't going to be short of those simple things and he provided well."

Times may have been tough during those bleak days of the early forties, but the family wanted for little and Jerry Fogarty's industrious ways rubbed off on the children, not least young Noel.

Upon leaving school in 1942, he joined up with his father and brother Brendan in the on-course bookmaking operation. And so began the ritual that would define his life over the next 52 years, working six nights a week at the capital's greyhound stadiums from March to November.

During the war, the Fogarty boys would head out to race meetings at venues like the Curragh. Cycling out in the morning, they put in a day's work at the races then cycled back to Dublin city, stopping off for a bite to eat in Wynne's Hotel and then on to work at the dog track in Harold's Cross or Shelbourne Park that night. After all of that, it was back on the bike to cycle home to Portmarnock, thinking nothing of it, for it was considered normal at the time.

If there was money to be made, then Fogo made it his business to be there, come rain or shine for two or three years, he even cycled to the Galway races. On one occasion he cycled to the Tramore races on his own, a mere 135 miles away. *"I cycled to Limerick Junction race course in Tipperary one year on a Wednesday, worked at the races on the Thursday and cycled home on the Friday, then headed straight to the dogs to work for my father. You can imagine what the roads were like in those days!"*

Tough times? Not a bit of it, as he told the Irish Press in 1966: "They were some of the most enjoyable times of my life. We were very fit and it gave us the opportunity to see the whole country...in slow motion!"

Needless to say, Fogo relished his days off on a Sunday when he loved nothing better than to feed his competitive juices with a cycle race to one of the various towns outside the capital. He vividly recalls one of those exhausting days out, which for him represented nothing more than a routine spin, given the mileage he was clocking up just for work!

"There was no Sunday horse racing back then and every Sunday morning we would be up and ready at maybe 7 o'clock. To put in a Sunday, you went to mass in the chapel and proceeded up to the old pub on the Navan Road, called the 1,500. It's right beside the old race course (Phoenix Park). We changed our clothes there and rode in a bicycle race to Delvin in County Meath (some 50 miles away). Rained all the way – when we got there, there was a van that had a change of clothes for us so we changed into our dry clothes. I think it was three and six pence or something for lunch, I got beaten by half a wheel in the race, and that was our pastime!"

After a mass crash in the heats of the 1-Mile Championship at the Iveagh Grounds, Dublin in 1944, Noel ran the final 300 yards while carrying his broken bike and qualified for the final, where he finished 2nd!

Not only that but Fogo and his fellow athletes re-mounted their bikes and cycled back home to Dublin, where he rang his girlfriend and now wife of nearly sixty years, Bella, and told her to get the bus into town. It was still raining as he cycled into Eden Quay. A date at the cinema was followed by an after-show ice-cream at Cafolla's. His future bride would then climb aboard the crossbar and Noel would cycle the pair of them home to Portmarnock via Baldoyle where he dropped off his young sweetheart. *"And I came on home here and that was a way of putting in a Sunday!"* he recalls.

It shouldn't come as a surprise to learn then, that Fogarty became National 440 yard Sprint Cycling Champion in 1945. With no real shortage of food, and a life spent in the fresh air, Fogo was as fit as a butcher's dog. His prowess both as a cyclist and also as an amateur boxer were gaining prominence (he was runner-up in the National Junior Boxing Championships at cruiserweight in 1951, losing in the final to Paddy Lyons who went on to become a national heavyweight champion).

However, the real turning point in Fogo's sporting life had, unbeknown to him, already taken place in 1945, when he decided to experiment with a new sport, now that he was 'working and doing nicely'. Alongside his brother Brendan, the pair joined the old Malahide Golf Club, which was then a nine-hole course, about three

However, the real turning point in Fogo's sporting life had, unbeknown to him, already taken place in 1945, when he decided to experiment with a new sport, now that he was 'working and doing nicely'.

miles away. The brothers were accepted for the princely sum of two pounds a year. It was to be the beginning of a love affair with the game that continues to this day, over sixty years later.

In time, he joined St Anne's Golf Club on the Bull Island and later on, Hermitage Golf Club in Lucan. His sporting ambitions became more focussed on golf and he was soon playing off single figures and beginning to enjoy a more intense level of competition.

Himself!

In 1953, by then a useful two-handicapper, the Dubliner came across an up-and-coming professional from Galway who was based in Bundoran called Christy O'Connor. *"This was one of my very first experiences playing with a pro in a pro-am. We played two rounds in the wet at Rosses Point and whatever language we spoke then, we are still speaking the same language together today, and that's for over 50 years now. We have remained very good friends".*

The pair became founding members of the ever-popular Links Golfing Society in 1966, alongside Cecil Whelan, who continues to run it over forty years later, with both O'Connor and Fogarty as Life Vice-Presidents and Des Smyth as its figurehead and President. (2007 Open Champion Padraig Harrington, who has been a member of the Links Society since he was 15, was awarded honorary life membership after his dramatic win at Carnoustie).

Portmarnock Golf Club, essentially across the road from the Fogarty home, never granted Noel Fogarty membership. Quite simply, his status as a bookie was not acceptable to those in power at the famous club in the late forties and early fifties. It's something that never sat well with Fogarty, but Portmarnock's loss was to be Royal Dublin's gain, where he was accepted as a member in 1958.

It's something that never sat well with Fogarty, but Portmarnock's loss was to be Royal Dublin's gain, where he was accepted as a member in 1958.

Not only did he become one of their most successful members, he was also one of their finest ambassadors, deriving enormous pride from his lifelong association with the world class Dollymount links. In 1959, O'Connor came up from Killarney to take up the position of professional at Fogarty's new club and their friendship grew even stronger. "*Christy O'Connor and I have been friends since 1953. I never called him anything else but the old pro and he was never very happy about it. In the middle of all that time we discovered, over a few drinks one night, that I was actually older! He said 'what date is on your birth certificate Fogey?' so I told him, and quick as a flash,*

Fogarty and O'Connor after winning the Gleneagles Foursomes Tournament in 1962.

Fogo shakes hands with the great Cecil Ewing after defeating the Co. Sligo legend in the quarter-final of the 1956 Irish Close Championship at Portmarnock.

he told me that he was born December 21st, so there were 16 days between us. He started calling me 'old man Fogey' from that day forward!"

Through his friendships with Carr and O'Connor, Fogarty was mixing with the best in the game. It did not go unnoticed that he too had a serious golf game. By 1956, Fogarty had reduced his handicap to scratch and made it to the semi-finals of the Irish Close Championship played at Portmarnock, beating Cecil Ewing in the last eight before going down to Dr Jim Mahon, who in turn lost to Joe Carr in the final. He was clearly playing to a very high standard and even contested the Open Championship that year, successfully pre-qualifying. He went on to play the first two rounds alongside triple Open winner Henry Cotton where he regrettably missed the 36-hole cut. The season did conclude on a high however with his first cap as an Irish International.

Life was certainly being lived in the fast lane. 1958 also saw him receive a call-up by the Walker Cup selectors for a trial, but a team spot did not go his way in the end, which disappointed not only Fogarty, but also his great friend Christy O'Connor, "I thought he was very unlucky that he didn't make the Walker Cup; I thought he was good enough to make the team. Noel was a very difficult player to beat because he had a magnificent eye on the green and was a very good putter, anything from 10 to 12 feet you could nearly give him. That was under pressure as well. He was a great competitor. I had many a good game with Noel."

On the domestic circuit, Fogarty became a formidable presence, contending in many Championships. A runner-up in the Irish Amateur Close at Portstewart to Michael Edwards in 1960, he was surprisingly omitted

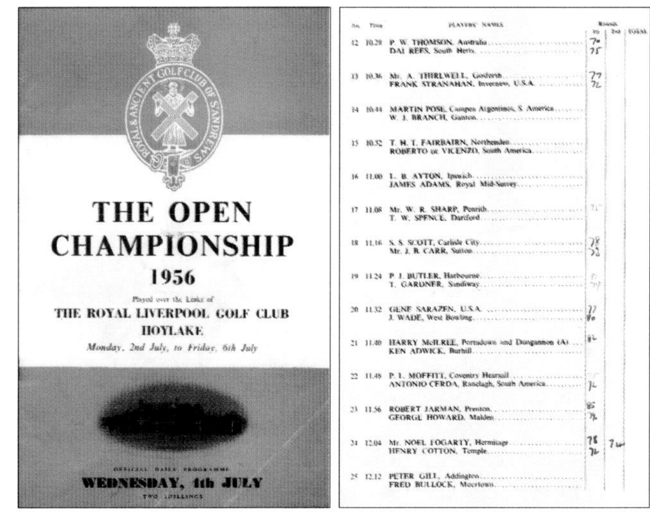
THE OPEN CHAMPIONSHIP
1956
Played over the Links of
THE ROYAL LIVERPOOL GOLF CLUB
HOYLAKE
Monday, 2nd July, to Friday, 6th July

OFFICIAL DAILY PROGRAMME
WEDNESDAY, 4th JULY
TWO SHILLINGS

No.	Time	PLAYERS' NAMES
12	10.28	P. W. THOMSON, Australia DAI REES, South Herts
13	10.36	Mr. A. THIRLWELL, Gosforth FRANK STRANAHAN, Inverness, U.S.A.
14	10.44	MARTIN POSE, Campos Argentinos, S. America W. J. BRANCH, Ganton
15	10.52	T. H. T. FAIRBAIRN, Northenden ROBERTO DE VICENZO, South America
16	11.00	L. B. AYTON, Ipswich JAMES ADAMS, Royal Mid-Surrey
17	11.08	Mr. W. R. SHARP, Penrith T. W. SPENCE, Dartford
18	11.16	S. S. SCOTT, Carlisle City Mr. J. B. CARR, Sutton
19	11.24	P. J. BUTLER, Harborne T. GARDNER, Sandiway
20	11.32	GENE SARAZEN, U.S.A. J. WADE, West Bowling
21	11.40	HARRY McILREE, Portadown and Dungannon (A) KEN ADWICK, Burhill
22	11.48	P. L. MOFFITT, Coventry Hearsall ANTONIO CERDA, Ranelagh, South America
23	11.56	ROBERT JARMAN, Preston GEORGE HOWARD, Malden
24	12.04	Mr. NOEL FOGARTY, Hermitage HENRY COTTON, Temple
25	12.12	PETER GILL, Addington FRED BULLOCK, Moortown

Souvenir programme cover from the Open at Hoylake in1956. FOGO is drawn with COTTON.

Through his friendships with Carr and O'Connor, Fogarty was mixing with the best in the game. It did not go unnoticed that he too had a serious golf game.

Noel Fogarty and his Irish team-mates at 1958 Home Internationals
Back row l to r: G.N. Fogarty, M. Edwards, G.A. Young, M.C. Dijon, J.W. Hulme.
Middle row l to r: G. McGlennon, T.W. Egan, Dr. R.E. Davitt (President G.U.I.), W.J.J. Ferguson, J. Harrington.
Front row l to r: C. Ewing, Dr. G.H. Owens (Captain), J.B. Carr, T. Craddock.

"To have taken the world's best amateur Jack Nicklaus down the nineteenth in the latter stages of an Amateur Championship says a great deal about his ability."
- Peter Alliss

from the Irish International team that year as he was considered, at 36, to be too old. He did however force himself back onto the team in 1963, having claimed his first major title at the East of Ireland in June of that year.

By the late sixties, Fogarty and Carr were "as thick as thieves", growing up around Portmarnock, they had always hunted in the same pack. From the earliest days playing golf on the three-hole municipal course bordering Portmarnock Golf Club, right through

"A brutish looking man with the most severe face. It was a face that belied his soft nature and I was ever so fond of him. Noel and his wife Bella were always wonderful company and I used to meet him a lot at tournaments like the Gleneagles Foursomes and of course, he played in several Open and Amateur Championships. To have taken the world's best amateur Jack Nicklaus down the nineteenth in the latter stages of an Amateur Championship says a great deal about his ability. A mightily talented golfer, he was unlucky not to have played Walker Cup but represented Ireland many, many times. Noel Fogarty was a terrific golfer and remains a good friend - Peter Alliss, May 2007 to Senior Cup battles and Championship action at home and abroad, their lives were intertwined. All in all, the two men only played each other in top flight competition three times and proudly, Fogarty was victor on two occasions, *"Joe always loved the one that he won, but I always liked the ones I won!. He beat me in the South of Ireland final in '69 (see Joe Carr chapter) and I won the South in '67, beating Joe in an earlier round.*" (Despite the obvious disappointment in losing, Carr just happened to have Fogarty in the sweep that year, so he was relieved that Fogo came through to win in the end, guaranteeing Carr a large payout!).

Noel with Scott MacDonald before the 1967 'South' Final.

1967 was arguably Fogarty's vintage year in Irish amateur golf. Winning 'the East' at Baltray over the Whit Weekend, he was in sparkling form as he headed to Lahinch for 'the South'. Taking the scalp of Joe Carr, as he did along the way, or in any Championship for that matter was always noteworthy, but for Noel Fogarty the real satisfaction came in winning the Championship outright for his second 'major' in a row. His opponent was a young Scotsman with a wonderful pedigree called Scott MacDonald.

Fundraising for the St Vincent de Paul, Fogo is pictured outside the Mansion House in Dublin with an assortment of Irish celebrities.
Front row l-r: Frankie Blowers (singer), Eddie Byrne (actor), Maureen Potter (entertainer) & JB Carr (Sutton GC).
Middle Row: Fogo, B.P.Malone (Sutton GC) & Noel Purcell (actor).
Back Row centre: Harry Perry (Boxer & Olympic Bronze Medallist 1956).

A Scottish international who would go on to make the famous 1971 Walker Cup winning team, he had every reason to feel confident against Fogarty given the age gap, and also the fact that he was playing well, having also reached the last four the previous year. In March of 2007, MacDonald reminisced on their encounter four decades before:

"Having beaten Pat Mulcare in an earlier round I was feeling fairly confident meeting Noel Fogarty in the 1967 final. He seemed 'old' at the time, but now that I am 62 myself, I would perhaps change my perception of old! The introductory handshake prior to commencing the match certainly made an impression. I have never felt such a strong grip and Noel's thick fingers almost crushed mine. I have no doubt he was not deliberately trying to injure or seriously intimidate me, but he definitely made me wince. The weather was a bit rough with a blustery wind and Noel's power

1967 was arguably Fogarty's vintage year in Irish amateur golf. Winning 'the East' at Baltray over the Whit Weekend, he was in sparkling form as he headed to Lahinch for 'the South'.

Fogo rips one off the tee.

play was perhaps more suited to the conditions. He drove better than me - at that time driving was the poorest part of my game - and I couldn't get enough of my iron shots sufficiently close to hole putts. I do recall that he made an eagle 3 at the second hole with a drive and 8-iron downwind and that rather set the tone for the round. Eventually he won 3&2 after a fairly close but ultimately, for me, disappointing match. We briefly met again socially at the Amateur Championship (Troon) the following year and I then discovered how full of life he was off the course!"

Scratch Cup Legend

Throughout the 1950's right up to the early '80's, the Scratch Cup was King! Every top golfer in the land aspired to victories in the big Championships, but very few emerged victorious. The Scratch Cups were hugely popular simply because they only took one day and, by and large, consisted of 36 holes strokeplay, usually on a Sunday.

From May to September, the Senior Scratch Cup circuit drew huge crowds of golfing enthusiasts to that weekend's venue, to gasp in awe at the shot-making ability of such big names as Joe Carr, Cecil Ewing, Jimmy Bruen, Tom Craddock et al. In those days, our leading amateurs were held in the highest regard, the play was very accessible for the golfing spectator and the standard very high.

Victories in the top Scratch Cups were coveted, and pilgrimages to Mullingar, Waterford, Killarney (for the famous foursomes tournament), Douglas and Castletroy, to name but five, were the lot of your typical scratch golfer of that era during the high season.

Noel Fogarty won and contended in a great many Scratch Cups and the stories of those great days are legend.

Noel Fogarty won and contended in a great many Scratch Cups and the stories of those great days are legion. One of his favourite tales concerns a very memorable Sunday adventure to Limerick City: *"It would have been in the early to mid-sixties and we always went down to Limerick for the Castletroy Scratch Cup. It was usually a two or three hour drive. That particular year, my brother John had a Mercedes 250 automatic. I was bringing a couple of lads down to Limerick so I asked him if I could borrow it for the weekend. He agreed and I swapped my Volkswagen for the Merc.*

We went to Mass at 7.30 in Gardiner Street. Joe Carr and Mick Fitzpatrick were going as well. I was driving with Tom Craddock, so out we went into the two cars. However, I had to go to Dolphin's Barn to pick up Dr. David Sheahan who had rung me and asked if he could have a lift.

Anyway, to make a long story short, I picked him up at 8:30 at the chapel in Dolphin's Barn. This was in the time before speed limits! I was full of petrol, so I picked him up and we got on to the Naas Road. I put the foot on the accelerator and sure nobody was awake at that hour going down the country, so it was foot to the floor all the way.

As Sheahan remembers it, "we were going down the old Naas dual carriageway, Noel was doing 120 miles an hour, because in his opinion, it was 60 on the left and 60 on the right, so that was the correct speed limit! Meanwhile Tom Craddock was reading the Sunday Independent upside down in the back seat!"

Fogarty continued: *"The roads were a lot different to now, you went through places like Naas, Newbridge, Kildare, and you never got below 50 miles per hour - you tramped on down the roads and you could rattle up a great speed. She was one hell of a car to go, I will say that for her, she could really motor. We pulled into the car park in Castletroy at 10 o'clock!*

Anyway, we played the Scratch Cup, which Tom Craddock won with a birdie on the 18th (Fogarty and seven others tied for second).

When racing and golf blended perfectly.
Noel is pictured receiving the 'Golden Ball' Trophy which he dominated in the sixties, winning three times before it became the Curragh Scratch Cup which he went on to win on two further occasions.
Making the presentation on this occasion in 1961 is the famous jockey Paddy Powell who was club captain. Given his success as a bookmaker, it shouldn't come as a surprise that his happiest hunting ground as a golfer should come at the Curragh Golf Club!

David Sheahan refused to come home with me, but Joe Carr decided he would take a lift. We were rather thirsty when we were coming across the Curragh and I said to Joe 'would you like a drink?' 'I wouldn't mind' he said. Now this is probably 10:45 at night, so we went up to the Curragh Golf Club (the scene of Fogarty's three victories in the famous 'Golden Ball' tournament) and I landed on my feet, as I always do. They had an extension so we got home at 4 in the morning. I dropped Joe home to Sutton and I came on home to Portmarnock!"

"we were going down the old Naas dual carriageway, Noel was doing 120 miles an hour, because in his opinion, it was 60 on the left and 60 on the right, so that was the correct speed limit!"
- David Sheahan

Fogo's distinctive Dublin brogue uttered the words 'Well, Jack, you never lost it!' Nicklaus turned around and upon recognising this character from his past, broke into a wide smile, and answered back, 'Noel, how are you?'

Life for Noel Fogarty was certainly busy in those great days. A successful bookie, he was in the unique position of affording golf the time it deserved, while attending to his career. *"Monday, Wednesday and Saturday evenings was Shelbourne Park for night-time greyhound racing. Harold's Cross was Tuesday, Thursday and Friday, so I was working six nights a week."*

In addition, there was also plenty of business for Fogo on the racetrack. Phoenix Park and Baldoyle (just a mile from his house) were popular race meetings back then but both have succumbed to closure and subsequent redevelopment as commercial parks and residential areas. Punchestown, the Curragh, Fairyhouse and Navan were all grist to the mill in what was a very full life. Fogarty loved every minute of it.

Not a man for an office job, if the weather was fine, he was down on the Royal Dublin practise ground hitting shots, meeting people and tuning up for a night at the dogs' or studying the form for the next race day.

Fogarty's ability to calculate the odds was honed from his earliest days when he collected his pocket money at the end of a week. He was no more than six or seven years of age and the remuneration was a six pence piece (the one with the greyhound!). *"My father used to give us our weekly money on a Sunday morning, at about midday. He would then play cards with us and win all our money off of us! When he had taken the money off you, he would give it back to you later and say that it was another lesson learned about gambling! To be honest, our life was gambling. I enjoyed all the racing. I worked at it. I suppose I would have to say I gave it as good a service as was possible. I started racing in 1942 and I finished in 1996. I worked for 54 years which is a good innings.*

Somebody said many years ago that no matter what you are doing in life, never neglect your business for pleasure. I said I always did it the other way round, I neglected my business so that I could have the pleasure, but that was only my joking way of playing! In my lifetime I did on a few occasions miss a race meeting, but it wasn't the end of the world. I missed as little as was possible. I made many friends and as far as I know I haven't got an enemy. If I have one, well then, it's their fault not mine. I just loved life and I loved people, I met everybody racing, from the Aga Khan to JP McManus and as I like to describe my career, I met the good, the bad and the ugly!"

As a footnote to an extraordinary tale and if there was ever a crystallizing moment in his golfing life and times, it came on Tuesday, July 24th, 2001, when Jack Nicklaus was warming up on the practice ground at Royal County Down. Not only was he playing in his first-ever Senior British Open but he was, at 61, making his competitive debut in Ireland.

There was a real buzz outside the ropes because the very mention of his name excited golf fans of all ages. Nicklaus is, after all, the most successful professional golfer of all time.

What was even more fascinating for those gathered there that day was that right next to the 'Bear' was Arnold Palmer, the player who brought the game to the masses in the late fifties and early sixties, by virtue of his swash-buckling style and magnetic charisma. The very sight of these two greats of the game, only yards away, was too good to be true. After striking some 15 to 20 balls with a mid-iron, the Golden Bear took a 'time-out' when a voice billowed out from beyond the rope cordoning off the players from the fans. Fogo's distinctive Dublin brogue uttered the words *'Well, Jack, you never lost it!'* Nicklaus turned around and upon recognising this character from his past, broke into a wide smile, and answered back, 'Noel, how are you?'

Fogo picks up the story, *"Jack dropped the club on*

the ground, came over, I stepped inside the rope and we shook hands warmly and patted each other on the shoulder. We talked for what seemed like a couple of minutes and the next thing Palmer turned around and said, 'what's all the noise here, I can't do my practise!' So he walked over. Jack said 'Noel and I are old friends, have you ever met Noel 'Foggerty'? (sic) and before he could reply I said 'Arnie and I met quite a few years ago at the Canada Cup in Portmarnock, Joe Carr introduced us'. Palmer said 'yes, I remember that and I remember Joe Carr telling me not to have a row with you, because you used to be a boxer!' said Palmer.

And who would doubt him? Noel Fogarty truly has met them all, in a life lived to the very full. These days, in his eighties, life is still very much enjoyed by Noel and his wife Bella. Rounds at Royal Dublin are a little sparser these days, but holidays in his caravan in Connemara and time spent with old friends like Christy O'Connor and his cronies at the golf club are savoured, along with the odd pint or two.

Gerard Noel Fogarty. A gentle giant who most certainly made his mark in Irish sporting life.

82 year-old Noel Fogarty pictured on the balcony of the new clubhouse at Royal Dublin in May, 2007. The famous 18th hole is behind him.

Jack said 'Noel and I are old friends, have you ever met Noel 'Foggerty'? (sic) and before he could reply I said 'Arnie and I met quite a few years ago at the Canada Cup in Portmarnock.'

CAREER HIGHLIGHTS

Name: Gerard Noel Fogarty

Date of Birth: December 5th 1924

Birthplace: Dublin

Family: Married to Isabella (Bella), 6 children: Isabella, Gerard, Caroline, Gregory, Noelle, David & Jill.

Club: The Royal Dublin Golf Club

Lowest Handicap: Scratch

CHAMPIONSHIP HIGHLIGHTS

British Open Championship
Played in Championship proper in 1956 alongside Henry Cotton, but missed cut. Failed to pre-qualify in 1957 & 1958.

British Amateur Championship
6 appearances

Best performance was in 1959, taking Jack Nicklaus to the 19th hole in the 4th round at Royal St Georges.

Irish Amateur Close Championship
Runner-up in 1960
Semi-finalist in 1963, losing to Eric O'Brien, who went on to lose the final to Joe Carr.
Semi-finalist in 1956 (losing to Dr. Jim Mahon, who was beaten by JB Carr in final).

Irish Seniors Amateur Open Championship
Winner in 1980 & 1981 (1st man to successfully defend title).

East of Ireland Amateur Open Championship
Winner in 1963 & 1967
Runner-up in 1957 & 1969

South of Ireland Amateur Open Championship
Winner in 1967
Runner-up 1969

West of Ireland Amateur Open Championship
Only played once in the early fifties as it always clashed with Easter Racing Festival at Fairyhouse and Irish Grand National.

North of Ireland Amateur Open Championship
Played 4 times but found that the excellent social life in Portrush had an adverse affect on his golf!

REPRESENTATIVE HONOURS:

International: 26 caps for Ireland between1956-1967

Walker Cup: Selected for trials at Fulwell GC, London 1958, but was unsuccessful.

Interprovincial: 65 caps for Leinster from 1956-1970

MISCELLANEOUS

Irish Senior Cup: Playing Captain of winning Royal Dublin team in 1969

Barton Shield: Playing Captain of winning Royal Dublin team in 1968

Scratch Cup Victories
Douglas (once), Dundalk (twice) Curragh (twice).

Killarney Foursomes
Victorious on 3 occasions with J.B. Carr: 1961, 1962 & 1966

Gleneagles Foursomes
Winner in 1962 with Christy O'Connor

Golden Ball Tournament (Curragh G.C)
Winner three times

Philomena Garvey

The Garvey Mystique: The sports shop manager from Baltray who won the British Open.

"Philomena Garvey set a standard of excellence in Irish golf that has never been equalled. In fact, such was her dominance over a twenty-five year period, it is unlikely that anyone will ever come close to her success on the fairways. Her contribution to golf on these islands has been immense and her strength of character, in particular in 1958, when she took on the Ladies Golf Union over the changing of the emblem for that year's Curtis Cup, is something that we in Ireland should be truly proud of and never forget. Philomena Garvey is a golfing national treasure."

ANNE TUNNEY, Centenary President of the Irish Ladies Golf Union, 1993.

"I loved matchplay. I didn't talk to anybody. I concentrated so hard, that the other person wasn't there."

The pride of Baltray Philomena Garvey signs autographs at the British Open Amateur Championship in Gullane, 1947. Beside her is Mildred 'Babe' Zaharias, the eventual winner and former double Olympic Champion. Zaharias described Garvey as 'the best they've ever produced over there'.

Queen of the Fairways

In terms of amateur golfing success, Philomena Garvey was the female equivalent of Joe Carr, dominating to such an extent in the same era, and for such a prolonged period that her record will never be surpassed. Her achievements as a golfer are simply astounding and her billing as Ireland's 'Queen of the Fairways' remains totally justified.

Making five British Amateur Championship finals in three successive decades and playing a key role in six Curtis Cup teams, in addition to her record haul of Irish Amateur wins gives some indication of her supremacy in the sport. What makes her even more intriguing however is that like Ben Hogan, there still remains a certain mystique about Philomena Garvey.

Whether it was contrived or not, Garvey had a real aura about her. In golfing terms, it was that rare quality which enabled her to strike fear into the hearts of her opponents and in some way too, it may have deterred many from even attempting to get close on a more personal level.

"I loved matchplay. I didn't talk to anybody. I hadn't time to talk to anybody during a match. Opponents probably thought that I was very unfriendly but I didn't mean to be. I concentrated so hard that the other person wasn't there, if you know what I mean. I remember playing Zelie Fallon in the Irish Final in Carlow. She was a lovely person, I was very fond of her and got on great with her, but on this occasion, we were going out to play the match and she turned to me and said, 'how am I supposed to beat you Phil, you're the British Open Champion'. I just responded that if that was how she wanted to look at it, it was up to her. In other words, she was beaten before we even went out. If you're not in the right frame of mind when you play a match, you can't give it your best shot. That's why I played in silence, because I knew that I produced my best golf when I was concentrating well and for me, there was only one way to do it!"

In talking to those who knew Philomena from those days of competitive golf (and having had the privilege to meet extensively with her in researching this book), all are united in acknowledging that Philomena Garvey is a very special woman indeed.

Beginnings

Born in 1926 in the golfing village of Baltray, she was reared in a house behind the well-known '19th' pub, a mere stone's throw from one of Ireland's greatest links courses, County Louth Golf Club. Garvey, like nearly all the locals, could not avoid the attractions of the game:

"We only lived a hundred yards from the golf club and my brothers were all good golfers. Kevin played off plus 3 and won 'the East' in 1942; Des and Nick were both low enough single-figure players. I just loved the game, it's as simple as that. From an early age, ten or eleven, I remember my father (James) coming out to the course looking for me - it was getting dark. I couldn't get enough of it. Kevin taught me at the beginning, but he gave me a dreadful grip! For the whole of my golfing life, I played golf with my left thumb resting under my right hand, down the right side of the grip. It was dreadful, but I was stuck with it."

In many ways, with an interlocking grip and her thumb in such a position, it gave her a very firm control over the club, but it was far from conventional. So much so that Henry Cotton, when seeing her at her peak in 1957, advised only one thing: 'to change the way that she held the club', but as Phil categorically states: *"I wasn't able!"*

Her initial entrée into the game came through the caddy ranks and via the encouragement of her older siblings. *"I caddied for Clarrie Reddan when I was a child. Clarrie was ten years older than me and had been Irish Champion* (in 1936) *and a Curtis Cup player* (1938). *She was the greatest thing since the high bike!"* As a child-caddy, Phil had a terrific eye for reading greens and selecting clubs, and both Clarrie and her future husband Val both availed of her talents as often as was possible.

Clearly inspired by her older brothers' proficiency at the sport, her innate competitive tendencies were developing through games with them. In fact, it was something that she would refer to in later years as her talent blossomed, acknowledging that her years playing against men was instrumental in developing her considerable length, matchplay skills and sound swing.

In many ways, from those early days as a youngster, she did her own thing with regard to learning the game's fundamentals. The love for the game was God-given, so a keen eye when watching good players taught her everything that she'd ever need to know. Garvey was finally accepted as a full member of the club in the early 1940's, when as a young teenager, it was obvious that she had a unique gift for the game. As her handicap plummeted, so too began an intense battle for supremacy between her and Clarrie, which would continue for many years.

When Garvey captured her first Leinster title in 1945 (at the age of 19), a changing of the guards was beginning to evolve. Irish championship golf resumed after the break for WW2 in 1946 and supporters were increasingly fascinated at the emerging rivalry between 'the Queen' and the heir-apparent.

A full 'hand-over' would not fully take place until the start of the 1950's however, so for the remainder of the post-war years, as the game was re-kindled in Ireland, these two club-mates engaged in regular combat for bragging rights. This was illustrated most notably when they contested the final of the Irish Amateur Championship at Lahinch in May of 1946. The game's biggest name prior to the outbreak of war versus this bright new talent – neighbour versus neighbour, club-mate versus club-mate.

The old class values of the era were very much in evidence when the majority of Baltray members who travelled to Lahinch seemed to be on Reddan's side. Unfair? Yes, but a reflection of the times more than anything else. As a former caddy, Garvey was not

Henry Cotton, when seeing her at her peak in 1957, advised only one thing: 'to change the way that she held the club', but as Phil categorically states, "I wasn't able!"

Clarrie Reddan and Philomena Garvey pictured when they contested the Irish Close final again two years later at Rosslare in 1948.

accorded the same respect as her clubmate, despite a breathtaking mastery of the game for one so young.

This of course, was no fault of Reddan's, who was not only the star of Irish golf in the years immediately before the war, but who also possessed a charismatic personality and had been brought up by parents who were long-established club members. Clarrie's mother May Tiernan, was a driving force at Baltray and Clarrie's husband Val Reddan was a long-time member and low handicapper. His father, Denis Reddan, had been a prominent town councillor and was very involved in the earliest days of the Co. Louth club. Garvey could not lay claim to such an established golfing background, but it did, undoubtedly, stir her competitive juices and in many ways, gave her the drive to succeed in the only way she knew how; with grit and sheer determination, to beat whomever crossed her competitive path.

Clarrie Reddan recalled that *"I missed a putt on the 36th hole from six feet, that I should have got really, but I didn't do it, so that was that."*

In the final itself, there was very little between the pair, and while they were on reasonably friendly terms, both were fiercely competitive. The 36-hole final at Lahinch was nothing short of spectacular, with Reddan shooting approximate figures of one under par to lead by 1 hole at the end of the first 18. What followed after lunch however was quite simply, the most exciting conclusion to a championship final that Lahinch and indeed Irish Ladies golf had ever witnessed at that time.

Garvey, displaying the sort of tenacity and fight that would become her hallmark in the years to come, proceeded to win the first six holes by shooting two under par and found herself 5 up in the match. After trading birdies on the 7th and 8th holes, she birdied the ninth to be 6 up with nine to play!

This was 1946 remember, and the huge crowds that had gathered on the County Clare links that day were being given a master-class by the sensational twenty year-old, who was taking the Championship by storm. The tenth hole was halved but then Reddan won the short 11th with a par. Her form did a sudden about-turn and she staged a miraculous comeback. With huge support from the gallery, she proceeded to play the back six in one under - she won six of the last eight holes to level the match and force it into a play-off. Garvey was absolutely stunned!

"Clarrie was a very good golfer and had a lot of experience, but I was 5-up and ended up having to hole a five-footer to half the match (on the 36th) and go into extra holes. I probably got nervous. It was my first big final. I had just turned twenty and Clarrie was ten years older and had won the Irish title a decade before. I missed a couple of short putts on the back nine that day which still annoy me!"

As the late Clarrie Reddan recalled to me in October of 2005, the title was hers for the taking on the final green, but her birdie putt slipped by and the match, proclaimed by many as the greatest ever played at Lahinch for its drama and quality play, went into sudden death. *"I missed a putt on the 36th hole from six feet that I should have got really, but I didn't do it, so that was that."*

After halves on the first and second play-off holes, the match continued to the 21st, the tricky par-three third (which is no longer part of the course). As Garvey remembers, "*I was on the green at the 21st and missed my long range birdie putt. The ball finished close to the hole. Clarrie chipped up from over the back of the green and left herself about eight feet away, but my ball was dead on her line, so she really had no option* (but to concede). *She could have tried to give her ball a wallop, in order to knock my ball out of the way, but she ran the risk of knocking my ball into the hole, so she had to concede, and we shook hands.*"

As Clarrie Reddan put it: *"it was a marathon all right. Phil won it with that stymie. She got away. We used to practise stymies a lot with a niblick (9-iron) that you pitched over the ball. Then you had to have a certain length of green beyond the ball to land on to get it into the hole. The stymie she laid me was unplayable, I couldn't play it. She was let loose there all right!"*

Garvey had won her first national title and was well and truly on her way. However, people could scarcely believe how quickly she would make a name for herself *away* from home, when she decided to test herself in the biggest championship of them all.

Her first British Amateur

Only weeks after her success at Lahinch, the twenty year-old Garvey was the surprise package in winning her way to a final showdown at the 1946 British Amateur Open Championship at Hunstanton on the Norfolk coast.

In making the final, Garvey had quite literally taken the Ladies' game by storm. It was the first major Championship since the war had ended and the international championships were only finding their feet again after such a prolonged suspension.
Her opponent was Jean Hetherington (née McClure); a great swinger of the golf club but it still took her until the last of the 36 holes to beat Ireland's brightest young talent, in a thrilling contest. Speaking 61 years after that first big break, Garvey proudly smiles when recalling her self-assurance at that time:

"I thought that I was a great golfer!" she says quite matter-of-factly, *"and I'll tell you why. I had great confidence in myself and my ability. I travelled to my first British Open feeling that I couldn't be beaten! I remember going into the pro shop ahead of that final at Hunstanton and buying four or five new Dunlop balls, they were number fives. Jean Hetherington was there and she immediately piped up, "you can't play those, I'm playing number fives!" I remember saying quietly to myself, that it doesn't matter one way or the other, I'll beat you anyway! That's how cocky I was, I was too young to have nerves."*

Clarrie Reddan, who followed her clubmate that day (and carried a bag of fruit as back-up, should Phil require sustenance) remembers being particularly annoyed by the antics of Hetherington's husband: "He was a nuisance. He was in the way everywhere, walking around and telling her what club to play and how to play this chip and that chip and the club would go back into the bag and another one would be taken out. It really was too much. I didn't like that business at all!" she said. For Garvey, her concentration was such that she was unaware of the commotion that her opponent's bagman was causing. *"I don't remember any of that at all, to be honest. I was too busy concentrating. If you are concentrating properly, you are completely focussed on your own game and you don't hear or see anything other than what you are supposed to be focussed on. For me, it was always about giving 100% to every shot. If my concentration was what it should be, then I was completely oblivious to everything else around me. However, there was one thing about her husband which I did notice and that was when he'd attend the flag. He always stood in such a way as to give his wife*

"I thought that I was a great golfer! I had great confidence in myself and my ability"

the line of the putt, but there was nothing I could really do about it."

Garvey lost to Hetherington, but while disappointed, she felt a great upsurge in confidence that she could compete for the biggest prizes: *"It didn't bother me. I was probably too young and reckoned that I'd win it another time, there'd be plenty of opportunities."*

It was the beginning of one of the most impressive periods of dominance of the women's game on these islands. The following year she defeated Kitty MacCann (née Smye) of Tullamore in the final at Portrush, before going on to claim an incredible hat-trick of titles, by once again defeating Clarrie Reddan in the final of 1948. The clubmates then enjoyed the notable distinction of both being selected to play in the Curtis Cup later that year.

While dominating at home, Garvey also received her second Curtis Cup cap in 1950 and while in America, made it to the last eight of the US Amateur Championship, losing to the eventual champion Beverly Hanson.

It was to be the beginning of one of the most impressive periods of dominance of the women's game in these islands.

Garvey, MacCann and Reddan were ***the*** biggest names in Irish Ladies golf at the time, and all were uniquely linked - they could each lay claim to having reached the final of the British Amateur Open Championship. Following Philomena's loss in '46, Reddan finished runner-up in 1949 at Harlech (Royal St David's), while MacCann became the first Irish winner of the title since May Hezlett in 1907, when she defeated Frances 'Bunty' Stephens by 4 & 3 to win in Broadstone, Dorset in 1951.

1953 was widely recognised as one of the greatest years in the golf world after Ben Hogan's remarkable treble of the US Masters, US Open and British Open. It is fitting, from an Irish standpoint that Irish golfers were also making their mark. Harry Bradshaw became

The Great Triumvirate of Irish Womens Golf. Kitty MacCann, Phil Garvey and Clarrie Reddan pictured at the Irish Close Championship at Baltray in 2000

the first player from the Republic of Ireland to play in the Ryder Cup, Joe Carr won his first British Amateur Championship at Hoylake and that June also saw Philomena Garvey's name back on the back pages when, once again, she came ever so close to joining the game's greatest achievers, by making the final of the British Women's Amateur Open at Royal Porthcawl in Wales.

It was not to be, regrettably, when for a second time, she was runner-up in the final, this time losing to the teenage Canadian sensation Marlene Stewart by 7 & 6. Two runners-up spots in seven years in the biggest Championship of them all left some observers wondering 'if' rather than 'when', she would ever claim that most elusive piece of silverware. As she reminisced at her home in Baltray she admitted: *"I think I would have been very sad if I didn't win it, because in those days it was* **the** *major championship to win. Everybody played in it in those days, the Americans, the Canadians and the Continentals. It was* **the** *one to win."*

The Golden Year

Ten years after beating Kitty MacCann (née Smye) in the Irish Close final of 1947, Garvey returned to her spiritual home and favoured Dunluce links at Royal Portrush, to once again stamp her authority on the ladies game here in Ireland. She accounted for Miss MacCann once more in the final, although this was a much tighter contest over two rounds. As Kitty MacCann recalled to me in November of 2005 at her home club in Tullamore: "it was a very close match. I had played against Phil at Portrush not long before the Championship and we finished all square after 18. I remember Stevie (renowned Portrush professional P.G. Stevenson) saying that I'd regret not beating her ahead of the Championship, it might have given me more confidence (ahead of the main event).

Phil was a lovely person to play against, there wouldn't be much chatting going on shall we say, but that was fine, you got on with your game and she got on with hers. Phil always played the course. In my view, you couldn't meet a nicer opponent. I have to say though that I used to out-drive her consistently by about twenty or thirty yards, but she was absolutely fantastic from fifty yards in, the ball was always dropping in around the flag."

Garvey eventually triumphed by 3 & 2 in the deciding match and knew that such a contest was perfect preparation for the upcoming British Open the following month.

Arriving at Gleneagles, she was not only brimming with confidence in relation to her game; she also enjoyed the splendour of the estate, with its hotel and facilities, which was offered to competitors at the reduced rate of three pounds a night. "*I had never been there before. It was a very posh place and I laughed to myself that this place is going to suit me! I was also feeling good about my game after winning the Irish Amateur Championship and I had practised for a couple of hours a day in the lead up to it".*

It should also be mentioned that anyone from the 'home countries' fancying their chances of making it all the way to the final would also want to be in good physical shape; the Home Internationals were being played in the immediate lead-up to the championship proper. The International matches began on the Thursday, with morning foursomes and afternoon singles. They concluded on the Saturday, before a rest day on Sunday, in readiness for the Open Amateur Championship which would begin on the Monday.

In making the final on the following Thursday, Philomena Garvey had played thirty-six holes a day for seven out of the previous eight days! *"It makes me laugh when I hear of professionals getting tired these days",* she says with a mischievous glint of the eye.

The whole of Ireland's golfing establishment felt that her time was now due and that it would be third time lucky but she still had to beat one of the greatest players of that era, in the final. Scotland's Jessie Valentine was already a two-time Amateur Champion and was a golfer of rare talent. In addition to winning the national championships in France and New Zealand, she went on to win the British Open one more time the following year and but for the war, would surely have added to her seven Curtis Cup caps.

It certainly looked good for the Baltray superstar when she negotiated the first eighteen holes without a 3-putt and found herself three up at lunch. In punishing, wet conditions, her previous experiences at this level gave her a crucial edge. *"I only wore waterproof slacks, I couldn't wear a top. I don't like making excuses, but it rained in that first British Open final in 1946, and I put on this waterproof top and I hit the ball and I missed it completely, it only went about 25 yards. I said to myself, never again!"*

Immediately after lunch, she produced a stunning escape from the unforgiving Dun Whinney bunker to force a half and remain 3 up. However, Valentine's

In making the British Open final on the following Thursday, Philomena Garvey had played thirty-six holes a day for seven out of the previous eight days!

class came to the fore when she reeled off two holes in a row at the 20th and 21st holes to narrow the deficit to just one. Garvey, regained both holes by the 24th before disaster apparently struck. Having successfully found the fairway at the seventh hole, she was walking over a small wooden bridge, when her foot got caught in one of the laths.

As she attempted to extract it, she knew immediately that she was in trouble - she felt a darting pain in her ankle. She was struck by the thought that all of her hard work could be undone in that instant and given that she had broken the same ankle some years previously, she feared that she would be forced to concede the match through injury.

Her opponent was seemingly oblivious to all of this, and was bounding on up the fairway towards her bunkered drive. Garvey was now under pressure not to lose ground and was completely unsure as to whether her ankle would withstand the obvious pressure of not alone walking, but the golf swing itself.

Luckily, amongst the spectators braving the wet conditions was her international colleague and friend Kitty MacCann, the 1951 champion. She was walking with the match alongside her husband Pat, who was a veterinary surgeon in Tullamore. In no time at all, he had removed Garvey's shoe and bound her ankle with his handkerchief. The damage wasn't as bad as was initially feared. *"It was sore for about ten minutes, then it was okay. Nevertheless I got a bit of a fright!"*

As the Irish Press reported, courtesy of Scottish journalist Willie Allison:

"This brief respite would prove to be enough, as she recovered to her feet and limped back into action, drawing approving rounds of applause from the already drenched spectators. Valentine had bunkered her drive and Garvey, despite the injury, managed to win with a four, to go four up with 11 holes to play. It was an especially trying day for both players, given that the rain was consistently falling throughout and there were thirty-six holes to contend with, as was traditional with the championship-decider. A small Irish contingent had made its way to Gleneagles, including Garvey's older brother Des, but as was reasonable to expect, the majority of spectators were Scottish and respectfully partisan."

Valentine, in a fighting display of real class, was far from finished however, and claimed the 26th and 27th holes to once more reduce the deficit to just two. The momentum thankfully, remained with the Baltray star. On the 435 yard 31st hole (the 13th), she rammed home her advantage with a terrific second shot to the heart of the green with a spoon (3 wood) to get back to three-up. Boosted immeasurably by this crucial forward move, she immediately claimed the 32nd hole, by getting up and down for a winning par from just off the green at the par three. Philomena Garvey was now four-up with four to play, and finally within reach of golf's Holy Grail.

Frank Moran, writing in the Irish Times, picks up the story:

"It was now virtually all over, for a certain war-weariness had crept into Mrs. Valentine. The straighter and stronger Irish player was too much for even will-to-win gallantry."

"It was now virtually all over, for a certain war-weariness had crept into Mrs. Valentine. The straighter and stronger Irish player was too much for even will-to-win gallantry."
- Frank Moran, *Irish Times*

Valentine's fighting qualities remained until the bitter end however, and she drew a huge round of applause from the soaked spectators when she holed a thirty-foot putt for par on the 15th green (33rd). *"She holed an absolute raker for her par and I was left with this crooked little five-footer for the match!"*

Unperturbed by her opponent's wonderful effort, Garvey stepped up to her putt and calmly stroked it home for a decisive half and the Championship, by the margin of 4 & 3. She had finally done it; the 'Queen

Double Champion.
Philomena Garvey with her British Open and Irish Close Trophies in 1957

of Irish Golf' had finally placed both hands on the most prized championship trophy in the Ladies game.

For Philomena Garvey, Valentine's was a notable scalp but no more than she deserved, having herself served an apprenticeship in this great Championship over 11 long years. Remarking after her hard fought 33-hole, ordeal, Garvey summed up her feelings by telling one journalist that *"it was worth getting drowned for!"*

Speaking to me on the fiftieth anniversary of her greatest moment, she fondly recalled the commotion that it caused: *"At the Railway Station in Drogheda, the Brass and Reed band were there to greet me with a huge group of people. It was a wonderful night."* Her jubilant homecoming also saw bunting draped across the road into Baltray reading 'Baltray's Pride, Phil'. There were celebrations too in Drogheda, where she was accorded a civic reception and of course at her home club, where she entered the front door of the clubhouse under a guard of honour, with members holding woods and irons aloft. A memorable occasion indeed, and such a worthy winner.

A guard of honour greets the new British Open Champion on her arrival at the clubhouse at Baltray in June 1957. Escorting her is club captain Noel McQuillan.

Her jubilant homecoming also saw bunting draped across the road into Baltray reading "Baltray's Pride, Phil"

Philomena makes her way through the jubilant crowds at Baltray on her homecoming from Gleneagles. On her immediate right are Club officers Peter McGuirk and Jack Gannon.

Curtis Cup

Philomena Garvey played on six Curtis Cup teams between 1948 and 1960 and was a key member of two winning sides, in 1952 at Muirfield and 1956 at Prince's. It should have been seven caps but for a dispute with the Ladies Golfing Union in 1958 over the changing of the Curtis Cup team badge to the Union Jack. The previous emblem signified the four countries, England, Scotland, Wales and Ireland, all of whom qualified to play in the Great Britain and Ireland team.

Garvey, in an effort to make a valid point and at the same time not deny herself a well-deserved place on the team, wrote to the LGU to outline her opposition to the new badge and offered instead to wear her old badge. After a further meeting, they voted to retain the new badge and as a consequence, she did not play in the matches at Brae Burn, Michigan. The team went on to retain the Cup, by virtue of a 4 ½ - 4 ½ draw. Ironically, Daisy Ferguson of Royal County Down, the President of the Irish Ladies Golf Union in 1958, also happened to be the non-playing captain of the Curtis Cup team that year. Ferguson was in an impossible position, but to her credit, gave her support to Phil Garvey when examining the situation, subsequent to the dispute. According to Garvey however, when Ferguson returned after yet another meeting in England, she called Garvey aside. "*She said to me that the badge will be a Union Jack... 'you won't let me down will you?' I said that I'd have to think about it and I thought and I thought and I thought.*"

"she said to me that the badge will be a Union Jack ... 'you won't let me down will you?' I said that I'd have to think about it and I thought and I thought and I thought."

In the end, with so much press speculation about the matter, Paul MacWeeney of The Irish Times convinced her to hold a press conference, which was hastily arranged in Jury's Hotel on Dame Street. The journalists asked if she was going to play in the matches and after a few seconds, as Garvey recalled it, she said, *"No I'm not. It's the original emblem or not at all."*

The ILGU's Central Council, headed by Audrey Donohue wrote a letter of protest to the Ladies Golf Union, 'deploring the fact that the question of a Union Jack was not put on the agenda of the February (1958) meeting of the Executive Council of the LGU. In view of the fact that it must have been obvious that the Union Jack badge could not be acceptable to many Irish Ladies Golf Union players, the Council considers that the ILGU should have been given an opportunity to put their case before a decision was reached'.

In any case, the ILGU urged Daisy Ferguson to continue as captain of the Curtis Cup side, despite her offer to resign. She did travel in the end and guided the team to that draw. *"In my view, nobody could play after me if I didn't take my stance about the Union Jack, not Mary McKenna or Ita Butler or any other Irishwoman, so I felt that as a player I had to make my views known."*

She is unrepentant, even fifty odd years later. *"I got a few rude letters from England, but I was happy with my stance. Even Reverend Ian Paisley wrote an article in one newspaper saying that I had a cheek causing such a fuss, given that I'd played so much of my championship golf in England!"*

In hindsight, had Garvey been on the team as she had deserved to be, and given that she was the previous year's British Amateur champion, it's fair to suggest that a first-ever victory on American soil would have been achieved.

Despite winning an astonishing six-out-of-seven Irish Amateur Championships between 1957 and 1963 and finishing runner-up in two further British Amateur Championships in 1960 and 1963, Philomena Garvey played on just one more Curtis Cup team, when the home side lost at Lindrick in 1960. It remains a sore point that she didn't get picked for the matches in 1962 in Colorado Springs. *"I think it was their way of getting back at me!"* Ireland would have to wait until 1966 before Ita Butler (née Burke) of Elm Park Golf Club was capped for the matches in Hot Springs, Virginia and four years later, the record-breaking run of Mary McKenna, who went on to play in nine consecutive teams, began in earnest.

Philomena (second from right) alongside her Curtis Cup team-mates in 1956 at Prince's Golf Club, Kent. Captain Zara Bolton is holding the trophy won by Great Britain and Ireland after they defeated the USA by 5 & 4.

In hindsight, had Garvey been on the team as she had deserved to be, and given that she was the previous year's British Amateur champion, it's fair to suggest that a first ever victory on American soil would have been achieved.

Matchplay

As a star golfer, Garvey had what all the great players possess: huge self confidence and the ability to intimidate. Like Joe Carr, as her legend grew, so did this aura of invincibility. To many players, the idea of lining up against her in a matchplay tournament in the fifties and sixties was not to be relished.

In ways she was ahead of her time. Like Joe Carr, she had a very gladiatorial attitude. It was simply a case of kill or be killed, in matchplay terms. *"Never show any sign of weakness, never give an opponent an opportunity to feel superior."* She clearly loved the combat aspect of the game.

Lining up against Garvey in the matchplay rounds of a Championship was unnerving. There was little or no chat, apart from the traditional handshake on the first tee and a mannerly "best of luck". Garvey would inform her opponent of the number of her golf ball and there would be no more conversation until the match was over. This was her way and boy did it work!

To many players, the idea of lining up against her in a matchplay tournament in the fifties and sixties was not to be relished.

The Garvey backswing.
In action in the US Open Amateur Championship at East Lake CC in 1950.

A Working Life

Philomena Garvey worked in Clery's from 1952 until 1988. Mary Guiney, who died in 2004 at the age of 103, was chairwoman of Clery's department store and was a great fan of Garvey, having herself enjoyed the game through her membership of St Anne's and Clontarf Golf Clubs. Knowing the demands of Championship golf, she facilitated Philomena's need in the early days to get time off from work to play at the top level events.

Talk to any aspiring young golfer in the early sixties and their faces light up at the memories of the legendary Philomena selling them their first golf club. Running the golf section of Clery's Department Store on O'Connell Street in Dublin, she took a great interest in youngsters and was known to be 'flexible' on price. As Ryder Cup player and 1982 Irish Open Champion John O'Leary attests, his life in golf began with a trip to town for a very special purchase. *"In 1962, my mother brought me to Clery's and Philomena sold me my first ever set of clubs. I was just taking up the game in that year and when she knew that they were for me, she gave my mother a nice bit of discount. She always knocked the price down a bit if a youngster was involved in the purchase!"*

Turning Professional

Having won the Irish Amateur Championship for a fourteenth time in June 1963 and after her fourth runners-up spot in the British Amateur Open the previous month at Royal Co. Down, Philomena decided to forsake her amateur status and turn

Philomena Garvey pictured with shop 'visitors' Dr. Patrick Hillery, President of Ireland (member of Lahinch and Portmarnock) and his wife Maeve in the late seventies at Clerys Department Store in Dublin.

professional. Such a move was unheard of in Irish ladies golf at the time and it most certainly raised eyebrows. There was no organised professional tour for women even in Britain at this point, so the rumour mill swung quickly into action that she would be heading to the United States to compete on the growing LPGA Tour. This however, was mere speculation.

Her decision to turn professional was not motivated by a desire to test her skills in professional tournament golf - it was more due to the fact that she had tired of the relentless grind of Championship and representative golf, and had achieved all of her goals. It's worth pointing out though, that some ten years earlier, Fred Corcoran, the driving force behind the professional game in America in the post-war era had attempted to cajole Garvey into the 'playing for pay' ranks. He knew how well respected she was at the time, in the eyes of his leading lights like Babe Zaharias and Patty Berg. Garvey resisted then and a decade later, in 1963, she was of the same opinion about going to play in the US.

As a great student of the golf swing, she believed that she still had plenty to offer the game and that a new career as a golf coach was a good option. So, at 37 years of age, she began a new chapter in her golfing life. *"I just thought that I'd like to do a bit of teaching"*, she recalled.

She was still working for the sports department in Clery's Department Store on O'Connell Street in Dublin, where she had been since 1952. The company was now free to advertise the fact that Philomena was on hand to give expert advice on their extensive golf range in stock, given that she had gone professional. In the past, any mention of her employment there for advertising purposes would have been in serious breach of her amateur status. Interestingly, when she first started working in the department store, she had to receive permission from the R&A in order to accept a job in sports retailing.

As she settled into life as Ireland's only woman golf professional, she began to receive offers from a variety of golf clubs around the country to conduct coaching clinics, usually for a day or so, at irregular intervals. However, she never became attached to any one golf club in a professional capacity, during her time away from the amateur ranks.

In addition, at the beginning of 1964, she contributed a special series of golf lessons on a twice-weekly basis for the Evening Herald newspaper. The club

As she settled into life as Ireland's only woman golf professional, she began to receive offers from a variety of golf clubs around the country to conduct coaching clinics, usually for a day or so, at irregular intervals.

Philomena Garvey-Shot Master.

manufacturers John Letters also brought out a set of irons bearing her name. Curiously, the Irish Ladies Golf Union never enlisted her to work with their national or district teams, which in many ways was a serious oversight, given her unparalleled input into the women's game in Ireland during her halcyon days as a player. However, as she was leaving the amateur ranks, the Union did acknowledge her unique contribution to Irish amateur golf, by making her a Life Vice President of the ILGU.

At 43 years of age, she was some way past her peak. However, her formidable reputation was such that she still commanded huge respect from players.

The Last Hurrah

By the mid-sixties, Phil had tired of teaching and the professional game. It had been a nomadic existence and in many respects, she had been way ahead of her time in taking this direction in the first place. *"After a couple of years, I got a bit fed up with it and I decided to give it up and look for re-instatement, but I had to wait another two years."*

In May of 1970, given that Royal Portrush was the venue, Philomena decided to enter the Irish Amateur Close Championship. Despite being a fourteen-time winner, her re-appearance in Championship circles caused remarkably little media speculation. At 43 years of age, she was some way past her peak. However, her formidable reputation was such that she still commanded huge respect from players.

Garvey wasn't exactly brimming with her usual confidence. *"In the lead-up to the event, I was playing really poorly. I nearly didn't go up there, it was so bad, but as soon as I got there, I played 18 holes and played great, and it continued through the week."*

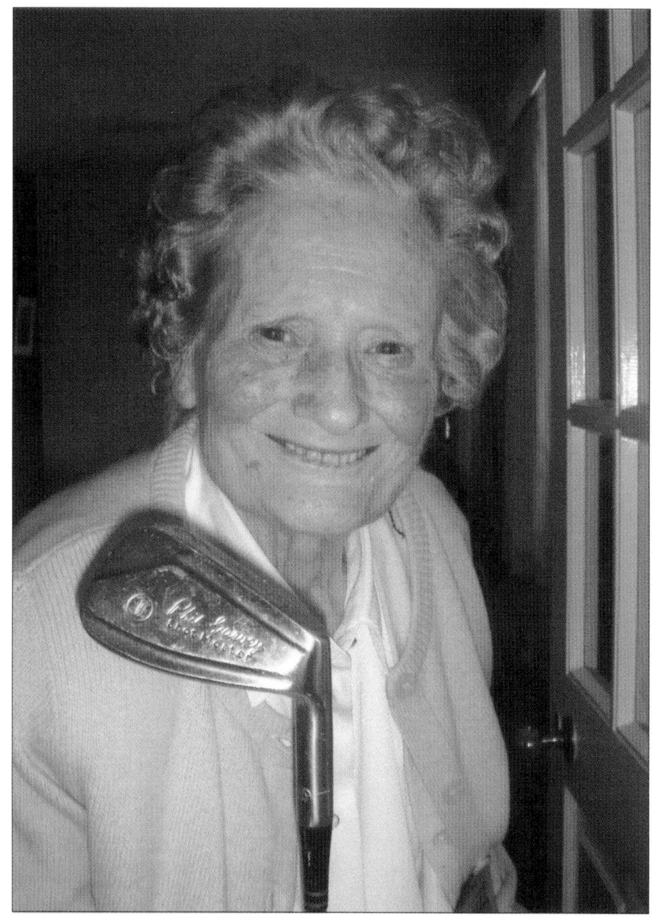

81 year-old Philomena Garvey pictured at her home in Baltray on the fiftieth anniversary of her win in the British Open in 1957 with the club that bears her name.

Undoubtedly, this sudden change of form had more to do with Garvey's primal instincts as a competitor - she just loved the smell of competition. The very thought of knuckling down to concentrate on just playing her game was like oxygen to her. She thrived on it, whether it was strokeplay, qualifying, or better still, matchplay battle - she couldn't wait to get into her cocoon of concentration. For her, it was the best place in the world.

In preparation for the trip to Portrush, she went to the new John Jacobs driving range at Leopardstown (run by Bill Hourihane, father of future Curtis Cup player Claire Hourihane) three nights a week, telling one journalist: *"it's tremendous to be able to belt the ball away, see what you're doing wrong and, best of all, you don't have to collect the balls!"*

As mentioned, Phil's first cut at the Championship since being re-instated was virtually ignored in the various Irish golf columns and that helped to inspire her to make a determined bid for a unique fifteenth title. Most of the pre-Championship articles devoted the bulk of their coverage to the defending champion Mary McKenna, Curtis Cup star Ita Butler and also twice former champion Elaine Bradshaw. These were the ladies who had 'taken over' from Garvey, MacCann and Reddan as the dominant triumvirate in Irish Ladies Golf.

Writing in the Observer newspaper, Garry Redmond wrote of Garvey: "She is unmistakably Irish. What perhaps is a little unusual in her Irish temperament is the enormous discipline which has moulded and preserved her game over a competitive career stretching more than 25 years. She is a completely natural player, but she has also benefited from the hard lessons of battle itself, and outside coaches."

What transpired over the next five days was nothing short of a master-class from a supreme competitor. Her second round match was against the defending champion, one Mary McKenna. Spectators and the media alike were licking their lips in anticipation of this encounter. McKenna was the rising star of Irish golf. The Donabate golfer, having beaten Catherine Hickey of Milltown the previous year at Ballybunion was also on the cusp of a Curtis Cup debut and the anticipation of seeing her taking on the greatest Irish golfer ever, was, as you can imagine, a script-writer's dream.

The match attracted huge crowds, despite the high winds, over the famed Dunluce course. For both competitors, there was much to prove. The Queen of Irish golf against her heir-apparent. It is arguable that Garvey had the upper hand, due to her greater experience over links terrain, and at 43 years of age, she had the ability to stamp her authority over the big-hitting McKenna, twenty-two years her junior.

As Eoin McQuillan, writing in The Newsletter put it: "controlling the ball expertly in tough conditions, Phil gave her highly talented but erratic young rival a lesson in the art of keeping the ball in play and recovered from two down after 11 to win on the 17th."

Phil herself recalled: "*It was very satisfying. I was two down at the twelfth and won the 13th to go one down and missed a putt for a win at the 14th. I won the 15th, 16th and 17th and beat Mary 2 & 1.*"

As Mary McKenna remembers it, it was a terrific match that could have gone either way. "Phil had this great quality of playing within herself, certainly over the opening nine and all of a sudden, she could unleash a drive and you'd find yourself thirty yards behind her off the tee! Her short game too was absolutely superb." She went on to defeat former Irish champion Elizabeth Purcell 5 & 3 and Malone's Ann McLean by 7 & 6 the following day, before disposing of Ita Butler in the semi-finals the next morning by 6 & 5! The 18-hole final was another all-Baltray affair and having beaten international Moira Earner for title number 14

What transpired over the next five days was nothing short of a master-class from a supreme competitor.

in 1963, she once again displayed her supremacy by defeating Earner one more time, this time by 2 & 1.

In her victory speech, she announced her retirement from both Championship and International golf. She was back on the front pages where she belonged and it's doubtful that we'll ever see the like of her again. Philomena Garvey, a supreme sportswoman and true champion.

Phil and the Babe

Mildred 'Babe' Zaharias (née Didrickson) was one of the greatest athletes, man or woman, of the twentieth century. Apart from being a gifted basketball player, she went on to win gold medals in the hurdles and the javelin at the 1932 Olympics in Los Angeles. She was deprived of a third gold in the high jump, for using an unorthodox method! She took up golf in 1935 and excelled there also, becoming the first American to win the British Amateur title in 1947. Turning professional not long afterwards, she was a founding member of the LPGA Tour and proceeded to win the US Women's Open in 1948, '50 and '54. She died of cancer in 1956, aged just 43.

"I made friends with the Babe in 1947 at the British Open, she was a great lady and an unbelievable golfer, who hit the ball farther than anyone I've ever seen."

Garvey and the Babe first got to know each other in 1947, when both played in the British Amateur at Gullane Golf Club in East Lothian. *"I made friends with the Babe in 1947 at the British Open, she was a great lady and an unbelievable golfer, who hit the ball farther than anyone I've ever seen."*

Garvey was one of the pre-championship favourites having been runner-up the previous year. Zaharias was obviously the star attraction, given her Olympic successes and her newfound mastery of golf. (In the picture on page 106 however, it would appear that Philomena Garvey was attracting more attention from autograph hunters than Zaharias!)

In 1950 she was asked by the Curtis Cup captain, Diana Critchley (commentator Bruce Critchley's

'Babe' Zaharias, the eventual winner and Phil Garvey, who was runner-up the previous year, pictured at Gullane GC, East Lothian in 1947.

mother), to play number one in a special series of matches at Sunningdale. Organised by the aforementioned Fred Corcoran, a team of top stars from the American LPGA would take on a team of the best lady amateurs in an exhibition event called the International Weathervane Cup (Weathervane was a ladies sportswear firm). As Phil recalls, *"I was always put at the top of the order, to be devoured!" It was going to be an 18-hole match, or so I thought, and I took on the Babe at number one! I won the (first) 18, one up, only to be told that it wasn't over, that we needed to play another 18 to decide it. As you can imagine, I was a bit annoyed. Anyway, we had a great match in the afternoon. She was hitting it incredible distances, and I wasn't short off the tee myself, but my short game was really good that day and the putter was working really well. She was one up playing the 18th and got an incredible kick from the big tree at the back of the green and the ball finished a foot away from the cup and won the match two up, but there was very little between us."*

The Washington Post reported the following day: "America's leading women completed a clean 9-0 sweep over the international women's team led by Diana Critchley at Sunningdale. Fair-haired Philomena Garvey, 24 year-old Irish champion was the only member of the home squad to offer serious resistance. Miss Zaharias won by 1 up over 36 holes."

Naturally, Phil was saddened to hear of Babe's untimely passing in 1956, aged 43. *"I was in America playing the following year, when I received a telephone call to the house that I was staying in. It was from George Zaharias, Babe's husband. She had died the previous year from cancer, but he took the trouble to look me up: 'I just had to talk to you, Babe spoke so often about you and thought that you were the best golfer ever produced over there.' They were his exact words and I thought that was extremely nice of him to go to that sort of trouble."*
Indeed.

THE GARVEY MYSTIQUE

ITA BUTLER

Curtis Cup player 1966. Curtis Cup Captain 1994 & 1996 (winning) & former Irish International.

"The only competitive match I played against Philomena was in the 1970 Irish Close Championship in Portrush, when, having decided not to continue in the professional ranks, she returned to the amateur game.

At that time, in order to be reinstated as an amateur it was necessary to serve a two year period in 'Limbo', which meant that one could not play in either professional or amateur events. As a result, over that period, Philomena did not have the benefit of competitive matches to sharpen her game.

However, it was a tribute to her outstanding ability as a player and her legendary powers of concentration that she went on to win that Championship.

For me it was the best lesson I was ever to receive in course management. Portrush was a long and demanding course and it was essential, on many holes, to be on the right side of the fairway in order to have a reasonable approach shot to the green.

Philomena's strategy in virtually every match that week, was to take an iron from the tee on several holes, which frequently left her with very long shots to the green. However, she was such an accurate and confident iron player that she made this work for her in two ways. In the first instance it meant that she was

Kitty MacCann and Ita Butler pictured at Tullamore Golf Club, November 2005.

'I just had to talk to you, Babe spoke so often about you and thought that you were the best golfer ever produced over there.'
- George Zaharias, Babe's husband

never in trouble off the tee and secondly, and equally importantly, it meant that she was first on the green every time and so she quietly exerted pressure on her opponent at every opportunity.

She had the effect of wearing her opponents down because she simply did not make mistakes - and in addition to all this she had a magnificent short game.

When I spoke to Philomena at the end of that Championship, which she was thrilled to win, she told me that on the way to Portrush she was about to turn back when she reached Belfast. She said 'I asked myself, what the heck am I doing this for? I don't need to put myself through all this pressure again. I have won the Championship so many times and I don't need to prove anything to myself. But, then I thought I would love to prove to myself that I can win another one'.

Philomena was one of the finest sportswomen that Ireland has ever produced and she really was ahead of her time in terms of practice routines and especially with regard to the psychology of the game. Probably one of her strongest qualities was her ability to concentrate and you really did get the feeling with Phil that she literally was not aware of anything or anyone around her when she was on the golf course. However, she was also one of the most helpful and supportive people you could encounter and when she finally retired from competitive golf she was more than generous with her time and advice to me and to other golfers."

I'll always remember her saying to me about winning the Irish Close that 'the hardest one is the first...when you've won that, you're away!'

MARY McKENNA (see page 155)

"Phil Garvey was **the** icon when I was starting out. She was the 'Queen of Irish Golf'". My mother and I went into Clery's to buy my first set of 'Playing Jane' irons from her. She was also good pals with Elaine (Bradshaw) and we would go up to Baltray together sometimes and Phil would take us out on to the course where she'd help us with our short games. Her attitude to the short game was phenomenal really. You just got up and down in a pitch and a putt. There was no question of not doing so, she was that strong mentally with her short game.

Mary McKenna, who assumed the mantle of 'Queen of the Fairways' when Philomena Garvey retired from top flight golf in 1970.

I'll always remember her saying to me about winning the Irish Close that 'the hardest one is the first ... when you've won that, you're away!' She had a point, but I'll always remember teasing her after I had won a few, saying things like 'I'll catch you one of these days' and we'd both laugh, but I did well to win eight! It doesn't really come near her fifteen wins though, which is phenomenal. She was the one that we aspired to. Elaine and I had a few of those sessions with her, playing the little shots and talking to her about the game. She was very highly thought of within her own era, having spoken to Kitty Butler and Kitty McCann about her. Kitty Butler only played for Ireland once but was an excellent Senior Cup player for Milltown and she used to tell me about playing County Louth in the Senior Cup - and basically it was a case of who would be the lamb to the slaughter, when it came to playing Phil. I think that during her peak years, everyone felt like that about playing her!"

CLAIRE DOWLING (née Hourihane).
5-time Irish Champion, International and 3-time Curtis Cup player and Curtis Cup Captain, 2000

"My mother was a trained singer with the RTÉ singers and in between also worked in the hat department in Clery's, selling and modelling hats. I was quite young when I first met Phil in the Sports Department in Clery's, long before I took up golf. Phil was very disparaging when she first saw me play, said I had a 'lavatory stance' and someone who was completely unsporty like me would never make a golfer. However she grudgingly changed her mind (I think)! She once gave me a lesson on chip and runs, hold the club down the shaft and belt it as near to the ground as possible. She didn't hold with all this airy fairy stuff up in the air, and there were no such things as lob wedges then, just ordinary pitching wedges. She would never take a wedge out of the bag unless she had to go over something.

I first made the Irish team in 1979 and Phil was a selector in 1980 when we went to Cruden Bay. She got so excited when we were doing well and when we had won (the Home Internationals). I was the last match left on the course, – even though the team had won I had to keep going, eventually the match finished on the 17th or 18th (can't remember) and I could start celebrating with the others. Phil came up and gave me a great big hug, and in her own inimitable style said: 'well done, you don't hit it so far but you're the best f......ing putter here!' Her words!

I always liked her even though her straight-talking could often be mis-construed. She was, and probably still is, a great friend of Liz Purcell's and the contrast was extraordinary, Phil down-to-earth and Liz, tall elegant and apparently snooty (though not at all in fact). Liz would invite Phil to dinner and Phil used to say, ok but none of your fancy muck, cook a decent pot of potatoes!"

ELAINE BRADSHAW
Three-time winner of the Irish Amateur Championship. In addition to many years of international duty for Ireland, she played in two Vagliano Trophy matches. Bradshaw more than deserved a Curtis Cup cap in 1968, having won the Irish Championship that year, defeating the champions of England, Scotland and Wales in the Home Internationals and becoming the first Irish woman to reach the final of the French Open, only to lose to the great Catherine Lacoste. One of Bradshaw's greatest influences was Philomena Garvey and her memories of the first time she saw the great Philomena Garvey are vivid:
"I was just a little girl when I cycled from my home in nearby Fairview to Clontarf Golf Club to see Philomena playing an exhibition with Harry Bradshaw, Joe Carr and Kitty MacCann. I hid my bike in the ditch, got in under the wire fence and followed the golf that day which was amazing. Little did I know that I would be playing alongside and become friends with these greats in latter years, but I got each of their autographs that day, which I still treasure.

"Phil came up and gave me a great big hug, and in her own inimitable style said – well done, you don't hit it so far but you're the best f......ing putter here!"
- Claire Dowling

Not long after, I took up the game, playing firstly in Corballis. My father would send me out onto the course to find balls, so that I'd have something to play with! I won my first Girls' Championship, with a five-iron, a seven-iron and a putter! It was an Eastern District Girls Championship at Malahide Golf Club and the prize was a voucher, which Ria Kenny presented to me, recommending that I go into Philomena Garvey in Clery's Department Store to get a new club for myself. I was desperate to get a nine-iron."

After a few more victories and several more vouchers, Elaine found herself with a growing set of clubs, but also a growing friendship with the great Miss Garvey. "Later on, after getting to know Phil, I got her to make a cardboard stance for me, indicating how to stand to the ball when playing a nine-iron chip shot. I kept it for a long time. I'd stand up like Phil and with the hands forward, the face closed, I'd play the shot like I would a putt, as she recommended. She was incredibly helpful, especially if she felt that you were keen, and I was. Phil was very strict on the rules of golf, how you behaved on the golf course, the etiquette and so on. It was something that she took very seriously.

Phil's powers of concentration were something else. She would get very annoyed at anyone who ever claimed to be distracted after playing a bad shot. That to her was sheer madness because, when you are concentrating as she said, you don't hear anything, 'and always remember that'. It's quite true you know.

As a swinger of a golf club she was magnificent. Absolutely and totally orthodox. She was self-taught and learnt the game through watching and caddying for people, but she also loved to practise, which was extremely important too. It made her very sharp and very competitive; Phil was extremely competitive when she was playing! She was also very enthusiastic. It was brilliant what you learned from her at that standard. I remember her saying to me in one foursomes match, 'it's your shot next, so concentrate on the next shot from the very time I hit mine; walk behind your ball from about 50 yards' and whatever it might be, 'you just concentrate walking behind that ball, looking at the direction you are going to hit it, where the bunkers are etc. You will have all that done by the time you get up to the ball; now it's up to you to choose the club and hit it.'

ANN HESKIN

International team-mate of Phil Garvey's in 1969. One of Douglas Golf Club's many great golfers was undoubtedly Ann Heskin. Having played for Ireland in six Home Internationals between 1969 and 1977, she captained Ireland in 1982 and most notably in 1983, when Ireland won the European Team Championships at Royal Waterloo in Belgium. Ann Heskin was President of the ILGU in 2004-2005:

"Phil Garvey was the best Irish female golfer in my lifetime. A beautiful striker of the golf ball, she had all the shots (and could use the odd legitimate bustle to her advantage if and when necessary!). It was a great thrill for me to be on the same team as her for the Home Internationals at Western Gailes, Scotland in September 1969, on my first outing.

I played against her in the Interprovincials in Tullamore that year and lost to her both morning and afternoon, on the 18th. Doubtless she was well past her heyday at that stage, but still a golfer to be reckoned with.

It was wonderful to see Phil getting such an enormous thrill out of being invited by Susan Simpson, the Ladies Golf Union (LGU) Director, to lead out the GB & I Team for the opening ceremony of the Vagliano Trophy at Baltray, her home course, in 2003. She clearly enjoyed meeting all the young players as well as Lally Segard, a French opponent of hers from days gone by (whose father Monsieur A. A. Vagliano

Philomena pictured alongside Susan Simpson of the LGU before leading out the 2002 GB & I Vagliano Trophy team at the opening ceremony at her home club.

"I had tremendous conversations with Phil Garvey about the golf swing. She was very much about the strike on the golf ball. Ball followed by turf, controlling it, and being able to work the golf ball from side to side. I always remember her saying that if you were playing into a wind, you must only hit the ball with 75% of your normal effort. You should never go beyond that and I've found it to be true. If you hit the ball at 75% into a wind, you put topspin on it and not backspin. In other words, if you hit it easy, then the ball flies under the wind. When it hits the green, even though you haven't put backspin on it, the ball will sit down easily enough, because it's using the wind to its own advantage. That was a shot she taught me how to play. There was no wrist break, just purely shoulders, arms and proper weight transfer, but with a controlled hit and controlled power. I learned that from Philomena. It stood to me for the rest of my life and it's one of the great golf shots. I don't think I met anybody afterwards who explained it to me or showed me how to do it as well as Philomena Garvey. She was a truly great player."

presented the original trophy). In many respects it amazed me that Ireland never won the Home Internationals back when we had the likes of Phil, Kitty MacCann, Pat O'Sullivan and Zelie Fallon in the fifties. That said, Philomena Garvey's record in Irish Championships will never be beaten.

ARTHUR PIERSE

Walker Cup player and Irish International. (See page 181) "Legend in his Spare time," Arthur Pierse was renowned for his ball striking throughout his amateur career and was particularly proficient in the wind. He is indebted to Philomena Garvey, whom he claims taught him the fundamentals of controlling the golf ball:

A willing pupil. Arthur Pierse in action at Baltray.

CAREER HIGHLIGHTS

Name: Philomena Garvey

Date of Birth: 26th April 1926

Occupation: Sports Shop, Manager,
Clery's Dept Store, Dublin

Club: Co. Louth, Golf Club

Lowest Handicap: +1

CHAMPIONSHIP HIGHLIGHTS

British Open Amateur Championship

Winner: 1957
Runner-up 4 times: 1946, 1953, 1960 & 1963

US Open Amateur Championship

Reached quarter-finals in 1950 at East Lake C.C. Atlanta, Georgia. Beaten in the last eight by the eventual champion Beverly Hanson. She was also introduced to Bobby Jones during her stay there. Reached quarter-finals in 1954 at Allegheny C.C. Pennsylvania. Beaten by the defending champion Mary Lena Faulk.

Irish Amateur Close Championship

Winner on 15 occasions (a record)

1. 1946, Lahinch. P. G. defeated Clarrie Reddan on the 39th
2 1947, Portrush. P.G. defeated Kitty MacCann 5 & 4
3. 1948, Rosslare. P.G. defeated Clarrie Reddan 9 & 7
4. 1950, Co. Sligo. P.G. defeated Mrs. T. Marks 6 & 4
5. 1951, Ballybunion. P.G defeated Dorothy Foster 12 & 10
6. 1953, Rosslare. P.G. defeated Girlie Hegarty 8 & 7
7. 1954, Portmarnock. P.G. defeated Dorothy Glendenning 5 & 4
8. 1955, Co. Sligo. P.G. defeated Audrey O'Donohue 10 & 8
9. 1957, Portush. P.G. defeated Kitty MacCann 3 & 2
10. 1958, Carlow. P.G. defeated Zelie Fallon 7 & 6
11. 1959, Lahinch. P.G. defeated Heather Colhoun 12 & 10
12. 1960, Cork G.C. P.G. defeated Kitty MacCann 5 & 4
13. 1962, Co. Louth. P.G. defeated Moira Earner 7 & 6
14. 1963, Killarney. P.G. defeated Elisabeth Barrett 9 & 7
15. 1970, Portrush. P.G. defeated Moira Earner 2 & 1

REPRESENTATIVE HONOURS

Curtis Cup

Capped as a player on 6 occasions: 1948, '50, '52, '54, '56, '60
(Selected but did not play in 1958)

Vagliano Trophy

Capped as a player on 6 occasions

International

Capped for Ireland:
1947, '48, '49, '50, '51, '52, '53, '54 (captain), '56, '57 (captain), '58 (captain), '59 (captain), '60 (captain), '61, '62, '63 & 1969.

MISCELLANEOUS

Irish Senior Cup

Member of 7 winning Senior Cup teams with Baltray (Co. Louth) 1946, 1947, 1948, 1949, 1953, 1957 & 1962

Course Record

Baltray (old 18 holes) 69, 6 under par.

Portrait of a Champion.

Garth McGimpsey

Ireland's greatest amateur since Joe Carr, Garth McGimspey displayed remarkable dedication to the game over a period of twenty-one years and all the while he managed to run a successful sports goods business.

"Garth was my golfing idol growing up. He was unquestionably the dominant player of his era and his record is astonishing. He set such a high standard and had such a presence that you couldn't but respect him. He was the best striker of a golf ball that I ever came across in amateur golf and his professional approach to the game, added to his ability to peak in so many of our major amateur Championships is quite breath taking. Garth always led by example, he was the one you looked up to and I wasn't in the least bit surprised that he became such a wonderful Walker Cup Captain. I'm proud to call Garth McGimpsey a friend."

DARREN CLARKE, September 2007.

Captain Garth McGimpsey receives the 2003 Walker Cup on behalf of his team at Ganton, a very special win in a career of superlative success.

Garth McGimpsey looked at the markings on the envelope, he too broke into a wide smile, knowing that it had originated from the most famous golf club in America

A Precious Invitation

Bangor, Co. Down, Christmas morning, 1985.

Having intercepted a letter to his son some days before, Hal McGimpsey could barely contain himself on that cold, bright morning as he looked forward to the arrival of his youngest son with his young family. Hal relished the prospect of producing that letter, which he would pass off as a Christmas present.

When the time came to swap presents, and the moment Garth McGimpsey looked at the markings on the envelope, he too broke into a wide smile, knowing that it had originated from the most famous golf club in America. The letter had been sent to Garth's parent's address, as that was the one on file with the Royal & Ancient. Hal, who had taken such an active interest in his son's development as a golfer, could not have dreamt of a finer moment, as his son received an invitation to play in the following April's Masters Tournament at Augusta National.

"Obviously my father took a huge interest in my amateur golf career, so he was on a crest of a wave at

this stage. He had also heard somewhere that Jack Nicklaus on occasion plays with the U.S. Amateur champion and the (British) *Amateur champion, so he wrote to Jack, to ask was it true and if it was, would he be so kind as to play with me. Jack wrote a very nice letter back to my Dad saying he would love to, and he would be around the putting green about 1pm on the Tuesday of Masters week!"*
An invitation to play in the Masters and a practice round with the Golden Bear... Christmas presents don't come much better than that.

A Dream Week

Garth McGimpsey, the 1985 British Amateur Champion, was the first player to arrive at Augusta for the 1986 US Masters. As the first invitee to register on that Sunday, he was allocated his player's badge, displaying the number two. Augusta National prides itself on its strict adherence to tradition, so despite being the first to check-in, the defending champion (that year it was Bernhard Langer) was always going to be allocated the player badge marked 'No.1'.

Not every aspect of his preparations had gone smoothly however. The day before, McGimpsey had wrenched a muscle in his back when lifting a six litre bottle of water from the boot of his car outside his rented home in Florida and was in some discomfort. A few days acclimatisation had come to an abrupt and worrying end.

Although disappointed to drive up Magnolia Lane carrying an injury, Ireland's leading amateur was keen to put the ailment to the back of his mind and sample a few holes at Augusta National. In the end, he played the back nine holes and had to continually pinch himself that he was indeed at the Masters and that yes, he was in the field!

Monday was a full day of playing and practising ahead of his date with the Golden Bear the following afternoon. This game was nearly becoming more important than the tournament itself.

Although desperately trying to appear nonchalant and just getting on with practising his putting on the practice green behind the tenth tee, he was secretly thankful to another young amateur called Peter Persons, who stopped by to say hello on that fateful Tuesday. Persons assured McGimpsey that the game with Nicklaus was about to happen and that he too, would be joining them along with another amateur, Chris Kite. Persons was runner-up the previous year to Sam Randolph in the US Amateur Championship final, and tradition there ensures that both finalists receive an invitation from Augusta National.

The introductions on the first tee between the great man and his playing partners were warm and a match was agreed, with McGimpsey and Persons taking on Nicklaus and Kite. The financial stakes were far from hefty, with the fourball playing for just one dollar on the front nine, a dollar on the back and two on the match!

Handshakes all round as Garth meets his idol ahead of their practice round at Augusta

An invitation to play in the Masters and a practice round with the Golden Bear... Christmas presents don't come much better than that.

Kevin McGimpsey, Garth's older brother (and as it happens, the author of a book called 'The History of the Golf Ball'), was in his white overalls, on caddying duty, as a thrilling round of golf and good chat ensued over five and a half hours. Proud Hal followed his boys' every move and took snaps from outside the ropes. All told, it was a memorable trip around the picture-postcard course for the McGimpsey clan, with Garth shooting a 73 to win the match for the pair against Nicklaus and Kite.

"Jack played okay, nothing special. It became evident that we had won the match and there were the traditional handshakes. In actual fact, there were a couple of opportunities where Jack could have said he was going in because the practice round had been delayed by thunderstorms and rain and we were sheltering under the trees to the left of the 6th tee. He could have said 'my back is sore, I am going to walk in', but he didn't, he was class. He was sort of saying where the pin placements would be on Sunday. I was thinking 'my God, I don't think I will need to worry – their position on Thursday and Friday was all I was worrying about!' I played well and my father obviously thought it was fantastic."

At the end of the match, Chris Kite paid his four bucks to Persons, while Nicklaus, it must be said, made no attempt to pay McGimpsey, nor did Garth mention it to the man who would, five days later, become the oldest-ever winner of a Major Championship!

There was more excitement to come. McGimpsey teed it up in the tournament proper alongside none other than 'The King', Arnold Palmer. Could it get any better?

"Now, that was a different experience, because obviously playing in a tournament you are concentrating on what you are doing and there was very little chat between me and Arnie. His game was faltering and he was trying not to look foolish. He

All told, it was a memorable trip around the picture-postcard course for the McGimpsey clan, with Garth shooting a 73 to win the match for the pair against Nicklaus and Kite.

Ireland's top amateur tees off, watched by the Golden Bear at Augusta

wasn't quite at the stage he is now where he was waving to the crowd and getting huge applause, he still wanted to do well.

I remember I holed a pretty sweaty six-footer at the second for a par, straight downhill, one of those which, if it doesn't go in, it's 30 feet away, and as we walked to the second tee, Palmer acknowledged my effort with 'nice putt, son'. The sweat was dripping off my hands as I was walking to the next tee. I will never forget that. I three-putted the last from nowhere to shoot 76 and I was gutted, while Arnie shot 81."

McGimpsey could actually have done so much better in that first round. Having arrived at the par three 16th two over par, he fizzed a six iron to 10 feet above the pin, which was perilously placed, tight on the right hand side. Tragically, he ended up four-putting for a five! *"It's a bitch of a hole that. I nearly holed the ten-footer for a two and then it goes right down the slope and you have got this 35 footer back up the slope again. I under-hit it and left it six feet short and then missed it. I finished 5-4-5. What looked like a 73 if I had holed the putt and two pars to finish would have been a pretty good score and then maybe you are talking about qualifying, but that's what Augusta is like. You are never in until you are in. 10 foot above the hole isn't necessarily a good shot. Augusta is unbelievable!"*

McGimpsey missed the cut and although it was obviously a fantastic experience, looking back, he does have some regrets (he also missed the cut again in 1987).

"The unfortunate thing is you do feel that your game is not in the best shape you'd like it to be, because it's quite early in the season and certainly you have no putting touch at that stage of the year."

Moreover, the fact that he never employed a local caddy annoys him too. Having always hired an experienced or local bagman when he was playing amateur Championships, one can assume that he simply never expected to shine at Augusta. Given the excitement that it generated amongst family and friends, the golfing element of the Augusta experience may not have been taken seriously enough, certainly if you are to compare it with his normally, meticulous preparations.

"My brother had a fabulous experience of caddying for me the first year and another friend caddied for me the second year, so if I had used a local caddy it would have taken that experience away from them, but I think it would have given me more of a chance. I definitely feel now, if I had to do it over, I would take a local caddy and they (family and friends) *would just have the wonderful experience of being there. Obviously a local caddy would be a huge asset. You can't possibly visualise where you have got to hit the ball. If it looks like there is a big break from the right, you still have no idea how far you have to hit it; you have actually to hit it away from yourself on occasions to let the weight of the ball take it down. The greens are impossible at times. What annoys me is that the top pros make them look reasonably normal, they putt on them so well. I promise you, the average guy would struggle big time!"*

McGimpsey missed the cut and although it was obviously a fantastic experience, looking back, he does have some regrets (he also missed the cut again in 1987).

The Famous Letter

Less than a week after arriving back to normality in Bangor after his first Masters, a letter arrived from North Palm Beach, Florida. It was from Jack Nicklaus, the newly crowned Masters Champion. It contained a cheque to settle his golfing debt to the reigning British Amateur Champion!

The following year, while practising on the tenth green at Augusta, Jack Nicklaus, who was waiting on the fifteenth tee, spotted his practice partner from the previous year and walked over to say hello. *"He even remembered my name, which was amazing. We*

"Garth was a terrific player, much better than I was," says fellow Bangor native David Feherty. "He won pretty much every amateur event that meant anything, and we were all really proud of him."

Jack Nicklaus

April 15, 1986

Dear Garth:

It was awfully nice to meet you, and I enjoyed our practice round at Augusta...even if I did lose our bet!

Here's my check for the $4...I hope this doesn't affect your amateur status!

Best wishes for continued good golfing. I hope our paths cross again soon.

Sincerely,

Mr. Garth McGimpsey
Bangor, County Down
NORTHERN IRELAND

/mk

Enclosure

The Masters Champion's letter to Garth McGimpsey, days after his success at Augusta

chatted briefly and he wished me well that week, he was just class!"

Father and Son

"Garth was a terrific player, much better than I was," says fellow Bangor native David Feherty. "He won pretty much every amateur event that meant anything, and we were all really proud of him. I was working as an assistant pro at Balmoral Golf Club in Belfast, when Garth's dad Hal brought him up to see Fred Daly for a lesson. Fred was my boss, and the only Irishman at that time to win the Open Championship (Hoylake '47). He was a very funny man, although I never learned a damn thing about golf from him, but he was a joy to be around.

Hal, who was kind of 'Earl Woods-ish' in his earnestness to see his boy succeed, was there with a pad and pencil as the lesson began. I watched as Garth emptied out his shag bag, and Fred told him to hit a couple of wedges, which he did. Hal was licking his pencil in anticipation as Fred said, 'here, give me that club.' He took the wedge from Garth and walked a few steps over to the corrugated iron fence that bordered the practice ground, and made a couple of back-handed swipes with it, at the thick grass at the base of the fence, saying 'see that?...... see that?..... that's it there,' and handed the club back to Garth. Hal, who by this stage was looking somewhat confused, stepped in and asked Fred how Garth could apply this demonstration in his swing, and was rewarded with, 'He can't......, that's that moss over there that's killin' our greens!' As the always entertaining Feherty recalled, "it goes down as one of my all-time favourite lesson moments."

Hal McGimpsey played a huge role in his son's extraordinary rise through the ranks of amateur golf. The odd bizarre lesson from an Open Champion not-withstanding, Hal, a two-handicapper in his own right loved plotting his youngest boy's evolvement from the

JACK W. NICKLAUS
BARBARA B. NICKLAUS
320
April 8 19 86
63-594/670
PAY TO THE ORDER OF Garth McGimpsey $ 4.00
four and 00/100 DOLLARS
BANK OF PALM BEACH AND TRUST COMPANY
MEMO for getting beat at Augusta National G.C.

The cheque that settled the debt

junior ranks at Bangor Golf Club to contesting the major amateur Championships - even on that special occasion, organising a practice round for his son with Jack Nicklaus at the US Masters!

They travelled many miles together, learning to cope with defeat and quietly revelling in the sweet smell of those precious successes. Essentially, Hal loved to plot and it undoubtedly rubbed off on his youngest son, who grew from being a great amateur to a respected and successful Walker Cup team captain, before retiring from the game with the biggest haul of prizes by any golfer on these islands in over thirty years.

Garth McGimpsey became the most dominant player since Joe Carr, and he too could beat opponents before ever stepping onto the first tee! 1982 Golfing Union of Ireland President Fred Perry, who spent many years refereeing the West of Ireland Championship at Rosses Point, vividly recalls one occasion when McGimpsey ground down an opponent in a final. "Garth was one of the all time greats, just a superb golfer. What was also great about him was that he never looked for a ruling! He just got on with it. He played the man and you could see that he had a strategy worked out for every game. One that stands out is the final of 'the West' in 1996. He was playing Sean Horkan, who was the slowest player imaginable. It took them an hour and a quarter to play the first three holes! McGimpsey was prepared for it though, and he deliberately slowed himself down in order to play Horkan at his own game and he won by two holes in the end.... but we were out there all bloody day!"

Few golfers will ever experience the kind of success that Garth McGimpsey has enjoyed, but then again, even fewer could strike the ball as impressively as him and combine it with an insatiable appetite for Championship success. Ryder Cup heroes Darren Clarke, Padraig Harrington and Paul McGinley all played for Ireland with McGimpsey during their own

Father and Son.

respective amateur careers, and McGinley and Harrington were also team-mates of the Bangor legend on the Walker Cup side that lost to the USA at Portmarnock in 1991. Darren Clarke meanwhile, was arguably the No.1 amateur in Europe in 1990, but turned professional at the end of that year.

Darren Clarke: "Garth was my golfing idol growing up. He was unquestionably the dominant player of his era and his record is astonishing. He set such a high standard and had such a presence that you couldn't but respect him. He was the best striker of a golf ball that I ever came across in amateur golf and his professional approach to the game, added to his ability to peak in so many of our major amateur Championships is quite breathtaking. Garth always led by example, he was the one you looked up to and I wasn't in the least bit surprised that he became such a wonderful Walker Cup Captain. I'm proud to call Garth McGimpsey a friend."

"Garth was one of the all time greats, just a superb golfer. What was also great about him was that he never looked for a ruling! He just got on with it."
- Fred Perry, GUI President

Padraig Harrington: "Garth was as good a role model as you could get for his 'professional' approach to the amateur game. He was a phenomenal ball striker, the best ball striker in Irish golf without a doubt. I had good success against Garth myself because I was so afraid of him. I would get hyped up and play unbelievably good golf against him because I feared him so much! He was a class act. The man at every tournament you knew was '**The Guy**!' "

Paul McGinley: "Garth was really stylish, with a great pair of hands. I can still vividly recall seeing his grip on the club, it was tremendous. Monty is a bit like that too. When Garth gripped a club, it looked like he was born to do it. It's a great asset for playing golf. He was also a tremendous wind player. The stronger the wind, the better he played. He was the only man I ever knew that when he hit his tee shot, absolutely flush on the sweet spot, it would literally skim the front of the tee box taking off. And it wasn't because he knocked it down, it was simply that he came down so steep on the ball and crunched it. Awesome!"

Having spent his teenage years and early adulthood enjoying the camaraderie of rugby, team games taught him a crucial lesson...how to lose!

Hal McGimpsey did a very good job in teaching Garth the fundamentals of the game from the very start. Fortunately, being a good golfer himself and a devotee of Ben Hogan, he gave his son a tremendous grounding in the game. *"He was really my modern day coach and taught me from an early age. I didn't really get coaching other than from my father. Sometimes he wouldn't let go though, when I wanted to try and move on a bit and he was a great one for always giving advice when, (at a young age) you think you know it all."*

Bangor Beginnings

Garth McGimpsey won fourteen major amateur titles in a top-flight career that lasted 21 years. It's unlikely that we'll ever see such a period of amateur domination again. What's remarkable about McGimpsey's golfing life is how late it actually began, despite Hal's best efforts to nurture Garth's undoubted talent as a boy. *"I probably focussed on golf later than you would imagine. I think I was a bit of a late developer. I was a reasonable golfer up until I was 18 or 19, playing off one or two handicap but was nothing special!"*

At school, rugby was the number one game and starting out as a scrum half, he developed into a very useful out-half, idolising his local hero, Ireland and Lions legend, Mike Gibson.

Garth went on to play club rugby with North of Ireland RFC, where Gibson reigned supreme. *"I loved rugby and I played it until I was about 25. There were about three years when I was playing both rugby and golf at a high level. I found myself getting my hands kicked and suffering all sorts of injuries, and when you're getting opportunities to play international golf, you soon realise that the two sports don't mix. I just decided that golf was going to be the way forward. Rugby probably held me back for a couple of years but I don't regret that in any shape or form. Amateur golf wasn't as serious as it is today, but a decision was made and I became a rugby spectator!"*

Having spent his teenage years and early adulthood enjoying the camaraderie of rugby, team games also taught him a crucial lesson...how to lose!

"In my 'teens, my father would enter me in the various Boys Championships during the summer months. I loved it. I got to the final of the Ulster Boys in 1971, not long after turning 16 but was beaten by Barry Brennan of Balmoral by 4 & 3."

Not long afterwards, while Garth and a group of friends were enjoying a short holiday on the Isle of Man, he received a call from his father one night, telling him that he had been picked to play for the Irish Boys' team. A few weeks later and he was at the RAC Club in Epsom, rubbing shoulders with the top juniors of the day, including England's Howard Clark and Scotland's Ewen Murray.

16 year-old Garth playing for the Irish Boys team at the RAC Club 1971

"I played with Garth when he was a young boy of 15 or 16 in the North. They talk about talent today - well the talent of that young boy at that time, which he carried through right up to his days as a top class amateur was outstanding, even as a young boy. He had the head, he had everything. He was made for golf." **Christy O'Connor Senior, Sept 2005**

These were heady days for Garth and his talent for golf was more than apparent. Crucially, he was being closely monitored by his father. Hal was the captain of Bangor's Senior Cup team and with team planning and tactics usually taking place at the McGimpsey homestead, it rubbed off on his youngest son.

"Bangor was trying to plot any victories it could. I was part of all this - back then there would have been team meetings with all my Dad's best friends and team-mates at our house and I would be in there making tea and listening to all their tactics.
Now that he was a junior international, there was plenty of gentle ribbing that he had yet to earn a place on the club's Senior squad, but that would sort itself out before too long!

Bangor Golf Club's Senior Cup team, like so many good clubs in Northern Ireland enjoyed a massive rivalry with the Belfast club, Shandon Park. With class players like Brendan Edwards, David Long and the Hoey brothers, Michael and Brian (father of 2001 British Amateur Champion Michael), Shandon was the class act in Ulster's elite team competition. (Shandon Park has in actual fact won the Irish Senior Cup a staggering 13 times since 1960. They also claimed the European Club title in 2000).

In 1972, he was again selected for the Irish team that competed in the Boys' Home Internationals at Moortown in Leeds.

There was also the important matter of deciding between a third-level education or a career in one of the various banking institutions. McGimpsey took the latter option and went with his local outfit, the Ulster Bank. For a good two years, he availed of their leniency towards the need of elite golfers for time off to contest Championships and of course, the annual inter-banks tournament.

"At this stage I was trying hard at golf, but wasn't putting in as much effort as I should have been, and hence the slightly late development at 22 or 23."

Having the confidence to play to a scratch handicap is as much a mental ability as it is a physical one - it is often found that the more natural golfers rely more on their competitive instincts during a round than basing their confidence on long hours at the range.

Undoubtedly, the harder workers usually win out in the long run, but for a natural player like McGimpsey, it took time for the penny to drop that he could really achieve so much more than just play to a high

"...the talent of that young boy at that time, which he carried through right up to his days as a top class amateur was outstanding, even as a young boy. He had the head, he had everything. He was made for golf."
- Christy O'Connor Senior, Sept. 2005

standard, and content himself with the 'best gross' in the monthly medal.

His breakthrough came in 1978 when he won the North of Ireland Amateur Open Championship (one of the five Irish amateur 'Majors'). It coincided with him leaving the bank and joining his father's sports goods business. Hal McGimpsey was the golf agent for Wilson Sports. He had recently suffered a heart attack and Garth didn't hesitate to leave banking behind him in order to help out the 'old man'.

When Hal recovered, Garth moved on and was offered a job with a rival, and over time he set up in business himself, becoming the distributor in Northern Ireland for the Acushnet brands of Titleist and Footjoy. Running his own business in the initial stages was, admittedly, a lot of hard work but it allowed him to make his own time for an increasing amount of practise.

That first major win was undoubtedly the catalyst in giving him a greater focus, ambition and crucially, the realisation of what he could actually achieve in amateur golf. A call-up for the Irish team to contest the Home Internationals at Ashburnham was further confirmation, if it were needed, that he could cut the mustard at the highest level.

That first major win was undoubtedly the catalyst in giving him a greater focus, ambition and crucially, the realisation of what he could actually achieve in amateur golf.

"Playing for Ireland and playing for Ulster were obviously huge ambitions at the time. To realise both of those quicker than I thought I was going to, (because I was still playing rugby at the time) while not totally devoting myself to golf, was huge."

Curiously, McGimpsey didn't get a cap for his province until the following year, because the team had already been picked by the time of his maiden Championship victory, *"so that was quite nice, to get picked for Ireland first and then play for Ulster the following year!"*

In 1979, at Ballybunion in County Kerry, Ulster won the Interprovincial Championship in absolutely horrendous weather. With team-mates like David Long and Johnny Dixon, McGimpsey was in serious company and its effect was a positive one. Long, a star of the Shandon Park Senior Cup team would himself amass four Irish majors, in addition to the prestigious Brabazon Trophy (the English Amateur Open Championship) in 1979. *"I really looked up to David, he was* **the** *class player at the time and we had a great rivalry for two or three years...eventually I took his crown, so that was all very exciting."*

I think I started to practise a lot harder after I got picked for Ireland and I am sure this is a familiar story. My business would open at 9am, but I would be on the practice ground at about 7:30 most summer days, hitting a few balls and trying to nip out at lunchtime too, to hit a few putts - then in the evening time I'd hit a few more balls. You are trying to do your day's work and do as much practise as possible and juggle all the balls at the same time and then have some sort of a family life. The family life probably suffered as a result of that."

Having his own job and being his own boss enabled him to work his schedule around tournaments that he wanted to play in. *"At that stage I focussed on the five Championships we had; one in each province and the Irish Close, trying to win one of those every year or two, but really just to try and make sure that I played for Ireland again, because I enjoyed it so much. If you win Championships then you are going to get picked and you're one of the best players. I went through a few lean years after that first win though!"*

Further victories were proving difficult to come by. In 1979, he was once again contending in 'the East' at Baltray, but he three-putted the final green to finish in a tie for the lead - he was beaten in sudden death by Tipperary's rising star Arthur Pierse.

"That was devastating. Arthur says he would have been heartbroken if he hadn't won but it was me that was crestfallen. He said 'I should have won that one because I three putted this and I three putted that', but it all boiled down to the finish on 18. Arthur had lost in 'the West' that year, so stupidly, I was sympathetic towards him and didn't really mind that he had won it. In hindsight I would have loved to have won 'the East' that year. I was then beaten in 1980 by Paddy Caul, so they were two bitter pills to swallow."

Despite those near misses, it was to be the beginning of a love affair with the Baltray links (the course had a par of 73 in those days, before it was decided to make the reachable par five 11th a long par four in 2002).

After that loss to Caul, he became a regular fixture on the Irish team and also made the six-man team that contested the infamous European Team Championships in St Andrews of 1981 (recounted in the 'Arthur Pierse' chapter of this book). There followed a very consistent period, as was becoming the norm, but a loss in the final of the 1983 West of Ireland Amateur Open Championship to Clandeboye's Colin Glasgow was cause for some concern. *"That was another massive blow to me. I think I would have been favourite going into the match, Colin played very well and I lost by 2&1 - I was getting a reputation for being a bit of a bridesmaid."*

What's worse, he was starting to believe it! Without delving too deeply into why it was happening, he comforted himself with the knowledge that he was getting into positions to win. *"Other people weren't getting into that position. I was in an elite group, I was playing for Ireland and I was playing for Ulster. If you start to win a few things you start to get the confidence and then you can grow from there, but those three setbacks were sort of a bad time for me, even though I was still playing good golf."*

The turning point was on the horizon thankfully. At the 1983 European Team Championships at Chantilly in France, McGimpsey was a key figure once again. Philip Walton had just returned from the US (where he was an Oklahoma State University team-mate of future PGA Tour players Scott Verplank and Willie Wood) and was widely reputed to be one of the best amateurs in Europe at the time. Arthur Pierse was to win a place on the Walker Cup team a little later in the year alongside Walton and completing the Irish side at Chantilly were Joe Carr's son John, (who had reached the semi-final of the British Amateur in 1981), Portmarnock's Mick Morris and Fermoy's Tom Cleary.

Garth played foursomes with Walton, which turned out to be a dynamite combination. Pierse and Carr formed another excellent foursomes partnership. *"Obviously the ideal situation is for everybody to be playing a part and the results just went for us and we qualified well. Philip was playing No. 1, Arthur was playing 2 and I was playing 3. Mick and Tommy played at 4 & 5 respectively. We had a really good week and I played particularly well."*

The pairing suited both men. It was very much a case of 'get the job done'; neither was the most talkative of individuals and it worked perfectly. *"We consulted on every shot and we were probably hitting the ball about the same distance with our iron shots, so we just seemed to click. I would like to think that I am an easy foursomes partner to play with because I don't get upset about whether I am in the rough or whether somebody has hit a bad shot. You can't afford to do that in golf obviously, you have got to move on. In many ways Philip was the better golfer of the two, but I was slightly more experienced, in that I had been doing it a little longer than he had. I think also in foursomes you have to be comfortable; you know the guy you are playing with is a good golfer and he is not going to let you down. We were unbeaten that week and the team won the European title!"*

It was the start of an unparalleled reign for McGimpsey. *It was only ever winning at amateur golf*

What's worse, he was starting to believe it! Without delving too deeply into why it was happening, he comforted himself with the knowledge that he was getting into positions to win.

that mattered to me. I was very focussed in the sense that all I wanted to do was play in what I classified as the majors, the five Championships that we had. I didn't play Scratch cups - I didn't waste time playing Scratch cups, if you like. I wasn't looking to try and win a £100 voucher to get the best gross over 36 or 72 holes!"

A family man, it was imperative that he limit his golf to 'the Majors', the Interprovincials and the Internationals. With a growing business, it was a demanding time and he was well aware that he needed to focus on quality over quantity and prepare wholly in that regard.

"I remember hearing that Jack Nicklaus concentrated on the majors, it was a bit like that with me in the sense that I would practise really hard before each Championship, put the work in and be very focussed. I would have all the right gear and a caddy. I wasn't going to leave anything to chance because obviously one shot determines whether you are winning or losing a match."

McGimpsey on his way to beating his idol at the time, David Long

It was only ever winning at amateur golf that mattered to me

It paid off when he took the first major of the year (1984) at Rosses Point, in a 5 & 4 drubbing of Co. Louth's Frank Gannon. The monkey was finally off his back. He went on to claim his second victory in 'the North' at Royal Portrush, when he easily accounted for his old nemesis David Long by 6 & 5. He also topped the Amateur Order of Merit, known widely as the 'Willie Gill Award' for most consistency throughout the season and if that wasn't enough, he took over from Arthur Pierse at number one for the Home Internationals later that September.

Such was his good form in 1984 that he was selected to compete on the four-man Great Britain and Ireland side that competed in the Eisenhower Trophy. This was a huge personal vindication for McGimpsey - he was now in exclusive company, amongst the very best players in the 'home countries'.

His team-mates included Peter McEvoy, the dominant amateur in Britain for seven years at that stage (who would go on to captain the Walker Cup Team in 1995). Colin Montgomerie was another – he had been beaten in the final of the British Amateur some months earlier at Formby by an up and coming Spanish teenager called Jose Maria Olazabal and completing the team, the reigning English Amateur Champion David Gilford.

"In many ways the Eisenhower was a much harder team to get on than the Walker Cup team because it's a four man team. It was also a Great Britain & Ireland four-man team, and to be considered in the top four was fabulous."

In point of fact, any chance of finishing in the top three at that event in Hong Kong was ultimately McGimpsey's responsibility - he was last of the four to play each day. Upon reaching the penultimate tee, he was informed that he needed a birdie-birdie finish for the team to claim the bronze medal. He succeeded at the 17th, but agonisingly, missed an eight-footer at the home hole to finish one shot away from a podium finish.

The GB & I team at the Eisenhower Trophy in 1984,
Charlie Green, Captain, David Gilford, Peter McEvoy, Garth, & Colin Montgomerie.

Bangor's favourite golfing son had now clearly moved up yet another gear, but little did anyone know what would happen next!

The Big One

The 1985 season got off to the perfect start with a trip for the Ulster Provincial side to Zimbabwe. A bit of warm weather golf in February or March was always welcome, given the Irish winters, and this was a perfect way for McGimpsey to kick start what would become his 'annus mirabilis'!

He was now more focused than ever on the ultimate task: following up his Eisenhower call-up with selection for the Walker Cup team. He arrived back from Zimbabwe in good form and in buoyant mood regarding the upcoming season. It didn't last long though, when Michael Hoey accounted for him in the second round of the season's traditional pipe opener, 'the West'. Hoey, twice a winner of 'the North' in the late sixties, was known to boast later that he was the last man to beat the 1985 Amateur champion and McGimpsey offers no contradiction!

Before heading to meet his destiny at Royal Dornoch, he had important business to attend to at Lahinch, when he led his beloved Ulster to victory in the Interprovincial Championship. There was no denying his impressive form, when he claimed a maximum of six points out of six, including a whitewash of another of our 'legends in their spare time', Arthur Pierse. Garth accounted for the stylish Tipperary man by a whopping 6 & 5!

He was clearly in the best form of his life and typical of his meticulous preparation, he was peaking at the perfect time for an assault on the world's oldest amateur title. He had focused all of his energies on it for a solid six months - his whole season was focused around making that Walker Cup team, and a good showing at Dornoch was imperative. *"My wife came with me and that was a very rare occurrence because we had a young family. I had obviously earmarked the British Amateur Championship as a big target for the year and I gave myself plenty of time for practise. I wasn't doing it on the cheap and we booked into a nice hotel. I gave myself time to make all the necessary final preparations, playing a couple of practice rounds with Peter McEvoy and a few of the other guys that were vying for the team at the time. I was playing nicely!"*

Few will forget that the summer of 1985 was something of a washout. A few weeks later Wimbledon would have serious problems with rain delays before Boris Becker's incredible debut win. The north of Scotland was particularly badly hit. For those who convened at Dornoch from all four corners of the globe to follow this classic Championship though, it was just another occupational hazard.

McGimpsey was fortunate to be on the right end of the weather, avoiding the worst of it in the first round of qualifying and playing his second at the tail end of a heavy downpour. He qualified easily for the matchplay stages.

He was clearly in the best form of his life and typical of his meticulous preparation, he was peaking at the perfect time for an assault on the world's oldest amateur title.

Given the weather, a player could never have enough gloves, dry towels and wet wear. In the practice rounds, he had employed a junior member of the club to pull the caddy car, complete with heavy bag. However, the youngster couldn't caddy for the tournament proper and suggested that his mother, a lady member, could help out. Reluctantly, McGimpsey agreed - he wanted every possible advantage and a caddy was top of that list. The problem was that Royal Dornoch is a remote enough place and there weren't many people that could help him out - he had no real choice in who could tote for him and so, the next day, Nell McDonald, the youngster's mother, was there, ready for duty...and it was the start of a magical week.

"She turned out to be fantastic. She was almost like a lucky mascot in the end and we still exchange Christmas cards to this day, she was fabulous. She wouldn't say anything, she just gave me the putter when I needed it and I would give it back to her. She was a very nice lady, very keen and she got involved in the matches. 'Keep it going' she'd say."

McGimpsey, a devotee of Ben Hogan like his father, was almost silent in his approach to his golf. It suited him to keep his thoughts to himself during a match and he was never one to waste words.

McGimpsey, a devotee of Ben Hogan like his father, was almost silent in his approach to his golf. It suited him to keep his thoughts to himself during a match and he was never one to waste words.

"Not that I would copy Ben Hogan, but Ben Hogan didn't say much on the golf course and I am not there to get anybody's life story either, all I am doing is trying to beat them. If I have a beer afterwards, that's fine. I very much keep myself to myself and try and get into that cocoon of concentration, to be as difficult to play against as possible."

McGimpsey had the kind of week that everyone dreams of: solid, precise driving, accurate iron play and crucially, a killer week on the greens. Quite simply, he holed everything. *"I putted like I never putted before and I haven't putted like it since!"* Being a lover of links golf, he was also falling in love with the Old Tom Morris designed golf course. Royal Dornoch is an old-fashioned links course, more or less straight out with the wind and straight back into it, *"an absolutely fabulous track."* McGimpsey was riding the crest of a wave and was utterly focussed.

He simply went through the field, picking them off one at a time. Germany's Thomas Schuster was the first to fall and in the second round he came up against a player from the area called Ernie Wilson. Local knowledge is always worth a few shots in matchplay, and so it proved.

Two down after five, McGimpsey bunkered his tee shot at the par three sixth, with his opponent already on the green. After leaving the second shot in the trap, he was in desperate need of a miracle or he was going three down. Without so much as a lingering moment to settle the head, he hit the shot and in she popped for an outrageous three! Wilson, in a fit of pique, promptly three-putted. McGimpsey, given his vast experience, knew full well that this was a turning point. He took control and cruised to victory. Nobody could take the Ulsterman even as far as the 16th green as he marched towards the final.

"My long game was as good as it usually was, without being big headed, because if you asked anybody, that was normally my strength. A steady draw up the middle, on the green, either hole it or it was a 'gimme'. Nobody really got close to me, it was all a bit surreal in many ways. I was obsessed with making the Walker Cup team and as every round passed I thought I must be getting closer now."

In the quarter final, he came up against future PGA Tour winner (and 2006 US Ryder Cup vice-captain at the K Club) Duffy Waldorf. The American recalled the match with great clarity, 22 years later.

"I remember being one of the top players from America over to play in the Amateur Championship

Duffy Waldorf tees off the first at Royal Dornoch, watched by McGimspey and Joe Carr!

that year and he was considered one of the top contenders from Great Britain and Ireland. One of the things that was said at the time was that it was tough we had to meet that early in the competition - I think a lot of people would have liked to have seen that as the final itself that year.

I had been playing well in the lead-up to the tournament and had played well in the earlier rounds at Dornoch. The weather had also been pretty good that week but I remember it being much colder the day of our match and I was struggling more to cope with that than Garth was. He was such a tough competitor and he handled the conditions a lot better than I did.

I had a few chances to get into the match but he was unrelenting, that is what I really remember most about him. He never gave me anything, never wasted any shots or any holes and anything I did get out of the match, I had to earn myself. It was a tough day to make birdies and I got behind early on and just couldn't get back into the match no matter how hard I tried - he eventually closed things out on the 15th green. I felt like my game was in good shape that week but he played really well and I would have had to play really great to beat him that day. It was no surprise to me that he went on to win that year," recalled the American.

McGimpsey kept notching them off. *"I kept saying to myself, 'it's going to be hard not to pick me now'. Then I got into the final!"*

Like most good golfers, he was obsessive about routine and that week he was clearly in the zone, so repetition was a key ingredient to his success. *"There wasn't much of a practice ground at Dornoch, but I found somewhere to hit a few shots. I would always walk across to the 16th green just to get the speed of the greens. I threw a few balls onto the green and circumnavigated the hole if you like, from 20-30 feet*

Like most good golfers, he was obsessive about routine and that week he was clearly in the zone, so repetition was a key ingredient to his success and practised my putting. I did that every day and as a result, I had a great feel for them. If it wasn't going in it was stone dead. Whatever the speed was, I think they were reasonably quick, I was comfortable; again, I wasn't even thinking."

For the first time in a long time, McGimpsey was enjoying stress-free golf, and what a week to do it! He wasn't going to be lacking in support for the big match either. *"Eight guys got into a car and drove across on the ferry to Stranraer and then travelled on through the night to be there for the 8:30 kick-off. There was a light aircraft hired as well and six people crammed into that and flew across, there was a wee airport beside Dornoch, it was fabulous."*

Graham Homewood, a strong county player with Middlesex was his opponent. McGimpsey, with all of his international caps and experience was the overwhelming favourite. Starting strongly, he was round in 69 in the first round of the 36-hole final and found himself five up. Never having been in the situation of contesting a 36-hole final, McGimpsey found it all a bit strange to be going into lunch five up when he would normally have been a 3 & 2 or 4 & 3 winner.

British Amateur Champion 1985

For the first time in a long time, McGimpsey was enjoying stress-free golf, and what a week to do it!

McGimpsey's classic style as he plays an approach shot in the 36-hole final

"The only game plan I had was to win the first hole that changed hands in the afternoon, to go six up rather than go four up. I managed to do that at the second and then just ground it out."

Homewood became desperate to turn around the deficit and it backfired, making the win a formality for the Bangor star, 8 & 7. *"It was really only when I had won the thing that I realised what I had done and everything that went with it."* Walker Cup was now almost a certainty, not to mention a spot in the following month's Open Championship at Royal St George's and of course, a prized invitation to the US Masters at the famed Augusta National the following year!

"Certain courses suit certain golfers. I am fortunate that we have all our Championships on links courses and the 1985 British Amateur, dare I say it, did feel like it came too easily. It was just my week."

The enormity of what he'd achieved didn't take long to register with McGimpsey, *"I remember I broke down during the prize giving, when I had to say a few words, which is so unlike me, I just cracked. The whole thing was just too much! It dawned on me what I had just done and the magnitude of the whole thing. Joe Carr had been the last winner (claiming his third Amateur title in 1965 at Portrush) and it was great to follow in his footsteps because he was a great hero of mine. The rest just fell into place. The next couple of years were taken up with playing in the Masters and playing in the British Open and still trying to do a job. It all went by very quickly."*

Proud Hal with his son at Dornoch

For someone who had spurned every opportunity to try his hand at the professional game, stating that he wasn't good enough, McGimpsey felt justified in aspiring to be at the very top of the amateur game and his success at Dornoch only validated that ambition - it couldn't have been more opportune. *"My business, Garth McGimpsey Sports, was going very well at that stage (1985). I was the distributor for Titleist and Footjoy. I had a warehouse, a salesman and myself and two girls in the office. It was a very small operation, but it meant that when I was away playing in a golf tournament the business was still going on.*

The next big date was the coveted exemption to the Open Championship the following month at Royal St George's. Irish golf was going through a period of unprecedented success, with the Curragh's Lillian Behan winning the Ladies' British Amateur Championship. Then, in the first round of the Open, Christy O'Connor Junior shot a stunning 64, six under the card to lead the world's oldest major. Junior eventually tied for third behind Sandy Lyle, while McGimpsey missed the cut.

Kevin McGimpsey, Garth's older brother was acting as caddy and things weren't going well, as the second round began to slip away. He was heading for a 79 and after making the notorious par-five 14th in three shots, he was left with a nasty 40-footer. Being a solitary type on a golf course, McGimpsey talked little to his brother over those opening two days, and now finding himself with a devilishly tricky putt, he decided to break his silence and consult Kevin. There followed much to-ing and fro-ing from the caddy, sizing up this long shot for a birdie. In the end, he sidled over and uttered: *"nasty, fucking nasty!"* The elder McGimpsey had gotten his own back, the two

McGimpsey felt justified in aspiring to be at the very top of the amateur game and his success at Dornoch only validated that ambition - it couldn't have been more opportune.

laughed, the par was achieved and a few holes later, the assessment that he wasn't professional material felt justified.

He played again the following year at Turnberry and while being reasonably pleased to have shot 76 in strong winds and rain in round two, Greg Norman, the eventual winner, who was two groups behind him, managed a 7 under par 63 around the Ailsa course, reinforcing Garth's own belief that he was much better off as an amateur!

The Open Championship always conflicted with his favoured North of Ireland Amateur Championship. *"I sort of begrudged it a wee bit because I loved Portrush, but in fairness, you only begrudge it when you have gone (to an Open) and not done well, you sort of think 'I could have been playing Portrush and winning a Championship!"*

McGimpsey had no selfish thoughts when he travelled to Pine Valley in August of '85 however, to compete alongside Peter McEvoy, Colin Montgomerie, 19-year-old Peter Baker and the rest of the GB & I team to take on the United States in the Walker Cup. Pine Valley would soon rate as one of his all-time favourite courses, but the Cup would stay with the Americans yet again.

On the US team were the likes of Davis Love, a hugely talented, long-hitting amateur, who would turn pro later that year, with almost immediate success. Duffy Waldorf, whom he beat at Dornoch was there as was the reinstated amateur Bob Lewis, with whom McGimpsey would lock heads both on the course that year and also later in 2003 and 2005 when both men would share the spoils in two tours of duty as respective Walker Cup captains.

"The target for the whole season was to get on that team, but playing No. 1 as amateur champion was absolutely fantastic. In the foursomes I played with John Hawksworth. We won one and lost one. In the singles I played Scott Verplank and he beat me 2 & 1, then I played Sam Randolph the next day and we halved. Randolph got an amazing half against me at the last so I could have won my match. A couple of half points makes all the difference."

Great Britain & Ireland lost to the Americans by 13 points to 11 and Randolph would actually go on to win the US Amateur the following week. McGimpsey qualified for the matchplay stages, but with a young family, it was just one week too many to be away and he was relieved to go out early and head back home.

A Different Level

The years 1985 to 1987 were undoubtedly McGimpsey's peak in the bigger league. For the record, he won a British Amateur Championship, played in two US Masters and two British Open Championships.

The years 1985 to 1987 were undoubtedly McGimpsey's peak in the bigger league. For the record, he won a British Amateur Championship, played in two US Masters and two British Open Championships.

Subsequent solo victories would elude him for a few years following his major moment in 1985 however, but having played in the Eisenhower Trophy team in 1986, he should have been in prime position for a second Walker Cup cap the following year. It never arrived, nor did it for Peter McEvoy, who summed it up as follows in his autobiography, 'For Love or Money': 'A couple of weeks previously, myself and Garth had played in the Eisenhower Trophy (in Venezuela), so that made us two of the best players in Britain and Ireland. In the space of a fortnight we had seemingly dropped out of the top 12 without competing against any of our rivals.'

McGimpsey was understandably very angry at the omission. "*It was a terrible thing at the time. It seemed like the end of the world had come. I remember speaking to Eamonn Curran and saying that I felt like giving golf up. He was captain of the Irish team and of course he was wetting himself that I would do that!"* In the end he didn't go to that extreme and displayed his frustration in the only way he knew how, by once again, letting his golf game speak for itself. He played a huge role in Ireland's magnificent victory in the European Team Championships at Murhof in Austria, where Ireland beat England in the final. He also played at number one for Ireland when they went undefeated in claiming the Triple Crown at the autumn Home Internationals later in the year at Lahinch, making his omission from the Walker Cup side even harder to take.

"We were pretty well miffed that we had been left off by the then chairman and the captain, Geoff Marks. We could never really get any sort of answer as to why we were left off. I think they were trying to pick a team of people that had never lost a Walker Cup before, so they didn't have the experience of losing. It was clearly obvious that they hadn't picked their best players because Peter was the best player available and I was maybe the fourth best player available."

For the record, Great Britain and Ireland were humbled by the Americans in that Walker cup. The only noteworthy victories coming from Ireland's John McHenry, Colin Montgomerie, Jeremy Robinson and Paul Mayo, three of whom had been attending American Colleges.

McEvoy went on to reach the final of the British Amateur Championship the following week, only to lose to Paul Mayo. *"He really wanted to win that badly. He just wanted to make a point if you like. (However) you can't beat the establishment,"* McGimpsey recalled.

In truth, the answer probably lies in McGimpsey and McEvoy's poor play in the Eisenhower trophy in Venezuela. The Walker Cup was to be played much earlier than normal in May of 1987 and the selectors based all of their choices on 1986 form, which more than explained John McHenry's justifiable selection.

Winning Eisenhower Trophy Team left to right Captain Geoff Marks, Peter McEvoy, Garth, Jim Milligan and Eoghan O'Connell

Fast forwarding a year to 1988, and with Geoff Marks still at the helm, McGimpsey and McEvoy were selected on the four man Eisenhower Trophy team that included new Irish prospect Eoghan O'Connell and Jim Milligan. All of a sudden they were back in favour and the team went on to record a memorable victory.

The event was held in Sweden, at a very difficult course called Ulna. McEvoy played out of his boots and also won the individual Championship, with McGimpsey tying for eighth place alongside O'Connell.

"To be on the winning team was absolutely awesome. I remember Peter and I were sharing a room and we were so tired. We said we should be out celebrating but we couldn't be bothered. I was too tired so we went down and ordered a bottle of wine from the bar. Because the R&A was picking up the tab we ordered the most expensive bottle of wine we could find and went up to our room, drank it and crashed out!"

McEvoy remembers it slightly differently: "Wine is not

"Because the R&A were picking up the tab we ordered the most expensive bottle of wine we could find and went up to our room, drank it and crashed out!"

cheap in Sweden and we certainly couldn't be seen to order another after Garth dropped the first one on the floor – and it was red! 'Never mind I'm exhausted anyway' he said, and got into bed!"

1988 was another golden year for McGimpsey, as far as dominance combined with victories was concerned. He returned to winning ways at the beginning of the year with a victory in his favoured West of Ireland Championship at Rosses Point. There was talk of a Grand Slam after he raced away to an eight shot win at 'the East'. However, he stumbled at the quarter-finals of 'the North' after leading the qualifiers and also fell at 'the South' at Lahinch.

Heading back to Portrush and his favoured Dunluce Links, McGimpsey fancied his chances of at last landing the Irish Amateur Close Championship. *"You know golf is going to knock you down at some stage, so when it all clicks for you, it's good to enjoy it. At certain times it scared me. Could I keep it going for all eight rounds? With two rounds of strokeplay qualifying and six rounds of matchplay, all you need is one bad round and you are gone. That's the difference, apart from the standard, between being a pro and an amateur. Most of our Championships are matchplay events and pretty much all of theirs are strokeplay; if you have one bad round in strokes, you might still squeeze it around in 73 and bounce back with a 66 or whatever. One bad round in matchplay and you're out!"*

The other difference, again apart from the ability aspect, is that if you win 'a North' or 'a West' or indeed a British Amateur, then you've had a great week. If you lose in a final though, that's a bad week and you go away gutted. However, if you are second at a pro tournament, you have gone away with a couple of hundred thousand Euros."

As Peter McEvoy confirmed, Garth had the whole package:

"I was lucky enough to play a lot of golf with Garth. He was a great player and also a great companion. If I had to sum him up I think I would point to his single-mindedness. He had loads of talent, of course, but then so do many players and not many combine this with the sort of determination Garth displayed. His determination was often misunderstood as aloofness or even selfishness. It was not the case...all good players are selfish to a degree – it's a prerequisite of being a winner that you want everyone else to lose."

That determination would pay off handsomely at Portrush as he defeated the young challenger David Mulholland of Castlerock by the margin of 2 & 1. He had finally added the Irish title to his haul of Championships, which now numbered seven.

'The South' at Lahinch would continue to elude him for the rest of his career. He came closest in 1986 when he lost out to arguably Europe's No.1 amateur that year, John McHenry of Douglas in Cork. That lack of success at 'the South' meant that he never achieved the grand slam of landing all five major titles during his astonishing career in amateur golf. It remains the single missing piece in his remarkable haul of Ireland's biggest prizes.

It's not that Lahinch was always unkind to him though. He was undefeated there during the 1985 Interprovincials and two years later he won every match in the historic Triple Crown winning Irish team that won the Home Internationals, but alas, the solo title of South of Ireland Champion could never be applied to the great man from Bangor.

"I got it in my mind that Lahinch was a course that didn't suit me. I always went down there early to prepare properly - but everybody wanted to beat me and that's fine. I just felt the course wasn't set up in a way that suited my game. It's very much a local knowledge course - people could out-putt you, they could hit it anywhere basically and still find it. It's a

Heading back to Portrush and his favoured Dunluce Links, McGimpsey fancied his chances of at last, landing the Irish Amateur Close Championship.

different story now. I think if I was playing at Lahinch with the redesigned course, with much more accuracy off the tee required and much more emphasis on second shots, then there would be every chance of a victory."

"I have no gripes. I think 'the South' got away from me a couple of times and I've had plenty of long drives back from there! Usually, you were beaten at around 5:30 in the evening and you had to make the decision whether you were going to drive back, which took about five and a half hours in the car. There was plenty of time to reflect, telling yourself that you'd never go there again, but you always did. Once I got to Ennis I was usually okay! I have had plenty of good times at Lahinch."

Victory on American Soil

McGimpsey went on to be selected on two further Walker Cup teams. In 1989, he and Eoghan O'Connell flew the flag for Irish golf at Peach Tree Golf Club in Atlanta, when Great Britain and Ireland made history in defeating the Americans for the first time on home soil.

He played Phil Mickelson in all of his three matches that week, two foursomes and one singles. Halving the morning foursomes alongside Stephen Dodd (2005 Nissan Irish Open Champion and 2006 Smurfit Kappa European Open Champion) against Mickelson and Danny Yates (a future Walker Cup captain in 2001 and son of Charlie Yates, who defeated Cecil Ewing in the British Amateur final in 1938), McGimpsey was outclassed in the singles, with the future Masters winner accounting for the Bangor-man by 4 & 2.

Captain Geoff Marks informed him after that singles game that he was being dropped from the following days singles, which was obviously very disappointing, but he also knew that he still had one more match to play, so he poured his energy into preparing for the following mornings' foursomes match, which was to be his last chance of a victory in that year's contest.

Phil Mickelson tries to figure out how to beat Garth and Stephen Dodd in the foursomes at Peach Tree

It went down to the wire. After blowing a five-hole lead against Mickelson and Yates, Dodd and McGimpsey found themselves one up with two to play. *"On the seventeenth, Stephen snap-hooked it into the trees. The hole was playing really tough, about 460 yards up into the wind and into the hill. I was away in these trees, so I said that I would just chop it out sideways. Stephen said no, that there was a gap up there and that I could hit a six iron through it. The gap was no wider than 15 feet and it was about 100 yards away, it was impossible! Anyway I took it on, hit this brilliant shot out and got it within about 70 yards of the green. They meanwhile had knocked it up on the right-hand side of the green."*

It went down to the wire. After blowing a five hole lead against Mickelson and Yates, Dodd and McGimpsey found themselves one up with two to play

McGimpsey promptly instructed his partner to 'get it into about 10 or 15 feet and I will hole it!' Bravado. Dodd knocked it 15 feet above the hole, and seconds later, the Americans fluffed their chip and ended up taking a five. *"I had this 15 footer to win the hole and the match. It was seriously downhill. I holed it and I just knew at that stage that that was me finished with the Walker Cup for that year. I had played my last shot. I took my visor off and I threw it into the crowd. It was totally unlike me, but it was such a big pressure situation. It was the last match on the course in the morning and that was me finished, barring somebody getting injured or something like that, which at that stage I hadn't even considered. It was one of the best moments of my life."*

"One of the best moments of my life", holing the winning foursomes putt against Mickelson and Yates in the Walker Cup

Despite being sidelined on that memorable afternoon at Peach Tree, McGimpsey's qualities as a future Captain were in evidence, and the 'walk' was in full view!

It proved to be a momentous day for Britain and Ireland's amateur elite. Garth's fellow countryman Eoghan O'Connell, who had looked up to Garth for many years, had the unenviable task of squaring up to Mickelson on the final afternoon. "We had never won on U.S. soil, but Garth, with his good friend Peter McEvoy, convinced us that we should win. If you look at the teams on paper now, they did a good sales job! However, they led the meetings with Geoffrey Marks, the captain. By the time we teed it up we were ready to win. We got a substantial lead going into the last day, needing only 1½ points out of 8 and Garth, as you know, played three matches, missing the last day singles. Not many people played all four games as it was 100 degrees and humid. This was back before golfers worked out! Garth walked some holes with me, urging me on. Many players would have been disappointed that they were not playing, but I walked down the fairway and noticed that Garth had the 'competitive walk' on the first fairway."

The previous year, when playing foursomes together for Ireland, O'Connell noticed the Bangor man's body language. "I noticed that he had a different walk when he competed. Call it his 'I mean business walk', which he did. If he played well or badly he walked the same pace with the same gait. He had short steps and walked quickly. I also walk with short steps and walk quickly so we couldn't be mistaken for gazelles from a distance, but you would see us 50 yards ahead of our opponents!"

Despite being sidelined on that memorable afternoon at Peach Tree, McGimpsey's qualities as a future Captain were in evidence, and the 'walk' was in full view!

O'Connell goes on: "Garth was there for the team and it was obvious. I was playing against Phil Mickelson, and Phil had beaten Garth the first day. Then for the second day's singles I was drawn against Phil. We had a great game. I was one down with two to go and Garth walked the two holes with me. I remember

The winning Walker Cup team, making history by claiming the Cup on American soil for the first time ever in 1989.
Back Row l-r: Jim Milligan, Darren Prosser, Jeremy Robinson, Craig Cassells, Stephen Dodd, Eoghan O'Connell & Russell Claydon.
Front Row l-r: Peter McEvoy, Andy Hare, Garth McGimpsey & Geoff Marks (Captain).

much of the conversation, basically saying, 'this is what it's all about...isn't this exciting?' Garth was enjoying the whole situation, which rubbed off on me. I was definitely more relaxed than I would have been if I had been left to my own devices. I managed to win 17 and we halved 18 for a half point. We needed one more half to win. Jim Milligan was three down with four to go against Jay Sigel, Garth was out working the magic again, and Jim managed to win three of the last four for us to win. There was some television footage and some photos from the seventeenth green when Jim Milligan chipped in against Jay Sigel that basically won us the Walker Cup. Garth jumped higher than Sergio Garcia after that cut two iron at Medinah against Tiger on 16 on that last day. He could have dunked a basketball! He

When Jim Milligan chipped in against Jay Sigel that basically won us the Walker Cup. Garth jumped higher than Sergio Garcia after that cut two iron at Medinah against Tiger on 16 on that last day.

was a great team-mate and allowed some of us to have a lot of team success. It isn't any wonder he was chosen as a Walker Cup Captain."

It was yet another great achievement to add to his already impressive CV.

He would play alongside budding Irish superstars Padraig Harrington and Paul McGinley in the Walker Cup matches at Portmarnock in 1991 against an American side that again included Mickelson, but also Jay Sigel, David Duval and Bob May. There was to be no fairytale ending on home soil however, with the Americans triumphing by 14-10.

As far as Championships were concerned, the McGimpsey golfing machine continued in earnest, notching up a further seven 'Major' domestic titles, making it fourteen in all! He continued to play for Ireland until 1999 and began to assume the role of mentor to the next wave of Irish golfing talent, as Padraig Harrington can testify:

"What I remember most about Garth is that he became a very good leader of the Irish team. He was a player's captain if you will. Obviously we had a Captain managing the team, but Garth was such a strong player that he also took on a very strong role throughout the Irish teams that I played on with him from 1990 to '95. He was definitely a good leader in the team. Again, his golf was very dependable, you knew what he was going to be like, but I think he gave more to those Irish teams off the course than people would have realised. I think earlier in his career when he was right at the height of his game, he was obviously a younger guy and just played the golf and produced the goods on the golf course, but certainly in terms of when I would have known him in the Internationals he definitely took on the mantle of player-captain."

What I remember most about Garth is that he became a very good leader of the Irish team. He was a player's captain if you will.

After 21 years of unbroken service and 202 caps, an all-time record, Garth McGimpsey retired from top-

Master tacticians: Garth and Peter McEvoy at Chicago Golf Club during the 2005 Walker Cup matches.

flight golf. He took on the captaincy of the Ulster side and also became a Walker Cup selector, eventually becoming the Great Britain and Ireland Captain. Although a man of few words, he was a terrific captain and was very decisive, as his great friend Peter McEvoy recalled fondly:
"Garth's straight talking used to keep me amused. One of the best occasions was when, as Captain of Great Britain & Ireland in a match for the St Andrews Trophy, Garth started the team meeting by saying that one player was going to be left out for the first day of the match. Ordinarily breaking such news would be a matter of some sensitivity and the unlucky player would be taken aside before the meeting to have the news broken to him. Garth, however, is far too matter of fact for such tactics and turned to Jonathan Lupton and said 'and Jon – it's you'!"

McGimpsey led the GB & I team to a fantastic victory at Ganton in 2003. The team included two young Irishmen, Noel Fox and Colm Moriarty.

Noel Fox: "Garth is a man of few words, as most people will agree. He just has the ability to say the right thing, at exactly the right time. When he speaks, it has meaning. Either as a captain, or as an opponent, he would always give thought to what he would say to you afterwards, over a handshake or whatever. It may only be a few words, but they'd always strike a chord.

We've been pretty good friends since we first played each other in the Irish Close at Lahinch in 1995 (Fox won). It's a person's right to be private, and anybody who says anything even remotely negative about Garth, really doesn't know him. Garth was the dominant player of his era and he carried himself in that way. You don't see Tiger Woods arriving onto the practice tee 'high-fiving' everybody, neither would Garth. I also think that he was very fair. He oozed class."

Colm Moriarty*:* "At Ganton, Garth just blended in, he wasn't intrusive at all as a team captain. He was so supportive and anything that you had to bounce off him you knew that he had been through it all before. Sometimes with managers who maybe know a little bit less about the game, they try and intrude more into it; Garth was always in the background, you knew he was there if you needed him, but he was never in your face, so to speak, you never felt as though he was hitting the shots for you. I have the utmost respect for him."

The win in 2003 was a poignant one. After the frustration of not being picked to play for the 1987 Walker Cup matches at Sunningdale, the irony was not lost on either McGimpsey or McEvoy, who were now captain and chairman of selectors, respectively. The tables had well and truly turned.

"That was for Hal!" Bangor's Garth McGimpsey holds his arms aloft in triumph after Captaining the British and Irish side that retained the Walker Cup against the USA at Ganton, Sept, 2003.

When Nigel Edwards secured the winning point on the eighteenth hole on that memorable Sunday evening, the home crowd erupted into a spontaneous bout of cheering, as Great Britain and Ireland secured their third successive victory in the matches.

In the moments after the result at Ganton was confirmed, Garth McGimpsey hugged Peter McEvoy and remembered his late father, who had died two years earlier. Having been inconsolable at his son's exclusion from the 1987 Walker Cup team, he would have been so proud of his son's achievement that day. No more needed to be said by his son, other than, *"that was for Hal!"*

Garth McGimpsey, one of the all-time greats.

You don't see Tiger Woods arriving onto the practice tee 'high-fiving' everybody, neither would Garth. I also think that he was very fair. He oozed class."
- Noel Fox

"To play in the Walker Cup is a tremendous highlight of any amateur golfer's career on either side of the pond. To then be asked to Captain your team is an incredible honour and it's something that I will never forget. My two terms as Captain coincided with Garth McGimpsey's stewardship of the British and Irish team and you could not meet a more decent guy. Garth is a straight-shooter and a thorough gentleman. Obviously when you're trying to win a Walker Cup there's tremendous pressure on you, so you can imagine how difficult it was to make a speech on the closing evening at Ganton after our side had lost by a point. Garth made it easier, by saying some very kind words about me and my team. He was first class. To reverse the roles two years later at Chicago Golf Club was quite something. For us to win by a point was truly dramatic, but that is what the Walker Cup is about, excellent competition and true sportsmanship. Garth was not only a wonderful golfer himself and tremendous Captain, he is a great ambassador for amateur golf." -

BOB LEWIS, *US Walker Cup Captain, 2003 & 2005*

CAREER HIGHLIGHTS

Full Name: Garth Michael McGimpsey, MBE

Date of Birth: July 17th, 1955

Birthplace: Bangor, Co. Down

Family: 3 Children: Jamie, Hannah & Jack.

Occupation: Company Director.

Home Club: Bangor GC.

Lowest Handicap: + 2

CHAMPIONSHIP HIGHLIGHTS

British Amateur Championship
Winner at Royal Dornoch 1985.
Semi-finalist at Royal Birkdale 1989.

Irish Open Amateur Championship
Runner-up to Padraig Harrington in 1995.

Irish Amateur Close Championship
Winner at Royal Portrush 1988.

West of Ireland Amateur Open Championship
Winner in 1984, 1988, 1993 & 1996.
Runner-up 1983.

East of Ireland Championship
Winner in 1988, 1994 & 1998.
Runner-up 1979, 1980.

South of Ireland Championship
Semi-finalist 1986.

North of Ireland Championship
Winner in 1978, 1984, 1991, 1992 & 1993.

Scratch Cups
Winner of Mullingar Scratch Trophy, 1985.

Willie Gill Award (Irish Amateur Order of Merit):
Winner in 1984, 1988 & 1993.

REPRESENTATIVE HONOURS:

GB & I *Walker Cup*:
3 caps-1985, 1989(winners) & 1991.
Victorious Captain in 2003, Ganton Golf Club.
Defeated Captain in 2005 at Chicago Golf Club.

GB & I *Eisenhower Trophy*:
1984, 1986 & 1988(winners).

GB & I *St Andrews Trophy*: **1984-1992**

International: A record 206 caps for Ireland 1978-1999 (this does not include 20 strokeplay qualifying rounds for Ireland at 10 consecutive European Team Championships 1981-99). On winning team in 1983 & 1987.

Interprovincial: 116 caps for Ulster 1979-1999.

MISCELLANEOUS

Awarded MBE in Queen's New Year's Honours list of 2004.

Member of the R&A.

British Long-Drive Champion 1980 (321 yards).

2008 Curtis Cup Captains, Mary McKenna & Carol Semple Thompson.

Mary McKenna

The Dublin bank manager who in her spare time became Ireland's most successful Lady golfer in the modern era.

"Mary McKenna is an ambassador extraordinaire for Ireland. Years ago when she came on a regular basis to play in American amateur tournaments, we all called her 'Irish'...not 'Mary', simply 'Irish'. No more needed to be said. She was the big hitter with the big game who never met a stranger. Mary exuded fun and enthusiasm, a wonderful combination to win so many friends here in the United States.

What a run she had: nine consecutive Curtis Cup Team caps for Great Britain and Ireland. That is a record that will never be broken. We crossed paths in Curtis Cup Matches four times. In 1976 at Lytham we battled to the 18th hole where she holed a 20-foot putt to close me out for an important point. I have no doubt that her record against me is very much in her favour."

CAROL SEMPLE THOMPSON,
holder of a record 12 Curtis Cup caps for the USA and Team Captain for the 2008 matches at St Andrews.

Living for the game

Mary McKenna's life has been dedicated to golf and the pursuit of excellence. It's over forty years since she picked up a golf club for the first time and began an amazing journey that continues to this day. In captaining the Curtis Cup side to face the Americans at the 'Home of Golf' in 2008, McKenna's golfing curriculum vitae is now complete and it's no more than she deserves. "She will make a fantastic Curtis Cup Captain because she engenders such affection as well as respect," says her friend and erstwhile rival Claire Dowling (née Hourihane, herself a Curtis Cup captain at Formby in 1994). Dowling saw McKenna up close during her peak years; they enjoyed an intense rivalry in the eighties and were members of the history-making GB & I side that beat the USA at home for the first time ever in 1986. For her, "Mary is possibly the best ball striker I have ever seen and was certainly ahead of her time in the way she played. A fantastic team-mate and a wonderful friend, she was a generous and sporting opponent and a wonderful partner when we played. One of a kind!"

'MAC', as she is known throughout the golfing world, became Ireland's most successful woman golfer of the modern era and achieved it all in her spare time. Her love affair with the sport has seen her walk the fairways of the world alongside the greatest players in the game. Her appreciation of golf's history has fuelled her dedication to pass on that awareness of the game's great traditions to the next generation.

'MAC', as she is known throughout the golfing world, became Ireland's most successful woman golfer of the modern era and achieved it all in her spare time.

As Maureen Madill, the 1979 British Amateur Champion, and her Irish and Curtis Cup team-mate told me, "Mary embodies the spirit of the Curtis Cup. You couldn't find anybody, even in that arena of such rivalry, who didn't light up at the mention of her name. It's quite extraordinary really. She always had a great sense of appreciation for the people who went before her, the Phil Garvey's, the Kitty MacCann's and the Clarrie Reddan's. What's great is that she is now passing that down to the next generation. She has

The Curtis Cup.
The pinnacle of every Lady amateur's career on these islands is to play for the prestigious cup donated by Harriot and Margaret Curtis in 1932. The sisters won four US Amateur titles between them. 2008 GB & I Captain Mary McKenna is proud to have met both ladies during her own storied association with the matches.

great respect for them and is never one to say that things were better in our day. For such a good player, to be as well respected as Mary McKenna is... well it's not normal to be honest, given the jealousy in the sport. She was always a very gracious winner **and** loser. McKenna is a very special lady and a very dear friend."

Mary McKenna's achievements in golf are immense and throughout her career, there have been many magical moments...those occasions in every top class golfer's career when absolutely everything clicks.

The "Magic Year"

The year 1979 stands out from all others, in her opinion, as a purple patch of note. *"I just really, really played superbly throughout that year. I won the Irish Close Championship in Murvagh and didn't go past the 14th hole!"* That was no mean feat given that big names like Claire Hourihane, Claire Nesbitt and Maureen Madill were all in her half of the draw. *"I played my 2-iron a lot then and I just had a feeling that I could actually land it whichever side of the pin I wanted to. It was a magic year; it was just a dream, an absolute dream year. I suppose I wasn't really giving it a lot of thought but was just playing well. The more you play well the more confidence you get. I got to the stage where I thought I would never miss a shot again!"*

It was only at the British Amateur at Nairn in Scotland in '79 that McKenna's unbeaten run since the Irish Close finally came to a halt, against her great friend and compatriot Maureen Madill in the semi-finals. *"I think it was probably her turn to win. She played super golf and I can still see my putt lipping out on 18. Needless to say it was disappointing as I had been playing so well, but as it was Mo, I guess it did not feel too bad. The greatest thing then was that she kept it going and got a win."* So it was Madill and not McKenna who became the first Irish winner of the title since Philomena Garvey over twenty years previously. Incredibly, that loss to Madill was the 2nd of four semi-final defeats for McKenna in the British Amateur.

In mid-August, just eight weeks after coming so close at Nairn, McKenna travelled to Moseley near Birmingham for the British Strokeplay Championship. *"I remember that we were in Porthcawl the weekend before, for a practise for the Vagliano Trophy and then drove up to Birmingham. I have to be honest, I played poor golf in the first round for an 83 and knew that if I did that again, I wouldn't make the cut and would be on my way home. The weather was very wet the next day and the practice field was a bit away from the clubhouse, so I decided to go into the practice room that they had. It was a building with 2 bays with nets and mirrors. I hit shots there and noticed in the mirror that the club was not pointing at the target on my back swing. I got that sorted out and went out and shot 72, to make the cut. I played steady golf for the next two rounds and ended up beating Vicki Rawlings (Thomas) by 2 shots. I vividly recall that there was a very quick presentation and I was then driven at speed to the airport to catch the last flight home. Only then did it sink in that I had won. It's a great feeling to have won a British Title."*

This victory, coming straight after her loss at Nairn confirmed her standing in the game, and underlined her two great strengths: confidence and consistency.

1979 also included an historic European Team Championship in Hermitage. McKenna played superb

McKenna and Madill.
Irish team-mates, British Strokeplay and Matchplay Champions in 1979

This victory, coming straight after her loss at Nairn confirmed her standing in the game, and underlined her real strengths of confidence and consistency.

"Having decided that my job was to pull the bag, hand her the club and otherwise shut up, I found myself saying 'hit the wedge and for Christ's sake don't dolly it'!"
- Claire Hourihane

golf and led the team to success. The year also coincided with Johnny McGonigle's appointment as National Coach to the Irish team. It was one of the first years that the Irish team actually had a coach who attended the events as well, and McKenna worked a lot with him at his own base at Co. Sligo Golf Club, Rosses Point.

Ireland defeated Germany 6-1 in the final fielding a side that included Claire Nesbitt, Maureen Madill, Rhona Hegarty and Mary Gorry, with Máire O'Donnell as non-playing captain. There was huge significance to claiming that title - it was the first major team Championship won by Ireland's Ladies since the Home International Championship 72 years before!

Along the way, McKenna recorded a memorable victory over the greatest amateur of the era, the iconic Catherine Lacoste of France. The elegant Frenchwoman, daughter of tennis great Rene Lacoste, had become the first amateur ever to win the US Women's Open, beating the professionals to the greatest title in the women's game in 1967. It is a record that still stands today. Two years later, she had the unique distinction of winning both the British and US Amateur Championships in the same year. She was essentially, a modern day Bobby Jones.

In 1979, Lacoste was still a formidable player with an enviable reputation in matchplay, but on a hazy day in late summer, over the testing Hermitage golf course in Lucan, County Dublin, she came up against Ireland's own amateur superstar, Mary McKenna.

It was nip and tuck throughout the match, with very little between them - standing on the tee of the downhill final hole, the Irish number one was one down. Her caddy that day happened to be Claire Hourihane, who was herself on the cusp of international recognition. She recalled a humorous exchange at that crucial point in the match: "Mary had made a cobblers of the 18th in each previous match. We were (usual caddy-speak – 'we') in the trees on the right against Lacoste and she said 'shall I hit a 9 or a wedge?' Having decided that my job was to pull the bag, hand her the club and otherwise shut up, I found myself saying 'hit the wedge and for Christ's sake don't dolly it'! She was still laughing as she hit it, fortunately on to the green and she went on to extra holes and a memorable win."

"I beat Catherine on the 19th," remembers McKenna. *"It was one of those dream wins against probably one of the greatest golfers that I have come across. I think Lacoste was one of the finest players and the lovely thing is we still keep in contact."*

The Frenchwoman continues to actively captain the French Senior's team and is heavily involved in the promotion of the National Seniors Championships of Spain and her native France. McKenna has been a visitor to her home during the Spanish event and during dinner one year, she noticed that amongst the various displays and mementoes on the walls was a framed draw for the British Amateur Championship of 1969, which Lacoste won at Royal Portrush. The draw included the name of one Mary McKenna. As Lacoste was crowning her own vintage year, our 'legend in her spare time" was making one of her early forays in golf's elite events.

For McKenna, looking back now, 1979 was a year of golf played in what she terms 'the bubble'. *"It's a dream actually and I suppose it's a frame of mind, it's an attitude, and the better frame of mind you are in, the easier it is to get into it. When you are in it, it's great and you don't see anybody, you don't see problems. All you can see is what the book says, 'what you are trying to do.' That whole year I just seemed to be very confident, played well, hit the ball well and I suppose success breeds success and you get more confident."* Irish Ladies golf was on a high.

The Early Years

Like so many parents of teenage children, Maureen McKenna, Mary's mother, knew that it was nearing the time to prepare for her offspring to fly the coop. Having devoted her life over the previous fifteen years or so to bringing up a son and daughter, running the family house and being a loving wife to the prominent Army officer, Lieutenant Colonel John McKenna, it was now time for her to get an extra curricular activity. It was time to reawaken her interest in a sport that she had only begun to enjoy before getting married.

Golf, as it happened, had brought John and Maureen together in the first place. She had joined Newlands Golf Club in west Dublin with some girlfriends, and it looked like becoming a regular pastime until a dashing young army officer came on the scene. McKenna was a nephew of General Dan McKenna, who played an important role in Ireland's army affairs during 'The Emergency'.

Newlands was a popular hang out amongst John McKenna's fellow army officers and so, although he was a non-golfer himself, he met Maureen at one of the regular social events so popular in Irish golf clubs, and love blossomed. After marriage, golf ceased to be part of their lives as two children came on the scene in quick succession. With the family settling in the farming area of Cloghran, a couple of miles northeast of Dublin airport, young Mary and Peter McKenna enjoyed the benefits of both country life and the proximity to the city of Dublin.

"Although we were six miles from the city centre, we were absolutely out in the middle of a field," recalls Mary. "My cousins, the Gannon's, lived 'next door'. There were four kids there and two of us, and the two houses were together so it was just like one community. It was a very happy childhood."

Sport was always a part of Mary and Peter's younger days; there was horse riding to be enjoyed locally and

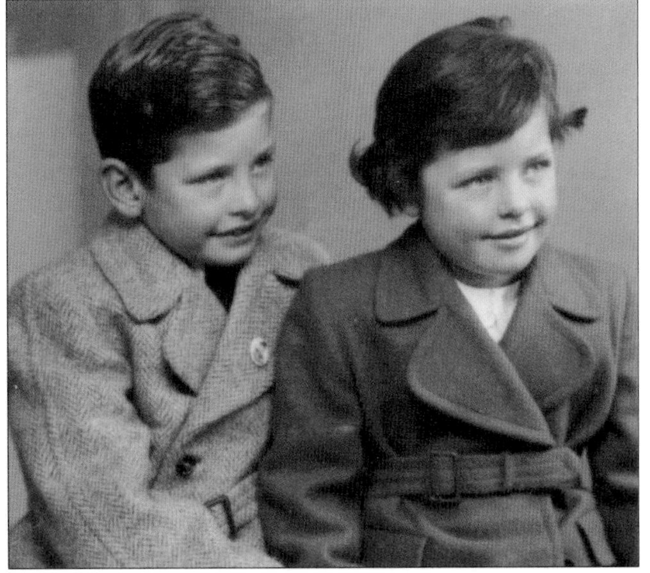

Mary and her older brother Peter in the early fifties.

there were fun-filled summer excursions by bus to the baths in Clontarf and Blackrock.

Attending secondary school at Loreto College in North Great George's Street on Dublin's north-side, Mary indulged in all the extra curricular sports activities. *"We played netball and then switched to basketball. We didn't have hockey or anything like that because we didn't have the grounds. There was a little bit of tennis, but again there was only one tennis court, which was also the basketball court! So basketball was really it."*

Midway through Mary's time in Loreto, that fateful first introduction to golf occurred. Her only prior 'golf experience' had been a few years previous, when she walked along some holes at Arklow Golf Club while making her way to the beach. However, she took a greater step towards the sport that would eventually define her life while on holiday in Rosapenna, Co. Donegal (the course where Jimmy Bruen also had his first game).

It was now time for her to get an extra curricular activity. It was time to reawaken her interest in a sport that she had only begun to enjoy before getting married.

On that occasion, Maureen re-ignited her interest in the sport, very briefly, with a round in the company of her cousins, with whom they were staying on holiday. Thirteen year-old Mary walked the course, alongside her mother but didn't actually pick up a club until the following summer (1963) when Maureen was accepted as a member of Donabate Golf Club, in Balcarrick, north County Dublin.

After her first year of active membership, Maureen decided that her son and daughter should join as junior members, now that the club was increasingly becoming a weekend haunt for the whole family.

Golf and Donabate were starting to become an integral part of the family's life and there was no shortage of encouragement when Mary began to show a natural aptitude for the game. There was regular competition for the ever-increasing junior membership and Mary also availed of coaching from the popular teaching professional, Watty Sullivan, at his base in the Grange Golf Club in Rathfarnham.

In essence, all the right steps were being taken when it came to giving her the best possible start in the game. Not to be underestimated either was the encouragement of Ria Kenny of Elm Park Golf Club. Kenny, one of the great administrators in Irish golf, happened to be an old friend of Maureen McKenna and she wasted no time in advising her of exactly what level of commitment was required of Mary, if she was to make the most of her undoubted ability.

The relentless charge of Mary McKenna through the ranks of world amateur golf was up and running.

This was all premature in many ways, because the fourteen year-old legend-in-the-making had just received her starter handicap of 36! The encouragement was well received though and Mary recalls her first proper competition at Woodbrook Golf Club that year:
"I played with a girl called Anne Finnerty from Kilkenny, (who became Anne Browne and curiously became a member of Donabate herself in later years). It took us five hours to play the singles competition. I had never played outside Donabate and we were late starters because Anne was delayed coming from Bettystown on the train, where she was on holidays. Of course everybody was in that little bit ahead of us and we were still plodding along, these two 'unheard-ofs'! I can still picture Ria Kenny saying to us 'sign those cards' and everybody was asking us how we did, but we hadn't a clue because she had taken the cards before we'd even added them up. Anne, off 29, was the winner and I was runner-up! She got three Fred Smyth irons and I got two. They matched my set because I already had 3, 5, 7 and 9 of the Fred Smyth 'Playing Jane' irons, which were the starter ones. That was my first competition."

The relentless charge of Mary McKenna through the ranks of world amateur golf was up and running.

Golf very quickly became more than just a school holiday pastime. Junior coaching was available to the best young talent in girls golf and with people like Ria Kenny supporting from the sidelines, Mary found herself on the right road to success. Moreover, she wanted it just as badly.

Peter McKenna vividly remembers his sister's early forays in the game: *"when we started to take golf lessons and started to play a bit with Mum first and later with Dad, it just seemed normal to me. Mary showed more aptitude for the game than I did, and she continued to play and progress, while I went from playing little to almost never. Her early success in junior golf did not seem anything unusual to me, at the time. It was not until she started to be picked on international teams, and bring home prestigious trophies that I realised that maybe there was more to this than I had thought!"*

Speak to any successful sportsperson about their path towards success and playing on the biggest stages and it all comes down to one word, DESIRE. Padraig

Harrington will tell you of his 'want', a force so strong from within that it manifests itself in an insatiable desire to improve. Read any biography or article on the great Ben Hogan and the oft-repeated quote 'you've got to dig it out of the dirt' jumps off the pages. It is something innate, it cannot be coached and for people like Mary McKenna, even at an early stage of their development, that desire is evidenced by a natural yearning to establish oneself amongst the better players, to make the grade and get on all the best teams.

Although she never managed to win a Girls' Championship, she was selected for international duty with the Irish Junior team for two years under the captaincy of Dorothy Glendenning and Audrey O'Donohue respectively. The Home Internationals were not established at the time for underage girls, so the highlight of the year was the annual match against the Welsh Girls' side. England played Scotland in a separate encounter.

Her first taste of the big time came when she played in the 1966 British Girls' Championship at Liphook Golf Club, an elevated heathland course on the Sussex/Hampshire border. She didn't excel that week but it provided her with a glimpse of a newer, better level of play, and one which she felt was attainable. She was also very comfortable with the solitary nature of the game, despite her solid grounding in team sports during her schooldays. *"I loved the game. I was very happy and contented to be able to hit balls and had no problems being in the practice field at Donabate on my own."* That practice, in addition to a flair for the game and a natural competitiveness, was really paying off - she was selected to play on Donabate's Senior Cup team at the age of 17.

The team's victory in the Eastern District division that year was a massive boost for the club and given that Donabate had many fine players to choose from, it was hugely encouraging for McKenna. *"Vivienne Singleton was an international and our top player. Maureen Moran (mother of 1986 Irish Close Champion Therese O'Reilly) was a low handicapper, so too was Brede Browne, who was a former international and also included were myself, Marie Nally and Bid Allen so we had some very good players in the club."*

Donabate reached the national semi-finals at Castlerock but lost out to the eventual champions Douglas, the Southern District Champions, whose line-up included internationals like Ann and Oonagh Heskin, Eileen McDaid (mother of future Curtis Cup player Eileen Rose Power), the legendary Zelie Fallon and Ann O'Brien.

McKenna had left school by this stage and, having undertaken a commercial course, had begun working for the VHI (Voluntary Health Insurance) Group. This was in the era of the permanent and pensionable job,

She didn't excel that week but it provided her with a glimpse of a newer, better level of play, and one which she felt was attainable.

but her move into the public sector had mixed implications. It was good because she was earning money with which to purchase new golf equipment, but it was bad when it came to getting time off for important tournaments like the Irish Amateur Close Championship!

Having travelled up North with her clubmates for the Senior Cup finals, it was frustrating to see all the other top golfers remaining in Castlerock for 'the Close', whilst she had to take the long and lonely road back to Dublin, where her new job required her first thing on Monday morning. It can't have been easy monitoring the progress of her new peers in the following morning's papers, but that was her predicament. In the Championship itself, Tramore's Pat O'Sullivan lost her fourth consecutive final, on this occasion to Gwen Brandom.

1968 finally saw McKenna tee it up in the biggest event in the Ladies amateur calendar. The Irish Close Championships took place that year at Lahinch and she wasted little time in making a huge impression. The McKenna clan descended en masse on the County Clare town, for a holiday as much as for the golf, and the relaxed spirit of the trip contributed hugely to Mary's easy-going attitude that week.

"The 19 year-old Miss McKenna is the most exciting prospect of the present time - and not only in this country."
- Paul MacWeeney, Irish Times

Quite simply, she sailed through the event and found herself in the final against Clontarf's Elaine Bradshaw, who had won the event two years previously at Rosslare. "*You get to the final, you keep playing day in day out and you don't think about anything until suddenly, you are photographed with the cup before teeing off so that the (national) papers will have it the next day. I think there was then a realisation that suddenly I was in the final, whereas beforehand I had just sailed along, oblivious to the fact!*"

McKenna's lack of big match experience was telling, as she never repeated the form of previous days and lost out to the wily competitive edge of Bradshaw, who was a dominant young player at the time.

Writing in the Irish Times after the final, Paul MacWeeney, the paper's golf correspondent heralded the arrival of Ireland's brightest new star:

"If Miss Bradshaw has gained notably in stature since her first success in the championship two years ago, and now is the complete player, the 19 year-old Miss McKenna is the most exciting prospect of the present time and not only in this country. She has rich assets- the build of an athlete, an excellent method and the desire to attack the ball, seeking for maximum length. All that remains is to acquire as much tournament experience as possible and then Ireland should have a regular Curtis Cup representative for years to come." Prophetic words indeed.

For McKenna, the whole experience only made her more determined. It gives us a glimpse of what makes great champions, in that she could only see positive things for herself in the game. She was certain that golfing success was in her future. She had proven her talent. Now came the hard work and she was more than prepared to get stuck in.

There was one slight snag however. While a whole new world was opening up for her through her success on the golf course, life as an employee of the VHI was less than perfect. The inflexibility of the job was exasperating and as a junior staff member, it wasn't likely to get any better, time-wise, for quite a few years. This prospect weighed her down and she had to seriously examine her options.

Fate, as it tends to do, lent a hand one evening in August of 1968, as McKenna concluded a round of golf at Dun Laoghaire, where she played in a mixed competition after work, opposite her good friend Pauline Martin and her father. Pauline would go on to play for Leinster and to captain the Irish Women's Seniors' side, but gained much greater prominence in the early eighties when she became Ireland's first ever female bank manager.

The Irish Team at the Home Internationals at Royal Porthcawl in September, 1968.
Back Row l-r: Zelie Gaynor, Ita Butler, Gwen Brandom, Joan Beckett, Mary McKenna.
Front l-r: Phil Garvey, Elaine Bradshaw, Sybil Moore (Captain), Carol Larkin (McAuley)

On that August evening as they concluded the round, the friendly banter veered towards Mary's inability to get suitable time off from work, despite making the final of the National Championship. *"Pauline wondered whether I'd like to work in the bank and I said that I didn't care where I worked, as long as I could get time off to play golf!"* Mr Martin was outraged that an emerging talent like McKenna should have to struggle to get days off and was particularly aggrieved that while the VHI would allow her time off for international matches, it was without pay.

In the clubhouse later that evening, Pauline introduced Mary to a fellow member by the name of Don Hogan. He was the Agent (Manager) of the Bank of Ireland in Dublin's College Green and knew of McKenna's impressive golfing credentials (that were about to include a debut at senior international level). He recommended that she apply for a job with the Bank of Ireland, and in no time, she found herself working for Hogan as a statement's clerk in the building just across the road from Trinity College. There would now be plenty of time off to play in Championships, with full pay! The stars were aligned, her home life was ideal and she had found the perfect career to fit in with her burgeoning talent on the golf course. To cap things off, the nineteen year-old made her debut for Ireland as a full international.

In 1969, McKenna once again reached the final of the Irish Close, this time at Ballybunion. At twenty years of age, and in her second consecutive final, there was already talk of a successor to Philomena Garvey. Premature perhaps, but she was, at least, better able to handle the big occasion this time around and won her first National title, beating Catherine Hickey of Milltown for the title.

She had also determined that it was for others to discuss how good she could be and whom she might emulate. Her primary focus was on improvement, goal-setting and achievement. McKenna was also very fortunate in that her parents, especially her father,

McKenna celebrates with friends after her first win in the Irish Close, Ballybunion 1969.
L-R: Valerie Hassett, Nuala Acton, "Mac", Pauline Martin, Kay Keating.
Front Row: Vivienne Singleton, Máire Mansfield.

She had also determined that it was for others to discuss how good she could be and whom she might emulate. Her primary focus was on improvement, goal-setting and achievement.

The curve remained upward. A debut appearance in the British Amateur Championship confirmed her exceptional talent as she made it to the semi-finals.

were in no way pressurising, nor were they living vicariously through their only daughter's successes.

"As far as Dad was concerned, if you won you won, if you lost, tough luck, it was about time somebody put you in your box! He was very proud and very supportive, but if you didn't win it didn't really matter. Not mentioning any names but it was true then and is even truer now that some people are nearly afraid to go home or to ring their fathers. For me, it's got to have played a huge part that they were so casual, yet hugely supportive about it all."

The year-on-year improvement in McKenna's standards and results was nothing short of exceptional. The comparisons with Garvey were no longer idle banter. After her success at Ballybunion, she was picked to play for Great Britain and Ireland in the Vagliano Trophy against the Continent of Europe at Chantilly in France. The curve remained upward. A debut appearance in the British Amateur Championship underlined her exceptional talent as she made it to the semi-finals. It was a huge disappointment to her not to be the first Irish woman to win the British title since Garvey in 1957, but she also knew, beyond doubt, that she had what it took to compete at the highest level, and set about aiming even higher the following year.

At around this time, McKenna became heavily involved in the Ladies Leinster Senior Alliance which allowed single-figure handicappers to play competitive winter golf and sharpen their games for the following season. The atmosphere was also one of the main attractions and great friendships resulted from those weekly gatherings, in mainly disagreeable weather. *"The Alliance was originally set up for low handicap players. There was a match nearly every weekend against a men's selection from some club. I played in that over the winters and there was hardly a weekend that I wasn't hauled out to play."*

In tandem with the Alliance, there was a splinter group that joined Baltray (Co. Louth Golf Club) as country members and this gathering did more than anything else to hone McKenna's competitive edge and matchplay prowess. *"Pauline Martin, Kay Keating, Eithne Scott, Valerie Butler, God rest her now, Vivienne Singleton, myself and Libby Byrne were all involved. It meant that if you weren't playing an Alliance match there would always be a fourball in Baltray. I think that's probably what stood to me most, was that kind of golf. It was money golf. You played for pittance, but it was the winning that mattered most."*

Keating and McKenna were regular partners in those winter battles. Pauline Martin was in the Leinster squad and a fourball completed by McKenna's clubmate and former international Vivienne Singleton was a regular weekend sighting at the Co. Louth golfing jewel. *"We were all single-figure players. You got your shots but you didn't get away with anything. In Baltray you never quite knew what could happen - the flag could drop or coins could rattle in someone's pocket when you were putting. It was probably the best training ever for matchplay. You were playing this type of golf on a regular basis so when you actually went out and you had a six foot putt, you were just immune to everything around you except the task in hand."*

There was also the Thursday evening ritual with former Curtis Cup star Ita Butler and other Dublin-based golfers at Elm Park Golf Club. A group of like-minded low handicappers would congregate at the club's driving range to practise together and afterwards make their way down the road to the Merrion Inn for banter and craic. The group, all members of the Alliance, were dubbed "The St. Judes division of the Merrion Road Sodality" by Butler, who enjoyed the fact that Thursday evenings were as much work as play, and in their almost religious devotion to practice, the pub afterwards became their little committee room!

Golf was now consuming McKenna in the best possible way. Her job with the Bank of Ireland meant that there was no chance of her life becoming one-dimensional. Making gradual progress in her career meant a great deal, but it also gave a better balance to her time, given the emergent demands placed upon her as a top class golfer.

She continued working in the College Green branch until 1980 and it should come as no surprise that her most bountiful period in golf came while working under golf-loving bosses such as Don Hogan, Des Magahey and Joe McGuire. As long as her work was done, there was never a problem getting time off; she was not working front-of-house, so finding adequate cover was never a problem.

McKenna's golfing status was underlined when she received the news that she was to get an opportunity to play for a place on the Curtis Cup team. *"In 1970, I was picked for the trials. They had 15 on the panel and it was a round robin event, with the top four automatically making the team. I played myself onto it! Again I suppose, I was not as well known as the others. Belle Robertson and I had made the team before the last morning's matches. She had 21 points and I had 19 and we couldn't be beaten. My golfing career now had a sort of progression to it. Playing in a top Championship, getting to the final, losing it, winning it the next year, making Vagliano, then Curtis Cup and Bob's your uncle. You just get into a pattern and then set your plans out."*

Would that it were so easy for lesser mortals.

Her debut in 1970 turned out to be the first of nine successive Curtis Cup appearances. Sustaining that level of excellence required incredible diligence, certainly when it came to practising the right method. Time spent working on her game had to have a certain quality attached. Time was precious, what with work and family life, so McKenna reasoned that she'd have

Raising the Irish flag at the opening ceremony for the 1982 Curtis Cup matches at Denver Country Club, Colorado. Belle Robertson is to McKenna's right. Vicki Thomas is to her left.

to make some sacrifices in order to work for a living and compete at the highest level.

"I had a ritual. I used to practise on the way into work. I practised in Clontarf (at St Anne's Park) for quite a while, there was a lot of time spent at Royal Dublin and I used to hit shots on the beach at

McKenna's golfing status was underlined when she received the news that she was to get an opportunity to play for a place on the Curtis Cup team.

Dollymount as well. I used to get to the course just before eight in the morning. Depending on what you were doing, if it was the short game you would just work on the putting, I mightn't even hit shots, I might just spend a half an hour or so on the putting green or on bunker shots or I would go out the course and play a few holes with the hares, usually 1, 15, 16, 17, 18 and then head on into the office. You can imagine at eight in the morning in Royal Dublin, (if the weather was half decent) it was absolute heaven. The key thing I think too was hitting shots off the sand on the nearby beach."

1970 also happened to be the year of the notorious bank strike. The Irish Bank Officials Association advised its members to take industrial action for better pay and conditions. The strike lasted for four months, which happened to fall during the summer, and McKenna found herself off work. Despite the obvious lack of pay, conditions were now just perfect for her! She had as much spare time as was required and her primary goal of making a solid impression against the Americans at the Curtis Cup seemed more attainable. *"I was living at home, being fed and watered and I continued to play in all the big events, no matter what it cost, because the deal was that I would make it up to my parents, who were funding me, when the strike ended and I got back to work, because there would be so much overtime!"*

Mary wins her third Irish title and celebrates with her parents Maureen and John at Lahinch, 1974

The call-up to play against the Americans again at Western Gailes in 1972 was a formality. McKenna was clearly a team player and supremely tough in matchplay. Her method was good and her mind even better. This was to be her dominant period in golf and there was no denying her charmed existence.

McKenna was clearly a team player and supremely tough in matchplay. Her method was good and her mind even better. This was to be her dominant period in golf and there was no denying her charmed existence.

"I suppose I was fortunate in having so many good teachers (from early days with Watty Sullivan to Irish squad coaching with Johnny McGonigle and onto Bernard Gallacher, when he coached the LGU Squads). It did come relatively easy. Probably the key thing is that I enjoy practising, especially on my own. I could go to Donabate and I would probably spend more time on the practice field even now, than I do playing on the course. We have a smashing practice field down there. You can just go down and practise to your heart's content. For me that was the key because a lot of people say 'I can't bear practising', but that was never a drudge for me."

She also acquired for herself a Honda 50 motorbike to get around, (with all the extra cash from the post bank-strike overtime!) and this allowed her a greater freedom, although it may have looked a bit odd to see a woman riding around on a motorbike with three or four irons sticking out from under the seat, as she headed to the practice ground at Donabate or the driving ranges at Elm Park or Leopardstown.

Mixing with the best of them

With such a flexible job, apart from international and Championship duty, there were also days off to play in an assortment of matches for the Leinster Alliance against pros like Christy O'Connor Senior and Des Smyth. Summer months were packed with endless golf; there was an assortment of open competitions at city clubs to fill her calendar and keep her game nice and sharp.

The seventies and early eighties also saw some memorable encounters with some of the great names in the game. With her status in amateur golf well and truly confirmed, McKenna availed of several opportunities to test her skills against the world's best professionals when they came to the UK for events like the Colgate International. 'The Colgate' was a massive tournament in Women's Golf in these islands and had a large purse which attracted the big names from the LPGA Tour in America.

The seventies and early eighties also saw some memorable encounters with some of the great names in the game. With her status in amateur golf well and truly confirmed, McKenna availed of several opportunities to test her skills against the world's best professionals.

Poetry in motion. "Mac" in action.

A gathering of Ryder Cup and Curtis Cup stars.
On duty at a Bank of Ireland-sponsored Links Golfing Society outing at Baltray, Mary is pictured with fellow 'greats': Ita Butler, Des Smyth, Christy O'Connor and Clarrie Reddan.

"Off I go with McKenna who was playing that day with Judy Rankin and the bloody thing took off – I nearly mowed down half the spectators. I reverted to a normal trolley next day!"
- Claire Hourihane

On one such occasion, her pal Claire Hourihane acted, once again, as bag-toter;
"I caddied for Mac, having failed to pre-qualify myself. I had to wear a caddy's bib and also happened to be the only caddy using a trolley. So this chap, who had just invented a power trolley called the Kangaroo Kart, asked me if I would trial it for him. Off I go with McKenna, who was playing that day with Judy Rankin and the bloody thing took off – I nearly mowed down half the spectators. I reverted to a normal trolley next day! Mary went on to win 'best amateur' and played on the last day with Nancy Lopez. Wonderful stuff!"

As McKenna remembers, *"it was a major tournament and the winner and runner-up from the four 'home' countries' respective national Championships were invited to compete for the amateur section. I went three times, winning the leading amateur that one time and I got to play alongside Joanne Carner (Big Momma), Kathy Whitworth and Nancy, which was a fantastic experience."*

In actual fact, it wasn't the first time that McKenna had rubbed shoulders with Lopez, arguably the most charismatic figure in Women's golf throughout those years. Mary had befriended Judy Bell (twice Curtis Cup player, captain in 1986 and more recently, President of the USGA) on her Curtis Cup debut in 1970. As a member of the GB & I team, she stayed on to compete in that year's US Amateur. Two years later, with the matches being played in England, McKenna received a further invitation from Bell to compete in a series of tournaments, culminating in that year's US Women's Amateur.

"Judy organised it. I went out and I played in the Western Amateur at the Broadmoor Country Club in Seattle and in three other events, before pegging it up in the US Amateur." In that Western Amateur Championship, McKenna came up against 14 year-old 'phenom' Lopez, who hailed from Roswell, New Mexico, the town famous for supposed UFO sightings.

"I played Nancy in the semi-final and she had been winning all around her. The trend continued, because she beat me too!" McKenna had shown good form to that point, accounting for another legend in the making, Amy Alcott, in the quarter-finals. Alcott, who was 16 at the time, went on to win five major titles including a runaway nine-shot victory at the US Women's Open in 1980. After 29 LPGA tour wins, she was elected to the World Golf Hall of Fame in 1999.

"I was about 23 at that stage and I was kind of ashamed coming home to say that I was beaten by a 14 year-old, because I was very young in Irish golf terms. When I came into international golf, Elaine Bradshaw would have been the youngest at around 25. Players like Zelie Gaynor seemed so much older, and here I was with this reality check, losing to a 14 year-old!"

Following through. McKenna launches another big drive.

Rubbing shoulders with, and taking on the biggest names in golf was becoming the norm for McKenna throughout the seventies and her Curtis Cup caps continued to accumulate.

The early spring also came to be dominated by participation in annual events such as the Avia Foursomes in England which was a four round strokeplay event, played invariably in snow and all kinds of weather over the St Patrick's weekend. Played over the famed Berkshire Golf Course, McKenna stayed with Elizabeth Jacobs, with whom she won the event on two occasions. (She also stayed there for the Sunningdale Foursomes, which is a matchplay event that she won once alongside her great friend Maureen Madill.) Admittedly it was a charmed life, and for McKenna, with her easy going nature and cheery disposition, there was always an invitation to stay as a house guest with one of her growing band of golfing colleagues, as opposed to the expense of hotel accommodation on her many and varied golfing excursions.

Amongst the World's Best

The dawning of a new decade saw McKenna leading from the front and setting a wonderful example to those who followed in her footsteps. She also went very close to winning the US Amateur Championship. *"Prairie Dunes was the venue in 1980 and Madill and myself went out for a three-week trip. We played the Broadmoor at Colorado Springs, staying with Judy Bell and Barbara McIntire. Judy organised for us to stay with friends of hers at the course in Prairie Dunes, Peter and Barbara MacDonald. They were tremendous hosts.*

Mary celebrates her win in the Hermitage Scratch Cup in the seventies with her parents Maureen and John.

The dawning of a new decade saw McKenna leading from the front and setting a wonderful example to those who followed in her footsteps. She also went very close to winning the US Amateur Championship.

"In the Championship I just played well. I kept getting through every round which was a bonus each time. When it came to the semi-final, I knew that if I had won, Madill and I would have had to change our flights home. In the end I lost to Patti Rizzo, missed out on the official presentation and flew home. I'm very proud of my bronze USGA medal though!" The great Julie Inkster won the first of three consecutive US Women's Amateurs that year, defeating Rizzo in the final. "Mac" was really mixing with the best of them, and holding her own!

In action against Patti Rizzo in the US Women's Open Amateur Championship semi-final, Prairie Dunes 1980.

The GB & I Team for the 1980 World Amateur Team Championship, Pinehurst Resort, USA.
L-R: Maureen Madill, "Mac", Belle Robertson and Máire O'Donnell, Team Captain.

Throughout the seventies, Mary McKenna had been Ireland's sole representative in the Curtis Cup and was called up on three occasions to be part of Great Britain and Ireland's elite, three-person team.

Throughout the seventies, Mary McKenna had been Ireland's sole representative in the Curtis Cup and was called up on three occasions to be part of Great Britain and Ireland's elite, three-person team, to contest the World Amateur Team Championships, known as the Espirito Santo Trophy.

A New Decade

In 1980, for the first time ever, Ireland had three representatives on the Curtis Cup team to take on the Americans at St Pierre in Chepstow. Claire Nesbitt (who had received an Espirito Santo call-up the previous year) joined McKenna and Madill in what was ultimately a losing side, but when looking at the bigger picture, it was a sign of things to come.

By the early to mid-eighties, a great rivalry had developed between Mac and Woodbrook's Claire

Hourihane. McKenna's wins at the Irish Amateur Close in 1981 and 1982 were followed by three successive victories for the Woodbrook star.
The pair also played on the same Curtis Cup side in 1984 at Muirfield and although GB & I lost agonisingly by a point, McKenna shared the stage with a young foursomes partner by the name of Laura Davies. At last, there was a prodigy to rival Lopez on this side of the Atlantic. Ladies golf was finally getting more attention and the young English superstar-in-the-making, was grabbing headlines at an enormous rate.

Davies, who went on to win the British and US Open Championship as a professional in 1986 and '87 respectively, speaks highly of her Irish friend: "My first memory of Mac was playing foursomes with her at Muirfield in those matches in 1984. I was terrified! Simply because Mac was **the** big gun at that time and was so far ahead of me. I quickly realised how wonderful she was however. Mary McKenna is the nicest person you'll ever meet."

For McKenna, there were to be more highlights, but not on as regular a basis as in her peak years of the seventies. When Lillian Behan, the 20 year-old from the Curragh, claimed the British Amateur title at Ganton in 1985, there was talk of a 'Big Three' dominating the Irish game. This was short-lived due to Behan's decision to turn professional. Before she made that switch, McKenna, Hourihane and Behan were all selected for the 1986 Curtis Cup matches at Prairie Dunes, Kansas. After 12 consecutive victories in the Cup by the Americans, Captain Diane Bailey was very upbeat and for good reason. Firstly none of the US

Laura Davies - one of Mary McKenna's biggest fans.

*"My first memory of Mac was playing foursomes with her at Muirfield in those matches in 1984. I was terrified! Simply because Mac was **the** big gun at that time and was so far ahead of me"*
- Laura Davies

team in 1986 had previous experience of the biennial matches and having lost by a single point at Muirfield, the GB & I side had a wealth of talented golfers who were familiar with the demands of Curtis Cup action. Consequently, the GB & I girls went into these matches both hugely determined and utterly focussed on the job in hand.

McKenna's recollections of that famous week are vivid: *"The weather in '86 was hugely hot. It was like walking out of the air-conditioning into an oven. Our captain, Di Bailey and our manager, Elsie Brown, had both done incredible groundwork in preparation for this."*

It was also the beginning of what McKenna describes as the 'isostar era'. *"Energy drinks were just coming onto the scene and Diane embraced the whole concept, given the heat that week. We were also encouraged to drink a carbohydrate liquid called Perform. For people who would be too nervous to eat you would drink this awful creamy stuff and it was full of carbohydrates so it saved you eating. You were weighed before you went out and then according to the amount of liquid that you would lose, you were given so much to drink. I don't know whether we psyched the Americans out of it with this move, but we were all going around with these bottles of energy drinks. Everywhere you went you had your bottle in your hand and whether it gave us the extra confidence or whether it worked, I am not sure, but we all came out of the traps and played well."*

"Everywhere you went you had your bottle in your hand and whether it gave us the extra confidence or whether it worked, I am not sure, but we all came out of the traps and played well."

Played well? The GB & I side had a massive lead of 6 ½ - 2 ½ going into the second day's play and ironically, the mood in the camp was almost one of trepidation. *"I think it was a little bit frightening. You would be nearly afraid not to play well for Diane Bailey. She just did so much groundwork; she was a very, very strong and good captain."* McKenna was paired for the foursomes on that second morning with the vastly experienced Belle Robertson, who was ten

History in the making.
Discussing the line of a crucial putt in searing heat with Belle Robertson at Prairie Dunes, Kansas 1986

years her senior and enjoying a comeback of sorts, having won the previous year's British Strokeplay title for the third time, at the age of forty five.

The Scottish great has fond memories of both the match, which was the final foursomes game that morning and of her friendship with McKenna, which remains undimmed:
"As I got older, I sometimes found myself voicing the old adage 'I hope I will not let you down' and immediately Mary would tell me 'listen, the rule in foursomes play is to hit the ball from where I put you and for me to do likewise!

A measure of our great understanding and familiarity with each other's games came to the fore when, near the end of our match that day, I raced a ten-foot putt uphill some five feet past on the 17th... unforgivable! Mary, to her great credit, holed the return to remain level. At the final hole, a long par four, I persuaded her to take her driver. She missed the fairway on the left, so I dug it out and then told her to put it on the green and I would hole it, and that's what happened! Diane Bailey rejoiced with the team at lunch, safe in the knowledge that history was about to be made, as our match result, ensured that no matter what happened in the six afternoon singles, we could not be beaten. That Curtis Cup was my last one (and for McKenna also), and we often rib each other as to who started the rot on those two final holes, or who contributed most in our unlikely win in that match. The delights of amateur golf and the pleasures of achieving success together as a partnership and as a team enrich us golfers with memories to last a lifetime."

As McKenna recalls, *"we needed one match from the afternoon and you were nearly afraid to talk about it because it was kind of a dream. I mean, we were never*

The history-making GB & I Team at Prairie Dunes
Back Row L-R: Mary McKenna, Elsie Brown (Manager), Lillian Behan, Trish Johnson, Jill Thornhill & Belle Robertson.
Front Row: Karen Davies, Claire Hourihane, Diane Bailey (Captain), Vicki Thomas.

The delights of amateur golf and the pleasures of achieving success together as a partnership and as a team enrich us golfers with memories to last a lifetime.

this far ahead before and when Trish Johnson won her match it was just fantastic. The first time on American soil we had the Cup back, beating the Americans by 13-5 - it definitely gave one hell of a boost to GB & I golf."

Johnson, now a multiple winner on the Ladies European Tour and a Solheim Cup player, remembers McKenna fondly: *"Mac as I've always known her, was my golfing idol growing up. Then I found myself on the same team as her (at Prairie Dunes) and found out that she was an even better player, and more importantly, person than I thought she was, and that took some doing!"*

Amongst the Americans were the likes of Dottie Pepper and Danielle Ammacapane, both of whom, like Johnson in Europe, made hugely successful transitions into the paid ranks. For McKenna the match was a record-breaking ninth and, as things turned out, her last appearance as a player, in the biennial contest.

McKenna's Last Stand

By 1989, Mary McKenna's reign at the top of Irish golf seemed to be on the wane. She was still a very prominent figure at this stage and featured annually on the Irish side that contested the Home Internationals. She also won the Leinster Championship twice, in '88 and '89 but it had been seven years since she had won her seventh National title.

Mac believed otherwise and prepared thoroughly for the Championship, to be played over one of her favourite courses, Westport in Co. Mayo.

The possibility of an eighth Irish title appeared to be beyond her, given the dominance at the time of Claire Hourihane and the increasing number of younger talents coming through. Luckily, Mac believed otherwise and prepared thoroughly for the Championship, to be played over one of her favourite courses, Westport in Co. Mayo.

"I stayed with my good friend Maureen Byrne, who had a house there. I came and went and did my own thing. I geared myself up to play and compete in the Championship, not necessarily away from everybody because you come in and you have your food and you eat with people, but I would stand up and I might go off and read a book or I might listen to my (psychology) *tape or watch TV. I had the comfort of the house and I could come and go as I pleased. It was just the way I competed and this arrangement suited me perfectly."*

Mary McKenna wins her eighth Irish title at Westport 1989.

McKenna was always a firm believer in the merits of a good mental approach when it came to maximising one's ability at the game and talks about those rare times when a golfer can eliminate all distractions and focus entirely on the job in hand. *"It's probably the last time that I was in 'the bubble', and it was my last Championship win. That was one where I had a 'feeling' all week. It wasn't that I was actually going to win it, but I wasn't going to lose. I know that sounds funny, but I just couldn't see myself being beaten."*

Laytown & Bettystown international Carol Wickham had come through a very tough half of the draw that week and looked odds-on to claim her first ever senior Irish title.

"She played super golf while I went through an iffy patch around 10, 11, and 12. I was two down playing 16 when we were both through the green. I pitched up and left it short and above the hole. I had about eight feet left, downhill! Carol was about 8 feet past. When I was standing over that putt, I wasn't really aware of what was happening. I was in the zone obviously but I didn't stand over that saying 'if I miss it and she holes I am dead, I am finished.' That didn't come into the equation. My frame of mind was just so good over it. Why, I don't know. I used to work with these 'play to win' tapes and listen to them: 'I am great, I am the best, I play like a champion and I play

Captain Fantastic!
Mary McKenna arrives home at Dublin Airport having captained the Irish team that won the Home Internationals at Cruden Bay in 2003.
Back Row L-R: Maura Morrin, Maria Dunne, Trish Mangan, Sinead Keane, "Mac", David Kearney (National Coach).
Front Row L-R: Claire Coughlan, Helen Jones, Ita Butler (President ILGU), Sheena O'Brien Kenney (Manager) & Tara Delaney. Missing from photo is Heather Nolan.

It certainly looked all over when she found herself two up on McKenna as they stood on the 16th tee in the final.

to win. My muscles respond with ease and flexibility to my mental commands.' I could nearly say it off. You just kept saying it and saying it...and it worked!" It worked alright, but, after Wickham holed hers, it meant that Mac was dormie two down and it looked all over. Think again.

McKenna's experience and class came boldly to the fore as she proceeded to birdie 17 and 18 to dramatically force a playoff. A sensational birdie on the 19th saw her claim an eighth Irish Championship! *"It was just one of those dreams and it's probably one of Carol's nightmares. It wasn't really that she lost, she didn't play 17 that well, but it was more that I just put the pressure on her and that's the way it goes. You can't account for it but it just worked."*

In the modern era, there is no Irish woman that can come close to McKenna's consistency and victory haul. She played on the Irish team for 24 straight years before being dropped in 1992. Fighter that she is, she claimed her 25th Home International cap in 1993, which happened to be the Centenary Year of the Irish Ladies Golf Union and a fitting time to retire from the international scene. Even as a 'senior' golfer, Mary continues to set goals, winning both the Irish and British Seniors titles in her first two seasons amongst the 50 year olds and over. In February of 2006, she added the Portuguese Seniors title to her incredible record.

"I don't really look back over what I've achieved. In 2002 I played on the first Seniors Home International team so I now have my three badges: my Junior, Ladies International and now my Seniors. I have achieved it all at that level. I have been very fortunate; God has given me so much. I have seen the world through golf. I have so many friends through golf and my whole life has been driven in a way, through the game. It's been very good to me. After the Curtis Cup in 2008, I will probably get back and play a little bit more club golf, which I really have been neglecting over the years, but I have had great support from them as well. I love Seniors' golf, I have to say, it's what keeps me going. As long as the feet keep walking I will keep playing!"

Mary McKenna, a modern-day golfing legend, in her spare time!

In the modern era, there is no Irish woman that can come close to McKenna's consistency and victory haul. She played on the Irish team for 24 straight years before being dropped in 1992.

Mac's Friends in Golf

MAUREEN MADILL
BBC Golf Commentator, former Ladies European Tour Professional. 1979 British Amateur Champion, 1980 British Strokeplay Champion and former Curtis Cup & Irish International:
"Mary was a great inspiration to me. She is the most selfless golfer that I've met and she always gave so much of her time to encouraging and helping younger players who were coming up. A lot of them were potential rivals, including myself! Whenever any of us were successful, there was never any remote bit of jealousy from her."

ANN IRVINE
British Amateur Champion 1974 and Curtis Cup team-mate of McKenna's in 1970 & 1976:
"Due to my leaving golf in the mid seventies, our time playing together was when Mary was very much the 'new face' of Irish golf. Her love of golf is passionate, and her love of her friendships, I think is even more important to her. Now that she's topping her fabulous career by being the Curtis Cup Captain, it is so right – and I believe she will be a great Captain.
I am just so proud to be a member of her International Selection Committee, and to have the chance once more, to walk the fairways with Mary – and enjoy her magnificent company. To be in Mary's presence (and I have said this to her) is like being in the company of a 'living legend' of Irish golf – the feeling only equalled, when with the late Joe Carr."

VIVIENNE SINGLETON
Donabate club-mate and former international team-mate:
"Mary and I played in many international matches together, and were virtually undefeated. We even beat Catherine Lacoste and Ann Marie Palli of France in the European Internationals. Mary was one of the most powerful golfers I have played with. I would say Mary was as powerful in her day as Nicklaus was in his *day.* If she had the advantage of the new equipment, I could only guess at how good she could have been.

She was a great ambassador for her golf club and for Ireland. She has a good sense of humour...when playing in foursomes together I would ask, 'Please put me on the fairway.' and I would end up one foot in the rough! It didn't matter, because she was so far up the fairway, I usually only had a short iron into the green!"

PETER McKENNA (*Mary's brother*)
"I left home in the early seventies, just about the time that Mary was really coming into her own. This is when I started to follow her career and successes more closely, especially when she came to play on international teams in the US. After the team

Peter alongside Maureen Madill.

"Mary was a great inspiration to me. She is the most selfless golfer that I've met and she always gave so much of her time to encouraging and helping younger players who were coming up."
- Maureen Madill

competition was over, most of the players would stay on and play in a few of the major US tournaments.

This is the part of her career that I was more involved in. For many years I would take holidays and visit her at whatever tournament she was playing in, sometimes even being talked into caddying for her!

One of the most memorable trips was when Mary and Tegwen Perkins from Wales came to visit me in Florida on their way home from the World Team Championships in the Dominican Republic. We had a great week visiting Disney World and all the other Florida attractions, including the beach.

Another great trip was to the Broadmore Golf Club in Colorado Springs, where we met up with Mary and a great group of Irish supporters. A great time was had by all in 'The Bee'. We will say no more!

At Lincoln City, Nebraska at another tournament, we met up with Mary and her great friend Maureen Madill, and I remember a great evening in the bar when the patrons realised that Mary was in fact that person who was being interviewed on the TV above our heads. That day she had just defeated one of the American favourites.

The patrons realised that Mary was in fact that person who was being interviewed on the TV above our heads. That day she had just defeated one of the American favourites.

There were other trips as well, but the one that means the most was in 1992, when Mary became Team Captain for the World Championships in Vancouver, BC, Canada. Six months after we moved to Vancouver, Mary comes to visit, and brings Mum along for the trip! On another trip to Vancouver, Mary played in the Canadian Seniors, and it was great for me to bring out some Canadian rent-a-crowd to cheer her on.

Mary provides us all with a lifetime of memories for which I am very grateful. However having Mary as my little sister and best friend is what means most to me.

The last thing I can say about Mary is that in her career she has met many wonderful people and made many friends all around the world, but her best friends are still the gang that were there at the beginning."

TEGWEN MATTHEWS (née Perkins).
Curtis Cup team-mate, 1974, 76, 78 & 80
Team manager of 2007 Vagliano Trophy and 2008 Curtis Cup teams:

"I have had the pleasure of knowing Mary since I was 17 years of age, feeling completely out of place on my first outing on a British Ladies Golf team. Mary and I very quickly became friends, where I think everyone else was English! And we shared a love of ice cream! It is no exaggeration to say that I look at McKenna (it's what I have always called her!) as my sister and we just have that magical friendship where you don't speak to each other for months but always pick up exactly where you were before and are always so comfortable in each other's company.

Her golfing record is immense and speaks for itself, but McKenna is the kindest, funniest, most helpful

Mary and Tegwen after winning the Avia Foursomes at the Berkshire, 1977

and caring person I know - she is also the messiest! Sharing a room with McKenna, you need a map to find the way out! On one occasion at a Curtis Cup in the USA, I drew a line down the centre of the room and told her that all her stuff must stay on her side - I kept the chocolates and sweets my side, so she was desperate!

One of my most treasured moments is winning the Avia foursomes partnering McKenna - it was even more special as we won it on St Patrick's Day and the pro at the Berkshire had decked the whole of his front display window in green golfing attire.

When McKenna phoned and asked me to be her Team Manager for the 2007 Vagliano Trophy and 2008 Curtis Cup matches at St Andrews, I was overwhelmed and took less than a millisecond to answer - I was completely honoured to be asked and it's the highlight of my golfing life. I would do anything for McKenna - no one can be as lucky as I am to have a friend like her."

CLAIRE DOWLING (née Hourihane)
Friend, rival and Curtis Cup and Irish International team-mate:
"I saw Mary McKenna at her best. We first met when I played her in a Senior Cup match at the Island. I remember standing on the first tee and was so nervous there was a roaring in my ears and I couldn't see. Needless to say I lost. I looked at her planting herself on the first tee and hitting it miles, and wished I was on another planet!

5 time Irish Champion & former British Strokeplay Champion Claire Dowling (nee Hourihane).

I roomed with Mary many times, but remember my first home international in 1979 at Harlech. She looked after me like a Mother. On the last night when celebrations were getting a little out of hand I was taken off to bed and tucked up with a cuppa and the 11 o-clock news. Our room overlooked the swimming pool and the Welsh, particularly, were a little the worse for wear and were chucking each other in, fully dressed. Mary has never drunk alcohol, and I didn't drink back then and it was nice to be out of the way when things could get a little messy downstairs!

McKenna was always fanatical about clean shoes and clubs, something she said was hammered in to her by Belle Robertson, so she passed it on to me. When I was Irish Captain I was always going on about it and after I finished I went to support the team the next year at Burnham and Berrow. They came off the course after the morning foursomes and surrounded me by the 18th green and said look down, we hope you're impressed? And I was ! 8 pairs of immaculate feet. That is McKenna's legacy!"

"She looked after me like a Mother. On the last night when celebrations were getting a little out of hand I was taken off to bed and tucked up with a cuppa and the 11 o'clock news."
- Claire Dowling (nee Hourihane)

CAREER HIGHLIGHTS

Name: Mary McKenna
Date of Birth: 29th April, 1949
Birthplace: Dublin
Family: 1 brother, Peter
Occupation: Bank Manager (retired)
Club: Donabate G.C.
Lowest Handicap: +4

CHAMPIONSHIP HIGHLIGHTS

British Open Amateur Championship
Semi-finalist 1969, 1979, 1982 & 1991

British Open Amateur Strokeplay Championship
Winner 1979
Runner up 1976 & 1984

British Seniors Open Amateur Championship
Winner 2001

US Open Amateur Championship
Semi-finalist in 1980

Irish Amateur (Close) Championship
Winner 8 times: 1969, 1972, 1974, 1977, 1979, 1981, 1982 & 1989. Leading qualifier 9 times.

Colgate European Championship (Professional) 1979
Leading Amateur

Irish Seniors Amateur Open Championship
Winner 2001

Irish Strokeplay Foursomes Championship
Winner in 1989 & 1993 (with Evelyn Hearn)

Spanish Seniors Amateur Open Championship
Winner in 2006

Leinster Championship
Winner 6 times:
1981, 1982, 1988, 1989, 1990 & 1993

REPRESENTATIVE HONOURS

Curtis Cup
GB & I Captain 2008
Capped as a player 9 consecutive times (GB & I record): 1970-1986

Vagliano Trophy
GB & I Captain in 1995 & 2007
Capped as a player 9 times: 1969-1983 & 1987

Espirito Santo Trophy (World Team Championship)
GB & I Captain 1986, 1990, 1992 & 2000
Capped as a player 4 times: 1970, 1974, 1976 & 1980

International: Capped for Ireland over 25 years, 1968-1991 & 1993

International Seniors:
Capped for Ireland, 2003-2006

MISCELLANEOUS

Winner of Sunningdale Foursomes
(Maureen Madill) in 1984

Winner of AVIA Foursomes
Tegwen Perkins (1977), Belle Robertson (1984 & 1986)

DAKS Woman Golfer of the Year (UK) 1979

East of Ireland Mixed Foursomes Championship,
winner 4 times with Eddie Dunne (1979 & 1984) and Paul Rayfus (1987 & 1989).

Winner of following Scratch Cups:
- Hermitage
- Woodbrook
- Castletroy
- Heath
- Shannon
- Tramore
- Waterford
- Cork
- Galway

Arthur Pierse

The garage-owner from Tipperary, with one of the greatest swings ever seen in Irish golf and the 2007 British Open Seniors Amateur Champion.

"Arthur Pierse was unquestionably the best driver of a ball that ever played in a left to right wind. The toughest wind for any right-handed golfer is a left to right wind and it was just uncanny how straight he would hit the ball in that wind, it was like it was on a tightrope. A great swinger of the golf club, he was unusual in terms of players of his era in that he had an orthodox golf swing!

His ability to swing the golf club and strike the golf ball was as good as any pro's was or is. Arthur had a strong presence on the golf course too. You worried about playing Arthur Pierse, you didn't want to give him the upper hand. I think Arthur wanted to look the part too; he always turned out well and would definitely be the one trying to assert himself over you in any match. He would like to be the guy leading off on each tee!"

PADRAIG HARRINGTON, January 2006.

The St Andrews Peace Agreement, April 2007!

It had been one of the most extraordinary rows ever in Irish amateur golf. So it was no surprise that when a group of fifty-somethings relaxed over a pleasant meal following a very enjoyable round at the Home of Golf that the topic of 'the small ball-big ball row' of 1981 should come up in conversation. Particularly when the man being asked about the infamous incident was none other than Arthur Pierse, one of the two main protagonists.

The other leading character that year was Ronan Rafferty. Widely regarded as Ireland's greatest golfing sensation since Jimmy Bruen, he was similarly very young (seventeen), had a unique swing and displayed remarkable ability when it came to shooting low scores on the toughest of courses; he was clearly a star-in-the-making.

And in that week back in May 1981, it was no ordinary, run-of-the-mill competition that the pair were playing in either; it was the European Amateur Team Championships. The six-man amateur team fielded by Ireland that week was generally considered to be the best ever assembled. Joe Carr, Ireland's greatest ever amateur, was in his final year as team captain and at the venue of his second British Amateur Championship victory, he was determined, and indeed confident that his team would win Europe's premier amateur team event.

During practise, Joe Carr asked me if I'd consider playing foursomes in the Championship with Ronan. I said that I wouldn't because he was playing with the big ball.

Pierse, who was a dominant player at the time, was joined in the side by the aforementioned Rafferty and another young prodigy, Philip Walton. Also amongst that elite Irish team were Mark Gannon, Declan Branigan and Garth McGimpsey. It just happened to be a Walker Cup year and therefore, several of the team had justifiable claims to a spot on the ten-man side. 'The Europeans' was in effect the final trial.

Unfortunately, Carr's high hopes soon gave way to

The 1981 Irish Team at the European Amateur Championships at St Andrews. L-R: Declan Branigan, Mark Gannon, Arthur, Joe Carr, Garth McGimpsey, Philip Walton & Ronan Rafferty

high dudgeon, after the 17 year-old Rafferty threw a spanner in the works. Declan Branigan recalled events over a quarter of a century later: "During practise, Joe Carr asked me if I'd consider playing foursomes in the Championship with Ronan. I said that I wouldn't because he was playing with the big ball. I'd never played it and it wouldn't have been a good time to start either!

Ronan actually said to me that it might improve my game but I was having none of it. I told him that from Sam Snead to Ben Hogan up to Nicklaus, Palmer and Watson, they all played the small ball when they came over here to play in the British Open. They had the option to play either ball and chose the small ball, despite playing the bigger ball all of their golfing lives. I said to Ronan that they obviously considered it an advantage over here and he could say nothing!"

It was a peculiar time for golf on these islands - the small ball (1.62 inches) was being gradually replaced by the bigger one (1.68 inches). At the time, it was allowable to play either size, but in foursomes, both partners had to play alternate shots with the same ball. Pierse normally used the small ball and had Carr's approval to do so in his foursomes match alongside Rafferty, against the top English pair of Peter McEvoy and Geoff Goodwin.

Rafferty, who could be petulant on occasion, absolutely refused to play with the smaller ball when the moment of truth came. The pair played with the big ball in the end, after Rafferty teed off with one at the first! On the fourteenth hole, Pierse reckoned that the best opportunity that the pair had of hitting the par five in two was to hit a "sloping-fade" off the tee. Without informing his partner, he proceeded to execute a perfect tee-shot, but with a small ball! Rafferty refused point blank to play his second shot. Pierse recalls: *"Joe Carr had to come over to sort it out but it was a bit unsavoury to say the least. In hindsight I should have informed him that I was changing the ball, but I didn't. Ronan got it home in two though, when he did eventually hit it!"* The mother of all rows ensued within the Irish camp later followed by threats to send Rafferty home. Any hopes for a unified team spirit were exhausted pretty quickly.

Having been part of two winning European Championship sides subsequently, Garth McGimpsey still considers the 1981 team to have been the best of all. "It was the strongest six-man team I ever played on. A lot of legends there, if you like, but Joe Carr was unhappy with Ronan. That was when Ronan didn't wear his team uniform the same way as everybody else, it was all unpleasant. I was sharing with Ronan at the time at the Rusacks Hotel. We were both in the room together (on one particular occasion) when Joe knocked on the door and stormed in and started laying into Ronan about the small ball/big ball. He was saying he was dropping him for the next day and I disappeared into the bathroom to try and get offside. Joe was very close to not playing Ronan next day, which would have scuppered his Walker Cup chances, but he didn't, and the rest is history."

Not surprisingly the Pierse/Rafferty partnership never ignited, small ball or otherwise. They were soundly beaten 3 & 1 and Rafferty went down in the afternoon singles to McEvoy on the 19th.

Rafferty's tantrums were forgivable to a point, given that he was only seventeen, but it had a hugely unsettling and divisive effect on the team, with Ireland losing to England in the matchplay round, effectively ruining their chances of overall victory.

Twenty-six years later, Pierse, by now a fifty-six year-old businessman, has softened somewhat in his view of the Warrenpoint star. Rafferty went on to become Europe's top golfer as a professional in 1989, in addition to playing in the Ryder Cup, before retiring young to pursue a career in golf punditry on television.

Some of that softening came about because who should walk into the restaurant on that April evening in 2007, barely minutes after Pierse had entertained

Friends again! Pierse and Rafferty pictured at Kingsbarns in April 2007, twenty six years after their infamous 'small ball-big ball' row.

Without informing his partner, he proceeded to execute a perfect tee-shot, but with a small ball! Rafferty refused point blank to play his second shot.

his friends with the tale, only the same Ronan Rafferty.

The former team-mates met again the following day, and on this occasion, one of Pierse's group, Denis Creedon of Lahinch had a camera, to put on record that the ice between the pair had indeed thawed!

The Early Years

Hailing from Tipperary town, Arthur Pierse was a student at Trinity College in Dublin when his golfing talent really began to shine through. Many afternoons were happily spent at Portmarnock Golf Club during those college years, in the company of the venerable old pro Harry Bradshaw. As eager to soak up the Brad's pearls of wisdom as the former Ryder Cup player was willing to dispense them, the friendship they built was to prove invaluable to Pierse as his golfing career blossomed.

Readily admitting to never having seen anybody like Harry Bradshaw when it came to putting, Pierse acknowledges the Delgany legend as having the complete short game package. *"He had a two-fisted grip which wasn't pretty to look at. He drew every golf shot he ever hit, didn't have a very nice set-up, but my God with a wedge in his hands and a putter he was absolute magic!"*

For a young man like Pierse, coming under Harry's wing was the golfing equivalent to striking oil.

If a golfer showed potential and was willing to work and learn, then Harry provided a rich seam of anecdotes and sound advice. For lovers of golf, his company and stories were a priceless joy. For a young man like Pierse, coming under Harry's wing was the golfing equivalent to striking oil.

Pierse however, had some previous form when it came to learning from the very best. Ireland's greatest ever lady player, Philomena Garvey, spent a few years in the mid-sixties as a professional and visited Tipperary Golf Club on one particular occasion to give lessons. One of her students was a then fourteen year-old Arthur. As Ireland's 'Queen of the Fairways' recalled to me in 2007: *"I remember telling Arthur when he was a boy in Tipperary that he shouldn't let anyone interfere with his swing. He had a perfect swing in my opinion and I don't think anyone would disagree with me. My advice was that he should keep doing what he was doing and to enjoy his golf!"*

Seven years later, Pierse was a different proposition altogether as a player. He had begun to take golf seriously in only his second year at University, having initially concentrated on tennis and rugby when he arrived in Dublin. Sidelined from both with a bad case of tennis elbow, he accepted the invitation of a few friends to play golf with the Trinity College second team, known as 'The Wedges'.

It was quickly evident that in golf, Arthur Pierse had found his perfect means of sporting expression. He went from a handicap of fourteen to scratch in a single year, winning his college Colours in the process and finding himself on a fast track to the elite level.

He began playing with a few of the first team members and it dawned on him that if he applied himself a bit more to working on the fundamentals of the game, and started to practise more, he could beat each and every one of them.

One of those fellow students, Graham Donald, was an excellent young prospect and Pierse began to play all of his student golf alongside him. Donald was from the Grange Golf Club in Rathfarnham, and having noted his solid performances in some major amateur Championships, Arthur found himself naturally inclined towards working hard at matching his friend's higher level of play. As Pierse testified: *"Every good golfer has a natural ability to a certain extent, but so much of it is hard work. I began to enjoy the hard work. If you don't enjoy the practise, I don't think you will ever be successful in golf."*

Pierse was also more than fortunate to have had parents who played and enjoyed the game. His father Gerry played no small part in presenting his identical twin sons, Gerry Junior and Arthur, with a precious introduction to the theory of the golf swing via Ben Hogan's celebrated work, '*Five Lessons: The Modern Fundamentals of Golf*', a book that has achieved biblical status over the years.

"I got that book at an early stage and I learned it, literally chapter by chapter. I must have read it hundreds of times and tried to understand it. What that gave me was the ability to understand the golf swing from Hogan's point of view - he was probably the greatest striker of them all. I think that if you understand that book then you don't need to see any coach. The game of golf has not changed in the last fifty or sixty years. Golf equipment has, golf balls have, but the golf swing hasn't!"

56 year-old Arthur demonstrating the "Hogan fundamentals" that have served him very well over the years, pictured in May 2007

Pierse had always been competitive, no matter what sport he played but it became clear to him by his early twenties that one game offered him the best potential to excel. He packed in rugby and tennis to focus his energies on becoming a winning golfer. As a genuine scratch player, he felt ready to take his game to the next level by playing in his first major amateur Championship. The year was 1972.

Moving up a gear

Pierse's debut in elite competition coincided with the Golden Jubilee of the famous West of Ireland Amateur Championship. Traditionally held over the Easter period, it is the first major Championship on the amateur calendar in Ireland. With high winds and rain such a regular feature at that time of year, it is always a very tough test for golfers. The standard of Pierse's accommodation certainly wasn't particularly high however - he slept in a tent with his mates Graham Donald and Sandy Dunlop, on the nearby beach at Rosses Point!

He did however bring a razor sharp game with him, and being something of an 'unknown' brought its own advantages. In the first round, the young Tipperary man found himself drawn to play Ireland's greatest ever amateur, Joe Carr.

The pair had never met, but Arthur knew of Carr's record from newspaper reports. In addition, he received a tip-off that the elder statesman of amateur golf was no slouch in the area of asserting his personality on a golf match, such was his competitive zeal.

Pierse had always been competitive, no matter what sport he played but it became clear to him by his early twenties that one game offered him the best potential to excel.

"In 1974, when I had been runner-up in 'the East', I felt that I didn't have either the playing ability or the mental ability at that stage to win."

"Joe was a pure legend and this was his comeback after suffering a heart attack. I vividly remember an incident on the tenth hole. Joe came over and said that he was in a rabbit scrape. Now, in fairness, he was in a rabbit scrape but I had heard so much about his ability to bustle that I told him that he wasn't in a rabbit scrape, even though I wasn't very well up on the rules at that stage!"

The imposing Carr intimated that they would send for a ruling, at which point Arthur, attempting a poker face, uttered firmly, *"fine, you can get a ruling, but I'm not giving you a drop!"*

Carr, as it happened, was perfectly entitled to a drop but decided to admonish his upstart of an opponent by saying, *'it doesn't bloody matter, sonny, we don't need a ruling, I'll beat you anyway!"*

That however didn't materialise for the twelve-time former champion, with Pierse emerging victorious on the 17th. After the handshakes and no shortage of back slapping from those in attendance, Carr's wife Dor came over to him with encouraging words: "Don't mind what Joe said to you, you are a lovely young lad and I am delighted you beat him!"

In the early seventies, Pierse, like so many of his contemporaries, sported long hair. His accommodation that week led to a slightly unkempt appearance. In addition, flared trousers were all the rage amongst the youth and his appearance was quite at odds with the accepted attire seen in golf clubs at the time.

Buoyed up by victory, Pierse decided to approach the imposing Carr in the bar afterwards, to see if he had any advice for the future. The Sutton great quickly looked him over and said 'yes sonny, dress yourself properly!' The amateur career of Arthur Pierse was off and running and although he didn't go on to win the Championship, his first round victory certainly helped to put him on the map.

Gerry Pierse had also promised his son a new set of irons while he was still a student and Harry Bradshaw even went as far as to order a custom-made set of blades for his young charge. As was his way, he wrote to the Hogan Factory in Fort Worth, Texas and included all of Pierse's specifications, including hand-size, lie angle and shaft flex. Such customisation was quite uncommon in those days.

"Those Apex Hogans arrived back a few months later and were just perfect. Hogan obviously was one of my real heroes and I went on to play with those irons for the next ten years. In those days Hogan actually designed the clubs himself. Harry assured me that they were absolutely identical to what 'the Hawk' himself played with. To this day I still look at those clubs and I can't think of an iron that is better than them."

Pierse's first significant run at a national title came in 1974 when over the June Bank Holiday weekend, he finished runner-up to Hugh Smyth in the East of Ireland Championship at Baltray. Leading by six shots at halfway and by four shots going into the last round, Pierse carded a one over par 74, while the City of Derry player shot a hugely impressive 68 to win the final by three shots.

"Once I got that far in a big tournament, I used to kind of look at those who were ahead of me and I decided then that I wanted to be number one! I had tremendous ambition; I wanted to win 'the West', 'the East' and 'the South'. I wanted to win as many of those as I could. In '74 when I had been runner-up in 'the East', I felt that I didn't have either the playing ability or the mental ability at that stage to win. I had to do so much more work on my game. In order to win I had to get way beyond where I was, so that when I came under pressure, things would happen naturally for me."

The improvements made over the next two years were obvious from his strokeplay performances, particularly when winning the leading amateur prize at the Carroll's Irish Open in 1975, when Christy O'Connor Junior won at Woodbrook. Pierse retained that honour at Portmarnock the following year when he joined Ben Crenshaw on the podium. Although he had yet to claim silverware in any of the Irish amateur Championships, provincial or national, his swing and ball-striking ability was drawing wide praise from all quarters. After impressive performances for Munster over a two-year period in the Interprovincial Championships, a first international cap finally came his way for the Home Internationals at Muirfield in September 1976. The endless practise was starting to pay off.

A Duo in the Sun!

The following summer, Arthur and a young Irish professional named Des Smyth took the ferry together from Larne to Stranraer in Scotland. They first came to know each other when Rockwell College (where Pierse attended) was beaten by St Joseph's CBS, Drogheda in the Irish Schools Championship at Baltray, and subsequently, through Pierse's challenges at 'the East' and in the Carroll's Irish Open. The pair had become friendly and as a cost-saving exercise, they, together with Arthur's twin brother Gerry, (along for the adventure as caddy) headed over to Scotland to attempt pre-qualifying for the British Open, to be held the following week at Turnberry.

It was the Championship that history now acknowledges as 'the duel in the sun' after Jack Nicklaus and Tom Watson's famous battle over the final two rounds that effectively spread-eagled the field. Smyth and Pierse both won their places in the starting line-up, with Arthur coming through qualifying with rounds of 70 & 74 at Kilmarnock Barassie. His goal was to make the cut in his first Open and to go on then and win the silver medal for leading amateur. He also hoped to meet some of his heroes, including a certain South African legend: *"I was named after my uncle, Arthur Darcy, who was a very keen golfer and also a big fan of Bobby Locke's, so I went up to Bobby in the locker room and introduced myself as Arthur Darcy Pierse and of course his real name was Arthur Darcy Locke! We hit it off and shared several minutes chatting about my uncle, golf in Ireland and of course, our mutual friend Harry Bradshaw."* The Brad had admitted to Arthur on one occasion that he had the best short game in the world bar one, conceding that Locke always had the edge on him! Interestingly, Bradshaw also reckoned that Mark Gannon was not far behind himself and Locke when it came to prowess with the wedge.

At one stage, during the build-up to the Open, Pierse and Smyth shared the practice ground with Nicklaus, Watson and Lee Trevino. *"It ended up with Dessie actually getting a lesson from Watson. We had a long conversation with him. He was telling us how important it was to build up our arms and our legs, that strong arms and legs were needed for golf and that we would have to do weights and we would have to build our legs. That was 1977, so all the talk about*

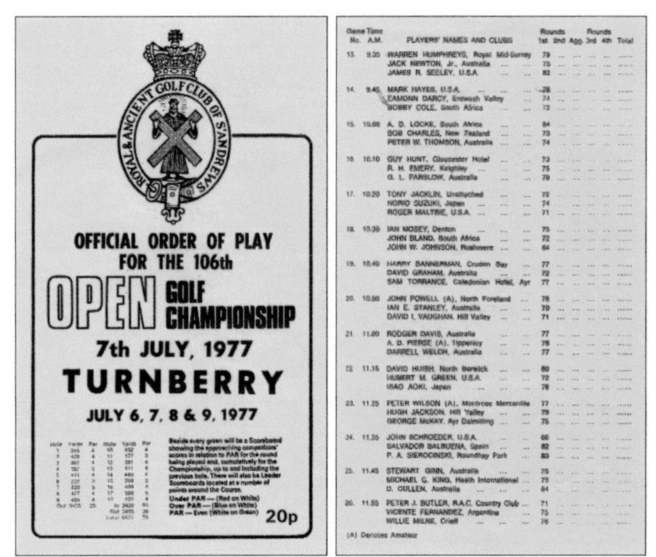

ROYAL & ANCIENT GOLF CLUB OF ST ANDREWS

OFFICIAL ORDER OF PLAY
FOR THE 106th
OPEN GOLF CHAMPIONSHIP
7th JULY, 1977
TURNBERRY
JULY 6, 7, 8 & 9, 1977

Under PAR—(Red on White)
Over PAR—(Blue on White)
PAR—Even (White on Green)

20p

Game No.	Time A.M.	PLAYERS' NAMES AND CLUBS	Rounds 1st	2nd	Agg.	Rounds 3rd	4th	Total
13.	9.35	WARREN HUMPHREYS, Royal Mid-Surrey	79					
		JACK NEWTON, Jr., Australia	75					
		JAMES R. SEELEY, U.S.A.	82					
14.	9.45	MARK HAYES, U.S.A.	78					
		EAMONN DARCY, Erewash Valley	74					
		BOBBY COLE, South Africa	73					
15.	10.00	A. D. LOCKE, South Africa	84					
		BOB CHARLES, New Zealand	73					
		PETER W. THOMSON, Australia	74					
16.	10.10	GUY HUNT, Gloucester Hotel	73					
		R. H. EMERY, Keighley	75					
		G. L. PARSLOW, Australia	79					
17.	10.20	TONY JACKLIN, Unattached	72					
		NORIO SUZUKI, Japan	74					
		ROGER MALTBIE, U.S.A.	71					
18.	10.30	IAN MOSEY, Denton	75					
		JOHN BLAND, South Africa	72					
		JOHN W. JOHNSON, Rushmere	84					
19.	10.40	HARRY BANNERMAN, Cruden Bay	77					
		DAVID GRAHAM, Australia	72					
		SAM TORRANCE, Caledonian Hotel, Ayr	77					
20.	10.50	JOHN POWELL (A), North Foreland	78					
		IAN E. STANLEY, Australia	70					
		DAVID I. VAUGHAN, Hill Valley	71					
21.	11.00	RODGER DAVIS, Australia	77					
		A. D. PIERSE (A), Tipperary	78					
		DARRELL WELCH, Australia	77					
22.	11.15	DAVID HUISH, North Berwick	80					
		HUBERT M. GREEN, U.S.A.	72					
		ISAO AOKI, Japan	76					
23.	11.25	PETER WILSON (A), Montrose Mercantile	77					
		HUGH JACKSON, Hill Valley	79					
		GEORGE McKAY, Ayr Dalmilling	75					
24.	11.35	JOHN SCHROEDER, U.S.A.	66					
		SALVADOR BALBUENA, Spain	82					
		P. A. SIEROCINSKI, Roundhay Park	83					
25.	11.45	STEWART GINN, Australia	75					
		MICHAEL G. KING, Heath International	73					
		D. CULLEN, Australia	84					
26.	11.55	PETER J. BUTLER, R.A.C. Country Club	71					
		VICENTE FERNANDEZ, Argentina	75					
		WILLIE MILNE, Crieff	76					

(A) Denotes Amateur

A.D. Pierse and A.D. Locke share the same page of the start-sheet for the 1977 Open Championship at Turnberry

At one stage, during the build-up to the Open, Pierse and Smyth shared the practice ground with Nicklaus, Watson and Lee Trevino!

Tiger being the lad who brought everybody into weights is absolutely untrue. All these guys did it and Gary Player was the first, of course."

Regrettably, Arthur missed the cut after rounds of 78 & 76 but made full use of his player's badge which allowed him inside the ropes to witness two of the greatest rounds of golf ever seen, with Nicklaus and Watson the stars of the show. *"Nicklaus' caddy was a guy called Rabbit Dyer. I had asked Rabbit before the final round to give me the golf ball if Nicklaus won the tournament. He says 'well, I don't think so, I can't do that.' When he came into the locker room afterwards, I just happened to be there! We were all allocated a locker in the clubhouse and mine was very near Nicklaus because I was 'P' and he was 'N'. After Nicklaus' famous birdie on 18 to lose by a shot, Rabbit came over to me in the locker room and he said 'he didn't win so you can have the golf ball' and he handed me the golf ball that Nicklaus had just holed out with!"*

He went on: *"It was a MacGregor ball and Nicklaus had his own name on it. I went up to Jack afterwards and asked him to sign a piece of paper. I showed him the ball and what I had written for him to sign: 'This ball was used by Jack Nicklaus to hole out on the 18th green in Turnberry in 1977.' He signed it and I gave the ball to a very good friend of mine in Tipperary called Tidgie Moloney and he had it in his pub for years. He made my first golf club (a three-wood) for me when I was only five or six years of age and it made a nice gift to a man who helped me when I started out."*

"I considered turning pro, but could I make a livelihood from playing golf?"

Career Amateur

By this time, a lot of people were asking Arthur whether he would consider following in the footsteps of Des Smyth and turn professional but the Tipperary-man wasn't driven in that way. *"In the 1970's, professional golf wasn't like it is today. Very few top amateurs, except for John O'Leary and Des turned pro, because the money wasn't in it. The Open was always live on television but the money only really started to grow in golf after 1980, when television started to do more outside broadcasts and that brought increased interest in the game. I considered turning pro, but could I make a livelihood from playing golf? I decided that I couldn't and that I probably had a better chance of being successful by going into a business."*

It should be remembered that in the mid-seventies, there was no such thing as a full-time amateur. All the top players combined their golfing activity with full-time jobs. Some were fortunate to be accommodated by employers when it came to international duty - the banking institutions were especially generous in this regard. As a consequence, many of the top young golfers in the 70's and 80's took up jobs in that sector. Nowadays the landscape is much more amenable to full-time amateurs, although the game, it has to be said, is lacking the same camaraderie and characters.

Pierse was fortunate in that his mother ran a successful antique business in Tipperary town. He worked in that trade for about four or five years before joining his brother Gerry in buying the business that evolved into Pierse Motors.

"Gerry had worked in Ballsbridge Motors (part of the MDL Group, which owns the Volkswagen, Audi and Mercedes franchises for the Republic of Ireland). *This opportunity came up to buy a main Volkswagen dealership and we decided to do it. That was how we started in that business."*

Slap bang in the middle of his burgeoning amateur golf career, Pierse found himself taking on a huge business commitment and were it not for Gerry's experience and diligence, Arthur's golfing ambitions would almost certainly have been curtailed. As it transpired, the brothers became a good partnership with Arthur combining his golfing aspirations with his obvious desire to succeed alongside his brother in the motor trade.

"I would make my way out to Tipperary Golf Club early in the mornings to practise from about seven until nine, before heading to work. Depending on how busy we were, I'd often head back at lunchtime just to do a bit of chipping for a half an hour. Then in the evenings, I would go out maybe at six or seven and I might practise until about nine and on a lot of occasions I'd then be back at the garage cleaning cars or whatever we had to do. That was how it was essentially, you had to do it. You had to get both ends right. If you wanted to be successful at golf you had to practise and the bank needed to be paid back what we owed them, so you had to work your business as well. Gerry and I always had that work ethic, it was bred into us. Times were very different than they are today. People who haven't lived through the seventies and eighties and been in business through those years don't really appreciate quite how difficult life was in the Ireland of that period. There wasn't any money around, you worked very hard for everything you had."

On the golfing front, Arthur's commitment to practice was about to reap some major dividends. Utilising the 9-hole course at Tipperary Golf Club, the sight of Pierse with a bag of balls, working on his game, was a daily one. *"I practiced very hard so that I had a swing that repeated itself under pressure. You can't really test your golf swing and how good or bad it is until you put it under the most pressure. If you can hit the golf ball well in a severe pressure situation then you know you have a good golf swing."*

It was something that Arthur worked very hard to achieve, particularly with the driver. Harry Bradshaw would never put anything in a junior golfer's hands bar a driver, a wedge and a putter. *'Master those and you have mastered the game of golf'* he was known to say.

Silverware at last

Pierse worked tirelessly on his long game and particularly at driving the ball well. As a result, he earned a great reputation for his ability to consistently hit fairways from the tees. So much so that he became one of the best strikers of a golf ball that the amateur game in this country had seen at that point. Even though major silverware continued to elude him, a welcome change in fortune was on the horizon.

The 1979 season began with a salutary lesson from Joe Carr. The Irish squad, of which Pierse was a member, had enjoyed winter training that year in Spain, with Carr as non-playing captain. He was to select a six-man team after 'the West' to represent Ireland in the European Championships to be held in Esbjerg, Denmark the following month. The Tipperary-man had led the Irish squad in individual scoring over the winter and looked odds-on to claim a spot on the team. He reached the final of 'the West' only to be beaten on the eighth tie-hole by David Long of Shandon Park and clearly felt that he had done enough to get on the six-man Irish team. When it was announced, the name A.D. Pierse was nowhere to be found.

"*Joe rang me and said, 'Arthur, sorry you are not on the team, you are first reserve. However, we are having a get-together in Portmarnock next weekend and I would like for you to come up and join in'.* Pierse accepted but Carr had a parting comment which resonated with the clearly disappointed Tipperary-man: *'I want to tell you one thing'*, he said, *'if your name is not the first name that goes on the team sheet you don't deserve to be on the team, is that understood?'* Difficult as it may have been, it was a message that was heeded.

Being the proven champion that he undoubtedly was, the underlying communication from Carr was that Arthur should put himself in the position to be the top amateur golfer in Ireland, practise to make sure of that

"If your name is not the first name that goes on the team sheet you don't deserve to be on the team, is that understood?" - Joe Carr gives it to Arthur straight

and when he **was** the top player, he would get on every team. Essentially, they wouldn't be able to keep him off it. Unless you are number one, you should never expect to get on any team. That decision is always at the discretion of the captain or selectors.

After the Irish team disappointed at the Europeans, some golfing scribes were more than keen to point out that it would be an embarrassment for Carr if Pierse, (having been left out of the Irish team by Carr) were to win the East of Ireland, and not to be surprised if he managed to do it.

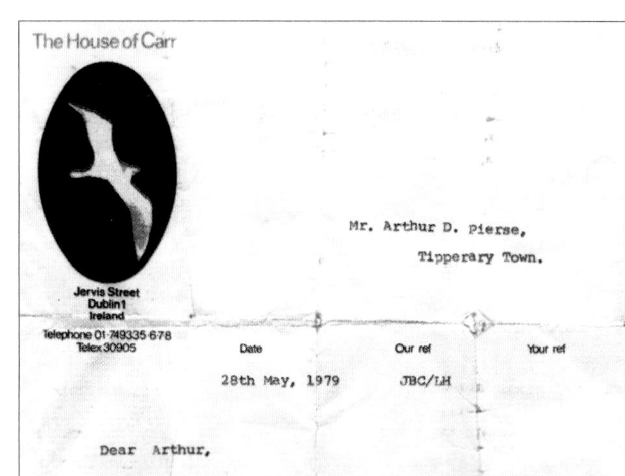

The House of Carr

Jervis Street
Dublin1
Ireland
Telephone 01-749335-6-7-8
Telex 30905

Mr. Arthur D. Pierse,
Tipperary Town.

Date	Our ref	Your ref
28th May, 1979	JBC/LH	

Dear Arthur,

I know you must be disappointed not making the six man team, but I know this is going to make you more determined to put beyond doubt any future selections. I would like to make one or two observations with regard to your play at Little Aston. It seems to me that if you have a weakness it is off the Tee and your short game seems to be a little sharper each time I see you. I think a championship might come your way this year if you keep working as hard as you have been.

I would like to thank you for your suppor in Little Aston and particularly your support of David in the closing holes of his win.

Kindest regards,

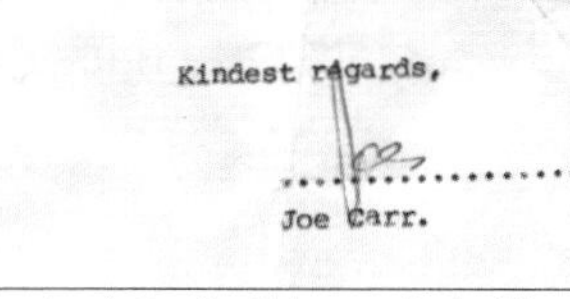

Joe Carr.

Joe Carr articulates his thoughts to Arthur in a letter. David Long, who had beaten Arthur at "the West", had subsequently gone on to claim the Brabazon Trophy (English Amateur Open Strokeplay Championship) at Little Aston.

Over three days of the June Bank Holiday weekend, Arthur Pierse did just that, finally claiming his first major amateur title.

Arthur, surrounded by his mother Catherine and father Gerry Snr, and brothers Morgan, Gerry and John after claiming his first 'Major' at the 'East' 1979.

Over three days of the June Bank Holiday weekend, Arthur Pierse did just that, finally claiming his first major amateur title, shooting four under par 288 for the four rounds and defeating Garth McGimpsey in a playoff!

"The first person that crossed the green to shake my hand after Garth was Joe Carr himself. He came over to me and said that I had proved him wrong. He said that he liked that in a player, that it was a good sign for me to win in the way that I did and that I was going to go on to greater things from there. In fairness to him we were very pally (sic) and he was the one golfer that I had the greatest respect for, both as a person and as a golfer."

The most successful years in Pierse's career were the early 1980's. There was a predictability about the contenders in the country's five major Championships. Quite simply, Pierse was now among a band of elite amateurs who controlled the era. Alongside the likes of Declan Branigan (Laytown & Bettystown), McGimpsey (Bangor), Baltray's Mark Gannon and two young prodigies, Ronan Rafferty (Warrenpoint) and Philip Walton (Malahide), Pierse helped to bring the standard of Irish amateur golf to a whole new level.

In 1980 he finally triumphed in 'the West', eight years after his debut and a year after his marathon final defeat to David Long. After a comprehensive win against Garth McGimpsey by the margin of 5 & 4 in the semi-final, he set up a Championship decider that afternoon against the rising young talent from Malahide, Philip Walton.

In the final, he accounted for the 18 year-old by the secure margin of 3 & 2. *"I always felt in control of the match and for some reason, Philip gave me the sense that he wasn't totally comfortable. Mentally I was much stronger that day."*

Tipperary Golf Club celebrates a double champion.
(l. to r.): Ven. Archbishop Ryan, President; Paddy Donovan, Captain; A.D. Pierse; Noreen Ryan, Lady Captain; Padraig O'Donoghue, Hon. Secretary.

Friday the 13th

The following June, at the British Amateur Championship at Royal Porthcawl, Arthur came closer than any Irish golfer since Joe Carr to bringing home the holy grail for amateur golfers the world over. Along with sixteen-year-old sensation Ronan Rafferty, he sailed through qualifying and marched boldly through the matchplay stages to a berth in the last four on the second last day.

Arthur at Rosses Point in 1980, when he claimed his first 'West' title.

Rafferty had dominated the headlines all week. Weeks after tying with Peter McEvoy for the Brabazon Trophy, the sixteen-year-old prodigy was on course to become the youngest-ever winner of the title and when disposing of five-time champion Michael Bonallack and reigning Scottish Champion Keith Macintosh on the Thursday, he had set up a quarter-final match with Wales' Duncan Evans.

On the morning of Friday the thirteenth of June in 1980, Rafferty bowed out of the Championship, losing to the strapping Evans by 2 & 1, so it was left to Arthur to fly the flag for Irish golf. He too would face Evans, this time for a place in the thirty-six hole final the following day.

"I always felt in control of the match and for some reason, Philip gave me the sense that he wasn't totally comfortable. Mentally I was much stronger that day."

At the long par five 12th hole, Arthur played two superb shots to be home in two and with his opponent in a seemingly unplayable lie in the rough, he was odds-on to go two up. He was sitting pretty.

Arthur tees off at Royal Porthcawl in the afternoon semi-final of the British Amateur Championship. He was just two wins away from an automatic spot in that year's Open at Royal St George's and the 1981 US Masters Tournament!

With Irish team-mate and former Walker Cup player Pat Mulcare as his caddy, Pierse teed off with high hopes and successfully found the fairway; Evans carved his tee shot onto the rocks to the left. *"Pat Mulcare gave me the news that he'd found the only bit of grass down on the rocks, which was unbelievable and he hit a magnificent recovery, just landing over the back of the green in two. He then chipped the ball to about six inches from the cup in three!"*

Pierse had made the dance-floor safely in two shots, and being only six feet away, he reckoned that with Evans' ball being so near the cup and fractionally left of his line, that he could easily canon off Evans' ball and into the hole, should he strike his putt ever so slightly off line. Leaving his opponent's ball unmarked, which he was entitled to do, Pierse attempted to hit the ball firmly, but the ball veered off line badly and in a cruel twist, knocked Evans' ball into the cup instead, which meant that the Welshman birdied to win the opening hole!

He remained one down at the turn until firing birdie-par at the next two to go to one-up. He was back in control against the six-foot five inch Evans, who worked in his father's (and caddy) fish and chip shop to finance his amateur career.

At the long par five 12th hole, Arthur played two superb shots to be home in two and with his opponent in a seemingly unplayable lie in the rough, he was odds-on to go two up. He was sitting pretty.

Again, the Welshman played a miracle shot just short

A poignant moment. Arthur makes a short speech at the conclusion of the 1980 British Amateur Championship after receiving the bronze medal for making it to the semi-finals.

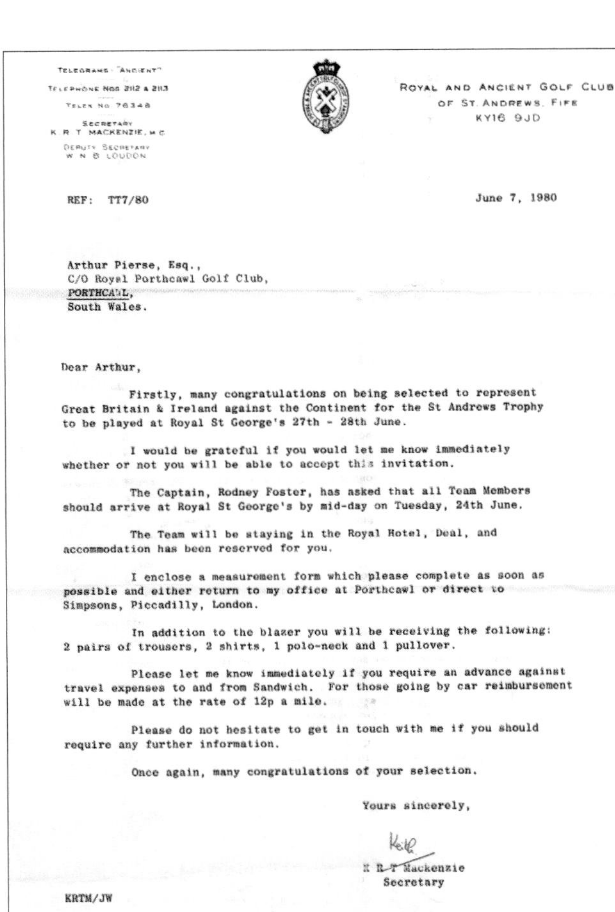

TELEGRAMS "ANCIENT"
TELEPHONE NOS 2112 & 2113
TELEX No 76348
SECRETARY
K. R. T. MACKENZIE, M.C.
DEPUTY SECRETARY
W. N. B. LOUDON

ROYAL AND ANCIENT GOLF CLUB
OF ST. ANDREWS, FIFE
KY16 9JD

REF: TT7/80

June 7, 1980

Arthur Pierse, Esq.,
C/O Royal Porthcawl Golf Club,
PORTHCAWL,
South Wales.

Dear Arthur,

Firstly, many congratulations on being selected to represent Great Britain & Ireland against the Continent for the St Andrews Trophy to be played at Royal St George's 27th - 28th June.

I would be grateful if you would let me know immediately whether or not you will be able to accept this invitation.

The Captain, Rodney Foster, has asked that all Team Members should arrive at Royal St George's by mid-day on Tuesday, 24th June.

The Team will be staying in the Royal Hotel, Deal, and accommodation has been reserved for you.

I enclose a measurement form which please complete as soon as possible and either return to my office at Porthcawl or direct to Simpsons, Piccadilly, London.

In addition to the blazer you will be receiving the following: 2 pairs of trousers, 2 shirts, 1 polo-neck and 1 pullover.

Please let me know immediately if you require an advance against travel expenses to and from Sandwich. For those going by car reimbursement will be made at the rate of 12p a mile.

Please do not hesitate to get in touch with me if you should require any further information.

Once again, many congratulations of your selection.

Yours sincerely,

K R T Mackenzie
Secretary

KRTM/JW

Although the week at Porthcawl ended in disappointment, there was good news at the beginning of the week. A sign of things to come, perhaps?

of the green and chipped to five feet. Arthur lagged his first putt sufficiently close to the hole to have his birdie putt conceded and Duncan Evans calmly stepped up and holed his for what had looked earlier like an unlikely half!

Still one up, Pierse safely found the green at the par four thirteenth, while his opponent's approach landed in a bunker. The momentum was back with the Tipperary-man, who knew that he could possibly win the hole, even with a par.

After studying his shot for a few moments, Evans settled into position in the sand and took a few waggles, visualising the stroke and committing himself to its execution. The ball exploded from the trap in a shroud of sand. It appeared that he had slightly over-hit it when, in an instant, it hit the flagstick, some sixty-feet away and dropped into the hole for another birdie! "It was an unbelievable shot, probably the most rewarding I've ever played. It turned the course of the match," Evans later admitted to reporters.

Pierse was shell-shocked. The match was now level and minutes later he was one down, after missing the fourteenth green from the tee, while Evans stitched his to short range for a birdie two and a win. There was no stopping the Leek golfer and he marched on to defeat Arthur by 2 & 1 before claiming the Championship outright the following day against Martin Suddards of South Africa.

Reflecting afterwards to Jack Magowan of the Belfast Telegraph, a gracious Pierse confessed: *"I always felt I was in control of the game but sadly that's not how it worked out. Even with two sixes chalked up against me, I was still two under par when the game ended. I couldn't have lost to a nicer guy..."*

The dream was over. He had come so close to scaling the highest peak in amateur golf, only to have it taken away, in the cruellest of fashion. "*There are a number of ways of looking at that whole series of events,*" he admitted to me in 2005, "*but I missed out on a golden opportunity to play in a match at Porthcawl to become the British Amateur Champion. What saddens me is that I never got the opportunity to tee it up in the US Masters which to me has to be the ultimate achievement.*"

At the Home Internationals in 1980 (in which Ireland disappointed), Arthur was given the honour of playing at number one. Ahead of the trip to Dornoch, Joe Carr sent this precious letter to Tipperary (see next page).

The dream was over. He had come so close to scaling the highest peak in amateur golf, only to have it taken away, in the cruellest of fashion.

PAUL McGinley: *"Arthur was a tremendous ball striker, a great driver of the ball. A classy player, but the reason that he wasn't more successful was that he wasn't a good enough putter. That's what held him back. He wasn't as comfortable on the greens as he was hitting a golf ball. He had a very successful career and he was undoubtedly a player that nobody wanted to draw in a Championship!*

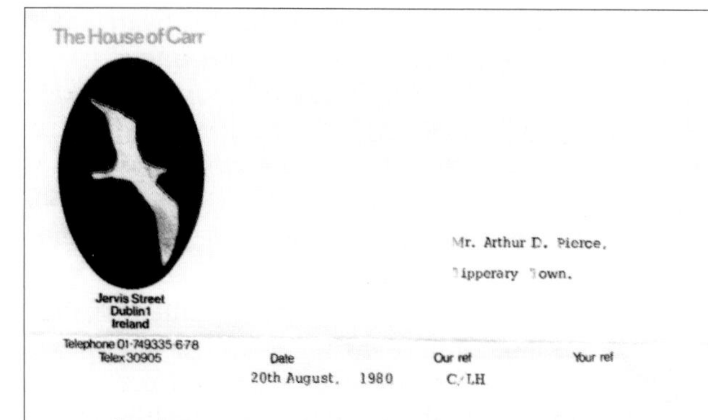

The House of Carr

Jervis Street
Dublin 1
Ireland

Telephone 01-749335-678
Telex 30905

Mr. Arthur D. Pierce.
Tipperary Town.

Date 20th August, 1980 Our ref C/LH Your ref

Dear Arthur,

Just a line to let you know how delighted I am to have you on this Team. As you know Ireland have never won the Triple Crown. This Team can do just that, but only with the full committment of every member to arrive in Dornoch at top physical condition and playing well.

As you know you are a very important part of this team, a place which I was in for many years, if you loose we loose. Now this is a heavy burden to bear Arthur, but you are the best player in the Country and there is no reason why you shouldn't carry it and carry it well. Also remember the results of these Internationals will have a bearing on next years Walker Cup Team.

We have all had a wonderful time at the expense of the Unions over the past few years, I feel this is payment time and the best payment would be to win the Triple Crown. You have got todrive well in Dornoch and you have got to putt well, and I would suggest to you that it would be no harm if you did a hundred drives a day and maybe one hundred irons and perhaps an hour on a good green and if you haven't got one down there do it on a carpet.

With Kindest regards,

Joe Carr.

Arthur and Ronan Rafferty (back right) line out for Great Britain and Ireland in the St Andrews Trophy not long after their respective disappointments at the British Amateur Championship. Duncan Evans, the Champion at Royal Porthcawl is seated front left. Roger Chapman is front right, Gordon Brand Jnr is next to him.

In 1981, there was no keeping Pierse off the six-man Irish team to compete in the European Team Championships at St Andrews. Regrettably, the whole 'big-ball/small-ball' incident marred what had looked like a Championship-winning team.

Ireland's capitulation at St Andrews was a low point and Pierse also had some near misses on the individual circuit also that year, particularly when he finished second to Roger Chapman in the Lytham Trophy, where he three-putted the last to lose by one. Despite the lack of silverware, Arthur still felt that there was every chance of a call-up for the Walker Cup matches the following year at Cypress Point in California. Instead, the selectors opted for Rafferty and Walton: *"They would never have picked three Irishmen at that time!"* claims Pierse.

*The GB & I Eisenhower Trophy team in 1982.
L to r: Philip Walton, Arthur, Andrew Oldcorn, George MacGregor and Rodney Foster, non-playing captain.*

F. Schlig		74	75	70
U. Schulte		73	77	71
	660	220	224	216
GREAT BRITAIN & IRELAND				
G. Mac Gregor		76	74	72
A. S. Oldcorn		74	74	75
A. D. Pierse		77	71	71
P. Walton		71	77	75
	658	221	219	218

Arthur makes his presence felt as he contributes to the GB & I cause in the World Amateur Team Championship known as the Eisenhower trophy

Pierse's status as one of the finest players on these islands was confirmed in 1982 when he was selected to play on the four-man Great Britain and Ireland team to contest the Eisenhower Trophy in Lausanne, Switzerland. Walton was alongside him, in addition to future Walker Cup captain George MacGregor and future BMW PGA Champion, Andrew Oldcorn.

He had, by that stage, reclaimed the West of Ireland title after comfortably beating Michael Malone of Belvoir Park by 3 & 1 in the final. Winning a place on the Eisenhower team however, also meant that he was a near certainty for the following year's Walker Cup matches to be held at Royal Liverpool, Hoylake.

Arthur was in the form of his life. He reached the last 16 of the British Amateur Championship at Deal in Kent, going unbeaten for GB & I in the St Andrews Trophy and claiming six points out of six for Ireland in the Home Internationals. He was at the very top of his game and the invitation to play in the Walker Cup duly followed. The golfing curriculum vitae of A.D. Pierse was now almost complete.

At Christmas, he was selected by the R&A to play in the Indian Amateur Championship and also teed it up in the Indian Professional Championship, where he led with nine holes to play. Fate then dealt a cruel blow.

"I had been fighting an illness for about twenty-four hours and it became worse all of a sudden and I began coughing up blood. I managed to finish down the field, but spent a fortnight in hospital when I returned and lost a stone and a half in weight."

The 1983 season began with a concerted effort to recover his fitness and get back to good health, given that he had some key goals to achieve that year. Despite still enduring bouts of ill-health stemming from a virus picked up in India, he was determined to take his place amongst the GB & I team that was to take on the Americans at Royal Liverpool in May of that year.

He travelled to Hoylake in reasonably good condition, but was far from perfect, health-wise. Nonetheless, it was an experience to savour as he joined his team-mates and opponents for the opening ceremony.

Tipperary's finest in action in Lausanne. Arthur's wife Margaret is partially hidden by her husband's follow through. Also watching, on the right hand side of the photo are Tipperary Golf Club supporters, Cathal McCarthy, the club captain and his son Karl.

Arthur was in the form of his life. He reached the last 16 of the British Amateur Championship at Deal in Kent, going unbeaten for GB & I in the St Andrews Trophy and claiming six points out of six for Ireland in the Home Internationals

Just about to seal victory on the 17th for his second 'West' title at Rosses Point in 1982

Despite his disappointment and obvious ill-health, (he spent three days in bed immediately after the Hoylake experience), he managed to regroup and without a practice round, qualified for the British Amateur Championship at Turnberry

An underweight Arthur lines out for the opening ceremony. Walker Cup team-mates Philip Parkin and Andrew Oldcorn are to his immediate right.

"I was still carrying the virus when I teed it up at Hoylake and didn't have great health. On the first day Stephen Keppler and I halved with Jay Sigel (the playing-captain) and Brad Faxon in the foursomes and I lost to Bob Lewis in the singles. The following day we lost in the foursomes on the 18th to Willie Wood and Rick Fehr and I was too sick to play that afternoon, so I withdrew from the singles."
The Americans won the matches by 13½ - 10½.

Despite his disappointment and obvious ill-health, (he spent three days in bed immediately after the Hoylake experience), he managed to regroup and without a practice round, qualified for the British Amateur Championship at Turnberry, eventually going out in the last sixteen.

The winner was his Hoylake team-mate Philip Parkin, who now works for the Golf Channel and Setanta Golf as a commentator and pundit. In 1983, Parkin was arguably the best amateur golfer in the world. A scholarship student at Texas A & M at the time, he was far and away the most dominant US collegiate player, leaving the likes of Steve Elkington, Scott Verplank and Colin Montgomerie in his wake on a regular basis.

Parkin's admiration for Pierse gives a great indication of the respect that there was for the Irishman's talent: "One of the main things that I remember about Arthur Pierse was that he was always incredibly friendly, he was everyone's best friend. I played amateur golf for about five or six years and he was always the one that would go to everyone else in the team, go into the other countries, talk to them, join them and sit down and just have a great time. He wasn't a very big guy, so to be as good as he was with his stature was incredible.

He struck the ball amazingly well. He was just so consistent, hardly ever hit a bad shot. I really think he was good enough to win the British Amateur not just once, but a few times. I think he was very unfortunate (in 1980), he came close a few times and with a little bit of luck going his way he definitely would have won the Amateur more than once. I was fortunate to win it one time and I think sometimes it's luck, and Arthur just didn't have the luck. He was definitely good enough, he was one of the top amateurs and when we played against him in the Home

The combined Great Britain and Ireland side with their American counterparts pose after the opening ceremony. Arthur is front right. Jay Sigel is seated in the centre. Seated left is future US Walker Cup Captain Bob Lewis. Seated in the middle row on the right hand side is the 1981 US Amateur Champion Nathaniel Crosby, son of crooner Bing. Back row third from the left is future PGA Tour star Brad Faxon.

"He struck the ball amazingly well. He was just so consistent, hardly ever hit a bad shot. I really think he was good enough to win the British Amateur not just once, but a few times."
- Philip Parkin, 1983 British Amateur Champion.

Internationals everyone was petrified, because he was a like an Irish Ben Hogan – his stature was similar to Hogan and he played like Hogan, with a swing that rarely went wrong.

The overriding thing I remember about Arthur is that you wouldn't find anyone nicer than him, he was a great guy and I like to think of him as being a really good friend of mine."

Pierse had recovered well enough by July to put in a very strong showing for Ireland in the European Amateur Team Championships at Chantilly in France. Ireland emerged victorious over Spain in the final and Arthur struck up a particularly successful foursomes partnership that week with John Carr. Big-hitting Carr, who was a son of the great JB, had been a semi-finalist at the British Amateur Championship in 1981 at St Andrews and the pair dove-tailed perfectly in France, winning all of their foursomes matches.

The winning Irish team return from their victory in the 'Europeans' at Chantilly. Back row l-r: Eamonn Curran GUI, Philip Walton, Garth McGimpsey, Tom Cleary. Front row l-r: John Carr, Arthur, Team Captain Brendan Edwards & GUI President Michael Fitzpatrick.

Gaining a precious Walker Cup cap and winning 'the Europeans' with Ireland represented the summit of the amateur game for the Tipperary-man.

Commitments

Gaining a precious Walker Cup cap and winning 'the Europeans' with Ireland represented the summit of the amateur game for the Tipperary-man. At 32 years of age he began to question his motivation to compete at the very top level. A less rigorous schedule was certainly beginning to appeal. Given the dedication required towards practise and all the demanding travelling, not to mention the expense of playing at the top level, the decision was made to reduce his commitment to the game.

The early eighties were particularly tough years in Ireland, with the country in the midst of a financial recession. Having married Margaret in 1982 and with Pierse Motors still in its infancy, greater priority was given to family and work; though he did continue to play in domestic Championships and figured annually on the Irish side for the Home Internationals.

It was not until July of 1987 that his class as a golfer was in clear evidence once again, when, quite literally, he took the field apart in the North of Ireland Amateur Championship on the classic links of Royal Portrush.

"In '87 our business was more established and I decided I would play in Portrush. I managed to go all the way to the final day and met Darren Clarke in the morning's semi-final. It was a very wet day and it was also the only time that my Dad ever came to see me playing in a Championship.

Dad had always felt that if he turned up, he would make me nervous. I saw him peering out from under the bush at one stage and I said 'Dad, come out of there and watch the golf.'" It was one of those precious days in golf, with Pierse taking just eleven holes to dispose of Clarke in the semi and twelve holes to see off Lurgan's Roy Hanna in the final!

"I played really well that morning, hit the ball very

Friends and family surround the 1987 North of Ireland Champion at Royal Portrush.

well, saw nothing but the flag, hit it close and scored well. There are times you get a day like that and I remember going to the turn against Darren, on a very wet morning, in 31! I did the same to Roy in the afternoon. I think I was out in 32 and both matches were played in very strong winds and howling rain. I hit the ball so well that whomever I played that day I'd have beaten them."

David Long, who had beaten Arthur in his first major final eight years previously, was the only player to take him past the 15th in the Championship that year. *"You get a week like that where your swing is good, everything is good and you are hitting every fairway, every green and your irons are finding the target."*

The season was capped most memorably when Ireland claimed the Home Internationals series for the first time on Irish soil at Lahinch that September.

In 1989 Arthur finished runner-up to Clarke in the East of Ireland at Baltray. He contested two more finals of his beloved West but his time as a major force in amateur golf was coming to an end.

"When Arthur Pierse was on song, he was, quite simply, outstanding! I had the misfortune to come up against Arthur in the semi-final of the North of Ireland Amateur Championship in 1987 and he was absolutely magnificent.

Arthur was and still is, one of the great ball-strikers in Irish golf, amateur or professional. He hits it pure. Thankfully in 1989, I was really getting into my stride and managed to stay ahead of him to win my first Major amateur title at the East of Ireland at Baltray. One of the great characters in Irish amateur golf, he was a great team-mate to have on Irish teams and was very supportive when I decided to

He contested two more finals of his beloved West but his time as a major force in amateur golf was coming to an end.

Darren Clarke, Arthur's Irish team-mate on the first ever Home Internationals winning side on home soil, Lahinch 1987
Irish team, back Row l-r, Paul Rayfus, Garth McGimpsey, Darren Clarke, GUI President Gerry O'Brien, Denis O'Sullivan, Liam MacNamara, Padraig Hogan.
Front row, l-r: Mark Gannon, Barry Reddan, Eddie Power, Team Captain Eamonn Curran, Neil Anderson & Arthur Pierse.

Twenty four years since first rubbing shoulders with Nicklaus, Watson et al, the Tipperary-man would again let his clubs do the talking as he made the cut and finished a very creditable 55th place and was third leading amateur.

turn pro at the end of 1990. While I've strived to carve out a successful career as a pro, I'm delighted to see that Arthur has kept his game in great shape and was thrilled to see him win the British Open Seniors Amateur Championship in 2007. You never lost it Arthur!"

- Darren Clarke, September 2007.

Golden Oldie!

As the twenty-first century loomed, so too did the prospect of Seniors golf for Pierse. The Irish Amateur Senior Open Championship is confined to golfers over the age of fifty-five, so initially he had to content himself with a few other 'challenging' goals.

Given that he had finished leading amateur at the Carroll's Irish Open on no less than five occasions during his peak years on the amateur circuit, he relished the prospect of again mixing it with the pro's upon turning 50.

In 2001, he criss-crossed the Atlantic and successfully came through two stages of qualifying in New Jersey to win an elusive place in that year's US Senior Open at Salem Country Club in Massachusetts. Twenty-four years since first rubbing shoulders with Nicklaus, Watson et al, the Tipperary-man would again let his clubs do the talking as he made the cut and finished a very creditable 55th place and was third leading amateur. In the third round, Pierse hit sixteen greens in regulation but 37 putts gave him a score of 76! In the end, Bruce Fleischer took the title ahead of Gil Morgan, Isao Aoki and Jack Nicklaus.

Turnberry clearly brought back happy memories of his debut in a professional major in 1977 and he returned to the Scottish venue in July of 2001 for his debut in the Senior British Open. He claimed the 'leading amateur' title at his first attempt, in a Championship that was won by Australia's Ian Stanley with Nicklaus in third.

He went on to win the 'leading amateur' prize at the British Seniors for three successive years and also performed with great distinction here at home, in the AIB Irish Seniors Open, part of the European Seniors Tour. From 2003-2005, he finished 'leading amateur' on each occasion and in 2004, at Adare Manor, enjoyed the distinction of finishing as leading Irish player, both amateur and professional!

2003 Senior British Open Champion at Turnberry Tom Watson alongside Arthur, who claimed the leading amateur medal for the third successive year.

In October of 2004 the golfing career of Arthur Pierse looked to be over when he was assaulted by a thug outside his business in Tipperary Town. There was no option but to undergo open surgery by Mr. Colville at the Blackrock Clinic for a full rotator cuff tear to his right shoulder. To regain any reasonable mobility, a year of physiotherapy was required. Any hopes of a return to serious golfing activity could not be guaranteed at that time.

The Big One

To his credit, and under the watchful eye of his wife Mags, who is a doctor, Arthur regained the necessary mobility and despite having missed out on the 2005 season, he surprised very few followers when he almost claimed the Irish Seniors Open amateur title at Limerick Golf Club in the summer of 2006. Suitably encouraged by his runners-up finish, he began to work hard again on his game and target new goals.

In August of 2007, he led the field from pillar to post at the hugely prestigious British Open Seniors Amateur Championship at Nairn in Scotland. Rounds of 67, 71 and 73 had given him the biggest international win of his career... or so he thought.

Standing on the 18th tee in the final round, the scoreboard told him that he was two shots ahead of his nearest challenger, Graham Cooke of Canada. Having just come off a double bogey on the seventeenth, he was in no mood to let this one slip (having let a few big ones slip through his fingers in the past). Taking a five wood off the tee, he drilled the ball onto the fairway. Making the green in three, he calmly two-putted for a par and although Cooke, who was playing alongside him had birdied, everyone was

Philip Walton: *"Arthur Pierse was a great player, one of the best ball strikers around at the time. He could manoeuvre the driver, he could hit left to right and right to left and he was a class iron player. His putting was a bit iffy, but he was a great player. He was a very fun guy to play with as well."*

Arthur and daughter Jill celebrate what they believe is victory.

On checking the scores, it was revealed that Cooke had actually tied with Pierse for the Championship and that their celebrations had been premature.

sure that the Irishman had won the Championship by a single shot. Spontaneous applause erupted amongst the crowd, Arthur was punching the air and hugging his daughter and caddy Jill, it was the crowing moment of his amateur career. Or was it?

On checking the scores, it was revealed that Cooke had actually tied with Pierse for the Championship and that their celebrations had been premature. "*The scoreboard had shown me to be four ahead playing the seventeenth. After I double bogeyed, it said that I was two ahead standing on the final tee. I was concentrating too deeply to be totally aware of Cooke's score. At one point during the back nine, I asked him how things stood and he just said 'take a look at the scoreboard'; that was the first time that I realised that I was four ahead and didn't give it another thought until the 18th tee, when I needed to be certain.*"

It appears that nobody was certain, although his partner, who was chasing the lead from the start of the day, must surely have known that he was closer than was indicated by the scoreboards.

"I was stunned when the official recorder told me we had tied and that a play-off was required to decide the Championship, but that was that. There was then a delay, as Cooke spent a long time warming up on the practice ground, so I headed out there to join him, telling myself that he wasn't going to take this one from me!"

At last! After no shortage of drama, Arthur Pierse looks skyward in thanks. He has finally claimed the British Open Seniors Amateur Championship.

Champion at last. Arthur Pierse, 2007 British Open Seniors Amateur Champion.

His brief few moments on the range had an immediate benefit as it allowed him to make a quick adjustment to his set-up for his tee shots, which had been a little wayward toward the end of the final round. With that sorted he proceeded to split the fairways as the sudden-death play-off went to the third hole. Pierse reeled off his third straight par, while the Canadian bogeyed. The title was finally his and the celebrations could begin, at last!

No more than four weeks later, having gained an exemption into the US Senior Open Amateur Championship in Kansas, Pierse was the only non-American to come through 36 holes of qualifying to make the matchplay stages along with 63 other contenders all over the age of 55.

In making the last eight, he could lay claim to having been the World's leading Senior amateur in 2007. It's also worth pointing out that five of the eight quarter-finalists in Kansas were re-instated amateurs, each having played on the PGA Tour!

Arthur Pierse has been playing to a handicap of scratch or better for over thirty five years and has been one of the dominant figures in the amateur game during that time. His ability to maintain such a standard into his senior golf career suggests that he'll be making the headlines for many years to come. Watch this space! Arthur Pierse, a bona-fide legend, in his spare time.

In making the last eight, he could lay claim to having been the World's leading Senior amateur in 2007.

CAREER HIGHLIGHTS

Name: Arthur D'Arcy Pierse.

Born: May 30th, 1951.

Marital Status: Married to Margaret, 4 Children, Arthur, Lorna Jill & Charles.

Educated: Rockwell College & Trinity College, Dublin.

Occupation: Company Director/Family Businesses.

Home Club: Tipperary Golf Club.

Lowest Handicap: + 2

CHAMPIONSHIP HIGHLIGHTS:

British Amateur Open Championship
Semi-finalist in 1980, Last 16 in 1982 & 1983.

British Open Championship (Professional)
Pre-qualified in 1977 at Turnberry, missed the cut.

British Seniors Open Championship (Professional)
Leading amateur 3 times, 2001, 2002 & 2003.

British Seniors Amateur Open Championship
Winner in 2007.

US Senior Open Championship (Professional)
Pre-qualified and made cut in 2001,
finishing 3rd leading Amateur.

US Senior Amateur Open Championship
Quarter finalist in 2007.

Irish Amateur Close Championship
Semi-finalist in 1982.

Irish Seniors Amateur Open Championship
Runner-up in 2006.

Carroll's Irish Open (Professional)
Leading Amateur in 1975, 1976, 1980, 1981 & 1984.

West of Ireland Amateur Open Championship
Winner in 1980 & 1982.
Runner-up 1979, 1990 & 1993.

East of Ireland Amateur Open Championship
Winner 1979.
Runner-up 1974 & 1989.

North of Ireland Amateur Open Championship
Winner in 1987.

South of Ireland Amateur Open Championship
Semi-finalist in 1980, 1984 & 1986.

Lytham Trophy
Runner-up 1981.

Irish Amateur Order of Merit (Willie Gill Award)
Winner in 1980.

REPRESENTATIVE HONOURS

Great Britain & Ireland *Walker Cup*:
1983.

Great Britain & Ireland *Eisenhower Trophy*:
1982.

Great Britain & Ireland *St. Andrews Trophy:*
1980 & 1982.

International:
99 caps for Ireland between 1976-1988
Member of Ireland's winning side at European Amateur Team Championships, Chantilly, 1983.
Team member in 1981 & 1985.

Interprovincial:
75 Caps for Munster 1974-1991.

David Sheahan

The Dublin based doctor who for forty five years held the record of being the only amateur to win a Tour event. He was one of the country's greatest shot-makers. Dr David Sheahan was a true champion during one of the most progressive periods in world golf.

"David Sheahan had a tremendous ability to move the golf ball from either side. He was a born winner. To achieve all that he did, and so young, points to a rather special ability. One time, when I was practising at the Grange Golf Club, in advance of the Irish Amateur Close Championship in 1970, he teased me that there was no point, that he was going to win anyway...and he did!"

JOHN O'LEARY, European Tour and Ryder Cup player, speaking in May 2007.

On that fateful final day's play, Sheahan and that year's British Amateur champion Michael Lunt (who sadly died in May of 2007, midway through his Captaincy of the R&A), were beaten in the morning foursomes by Coe and Beman.

David Sheahan

Turning Point at Turnberry

On the 25th of May 1963, a real upset was on the cards at the Walker Cup matches in Turnberry, Scotland. Only once before had the cup been won by a British and Irish side and that had been back in 1938, when Jimmy Bruen and Cecil Ewing were the Irishmen on a team that beat the visiting Americans, who were led on that occasion by the famed Massachusetts amateur Francis Ouimet.

At Turnberry, the home side this time featured three Irishmen. The irrepressible Joe Carr had been joined by a soon-to-graduate doctor called David Sheahan of the Grange Golf Club in Dublin and Royal Belfast star David Madeley. It had been absolutely inconceivable that the Americans could lose. In their ten-man team, led by Dick Tufts, were stars like Deane Beman, a winner of both the British and US Amateur Championships and Charlie Coe, a former US amateur champion and runner-up at the US Masters the previous year.

Coe was considered by many to have been the greatest American amateur since Bobby Jones. And that's not to forget the bespectacled Billy Joe Patton, the man who missed out on the 1954 US Masters in a playoff with Hogan and Snead, by a single shot!

Recalling the matches over forty years later with great clarity, it is the considered view of David Sheahan that the home side were never given enough credit for their play on the first day of the contest. The Americans were victorious in only one of their eight singles matches, with Sheahan taking the notable scalp of the reigning US Amateur champion Labron Harris and the USA ended up trailing by three points. According to Sheahan, what was significant about the American turnaround on Day Two was that Patton, assuming all of the battling qualities of his wartime namesake, had rallied his troops that night into such a patriotic frenzy that lives were willing to be put on the line the following day, in order to retain the cup.

On that fateful final day's play, Sheahan and that year's British Amateur champion Michael Lunt (who sadly died in May of 2007, midway through his Captaincy of the R&A), were beaten in the morning foursomes by Coe and Beman. Sheahan was one of the few successes against the rampant Americans on day two, when he later dispatched the previous year's British Amateur champion, the eccentric American

A rare photo of both the British and Irish side with their American counterparts. David Sheahan is on the back row, 5th from left.

antiques dealer Richard Davies by one hole in his singles match.

The Americans had conspired to stage a marvellous comeback and won in the end by 12 points to 8. Many years later, while playing against each other in the traditional 'ex-players match' ahead of the 1993 matches at Interlachen, Patton confirmed to Sheahan that he had indeed assumed an unofficial captaincy of sorts on that famous night in the Turnberry Hotel. Clearing a room of its patrons and filling it with his team-mates, he shut the doors and in a maniacal, passionate speech to his countrymen, imbued them with the confidence and belief to turn the matches around the following day, which they did, in no uncertain terms.

The Walker Cup was David Sheahan's crowning achievement. At the tender age of twenty-three, he had accomplished so much in the world of golf. His qualification as a doctor was only a week away and his two very separate lives briefly converged and brought the young star to a crossroads. Would he postpone his career in medicine for a life as a professional golfer, now that he had achieved so much as a top class amateur? Or would he continue a family tradition, and at 23, allow golf to take a back seat in favour of a medical career?

The Walker Cup was David Sheahan's crowning achievement. At the tender age of twenty-three, he had accomplished so much in the world of golf.

There really was no great decision in the end: *"it never seriously entered my mind to be honest. Firstly, I wasn't good enough and secondly, there was no money in it!"*

History Maker

Until Pablo Martin's breath-taking win in the 2007 Open de Portugal on the European Tour, David Sheahan's name was alone in the record books for forty-five years, as the only amateur winner of a Tour event in Europe. He will forever be remembered as the young amateur who defied all the odds to beat the pros in a top Tour event held in Royal Dublin in 1962. The key to his prowess was his tremendous ability to shape the shots with a golf ball which, when allied to a sublime short game, could kill off top class opponents in the biggest amateur championships and the Walker Cup. That he achieved most of it while striving to attain a medical degree at University College Dublin makes his achievements all the more remarkable.

One of Sheahan's greatest golfing attributes was undoubtedly his self-belief. The game is well known as being a great leveller, but ask a proven winner like Sheahan about the defeats, the near-misses in his golfing life and you're guaranteed a hardy rebuke!

"As far as I was concerned, when it came to matchplay, the opponent never beat me!"

"As far as I was concerned, when it came to matchplay, the opponent never beat me!" Not only that, but such is his sense of conviction, David Sheahan is certain that he was only ever beaten twice in his competitive life...by golf that he would have great difficulty dealing with! In order to emphasise the point, he is adamant that it was he, and he alone who contrived to lose 95 per cent of his matches. With a wry smile he added, *"I am absolutely convinced of it and anybody who thinks otherwise, is fooling themselves!"*

Idolising Joe Carr and his exploits from a young age also gave him much to aspire to and over time, the elder statesman of Irish amateur golf shared many of his thoughts with regard to maximising Sheahan's undoubted potential as a golfer. Effectively, as he admits himself, JB Carr taught him how to play the game. *"Not in terms of technique or anything like that but in terms organising yourself to win a match, he was exceptional."*

Sheahan's growing prominence amongst his golfing peers in his late teens and early twenties led to several matches against Carr, most notably in the Senior Cup and at the odd Championship. Having been *"hockeyed the first few times"*, he began to question why Carr kept beating him so comprehensively and it dawned on him that it was *he* who was losing the majority of the games, either through silly mistakes, bad concentration or trying too hard to get one over on JB. Joe invariably didn't have to play fantastic golf to win his matches, his reputation was such that opponents, himself included, tended to focus on everything but their own games when playing the Sutton star.

Learning from the Master.
Sheahan and Carr during a Senior Cup battle at the Castle Golf Club, 1964.

"In a professional field, it's quite different. You have so many good players, all grouped together over seventy-two holes; you come to the last eighteen and there are so many of them separated by only a few shots, you can do your best, but there's always a chance that a guy can have a hot spell and there goes your chance, despite not doing anything wrong yourself. However, in an 18 hole match in an amateur competition, if you're good enough, you should be in control of the situation more than ninety per cent of the time. If you lose and you look at all the mistakes that you made over the round, and the number of times that you got away with a bad shot, you must say to yourself, that I **lost** *that match, not that your opponent played better, but that I lost it. There are times when you'll win despite playing poorly, but be honest with yourself and admit that it was luck!"*

Luck had very little to do with David Sheahan's ascent to the top flight of Irish golf however. He was undoubtedly fortunate to have been born into a middle-class, professional family, and one that enjoyed the game. As you'll see, fate played a great role in allowing the boy Sheahan develop his own game and allow him to dream the impossible dream, of glorious days on the greatest links of the world.

The Early Years

Born in Portsmouth to Cork natives Dr Hubert and Ita Sheahan, the family's blissful lifestyle in their adopted country was interrupted by the outbreak of World War 2. Not long after David's birth in 1940, Hubert reasoned that it would be wise to send his wife and two sons, Gerry (now a pathologist) and baby David home to Ireland for safety reasons. Hubert himself returned home for good some months later, having finished up his commitments, where he had enjoyed a thriving general practice with his uncle, Denis Sheahan.

The family settled in Tyrellspass in County Westmeath, a sleepy little village on the Dublin to Galway road. Dr. Sheahan became the local GP and in nearby Mullingar, the couple often socialised, mainly through their membership of the local golf club. In due course, a love for the game was passed on to their youngest son.

"Golf seemed to come naturally to me. My father would always head to Mullingar on Wednesday mornings for meetings and during my summer holidays I'd join him, because he could drop me off at the golf club on the way into town and I'd play 18 holes in an hour and a half."

Those first unconscious steps toward golfing stardom were taken at the famous Westmeath course. Being a smart lad, it didn't take long for the penny to drop when he began to analyse how best to score at the game. *"Some days I'd just practise, but I figured out very early on that pitching and putting was the solution to golf, particularly at amateur level, because there was no amateur, in my time, who was good enough from tee to green to be unbeatable."*

Unwittingly, Sheahan was also playing predominantly with a three iron. He used it constantly, from the tee, the fairway, for chip shots and at times, out of bunkers! All in all, it led to a very inventive approach to shot-making, which would become his hallmark in the years that followed. *"I didn't realise what I was doing, but I was learning an innate skill of the game. It was more by accident than design and that really stood to me, that ability to manoeuvre the flight of the ball."*

Nowadays, there's a club for every conceivable shot, but in those formative early years of his evolvement as a golfer, creativity with hickory and persimmon was commonplace. His flair with that three-iron reaped rich reward and his advances at the game saw his handicap plummet to two by the time he was 16 years of age.

"Golf seemed to come naturally to me. My father would always head to Mullingar on Wednesday mornings for meetings and during my summer holidays I'd join him, because he could drop me off at the golf club on the way into town and I'd play 18 holes in an hour and a half."

The 16 year-old Sheahan in action at Dun Laoghaire in the final of the 1956 Leinster Boys' Championship, where he lost to Frank Fagan of the Castle.

"Bob Shaw was in charge when I turned up that morning in 1958. He raised his hand to his forehead with a sigh saying, "'another one of these bloody students!'"

Sheahan's involvement in junior golf revolved around club competitions and the odd Boys' Championship during his summer holidays (from Rockwell College near Cashel in County Tipperary). In 1956, he was runner-up to Frank Fagan of the Castle Golf Club in the Leinster Boys at Dun Laoghaire.

Although a successful wing forward on two Junior Cup winning rugby teams in the Munster School's Cup, golf was increasingly becoming more of a priority. Always good academically, it was inevitable that he would follow in his father's footsteps and study medicine, eventually settling on UCD.

At around this time, when planning to head away to university, the family was rocked by the death of his father, Dr. Hubert Sheahan. Life in Tyrellspass was swapped for a move to the capital, his mother reasoning that it made more sense, given that both her sons would be attending third level there.

In time, as the Sheahan's settled into life in Terenure, the need for more regular golf became a priority, especially for young David. There was a good bit of activity in the UCD Golf Society, but with nothing like the regularity required of a low handicapper, a meeting was arranged with the all-powerful Secretary of the Grange Golf Club in nearby Rathfarnham.

"Bob Shaw was in charge when I turned up that morning in 1958. He raised his hand to his forehead with a sigh saying, 'another one of these bloody students!' In any case I asked the Colonel if it would be okay if I joined the Grange; he asked my name and then asked what my handicap was, to which I responded that it was two. He immediately changed his tune and urged 'sign here', pointing to a membership application form!" Not batting an eyelid, Sheahan swiftly asked if his mother and brother could join too and the imperious Secretary paved the way for the newcomers to be welcomed into the illustrious club at the foothills of the Dublin mountains.

David and his UCD team-mate Tommy McAleese (Portmarnock) pictured with the legendary Harry Bradshaw and young professional Michael Murphy ahead of a UCD versus Leinster Pros Challenge match.

Northbound Train

With his studies taking up so much of his time, the only championship that would allow him sufficient preparation happened to be the North of Ireland Championship at Royal Portrush. Given the travelling required and the general attitude amongst many southerners to the 'six counties', it wasn't a typical move by a rookie from the Republic to venture northward, but Sheahan's focus was squarely on the golf. It was also a bit of a holiday after the toils of First Med and this was no more than an adventure for a wispy teenager, who just happened to have a serious golf game.

The trip north in 1959 however would be his only visit to Portrush to play in their historic Championship. *"It*

Onward and Upward

David Sheahan had all the attributes required to be successful at golf during his peak years in the sixties. As a direct consequence of those formative days playing with just a three-iron around Mullingar, he had an uncanny ability to manoeuvre the flight of the golf ball in every possible way from the fairway. He was a wonderful exponent of the all-important short game, and with a deep-rooted competitiveness, he was more than able to maximise his performances when playing at the highest level. Small wonder then, that he achieved all that he did, in such a short space of time.

His two-handicap was swiftly reduced to scratch by virtue of some sparkling golf in the Leinster Alliance, in addition to a mastering of his new surroundings at the Grange. The real elevation however, to that rarefied air of the elite golfer came in 1959, when the nineteen-year-old undergraduate was encouraged by his intuitive mother to challenge himself by playing in an upcoming Championship, with the proviso that she would pay his way.

UCD star. D.B. Sheahan, 1959.

His two handicap was swiftly reduced to scratch by virtue of some sparkling golf in the Leinster Alliance, in addition to a mastering of his new surroundings at the Grange.

was a whole new experience for me, and with fifteen pounds, given to me by my mother, I set off alone on the train from Connolly Station to Belfast and caught another train onto Portrush, where I found a B & B for seven and sixpence. It was an extremely organised Championship and Portrush as a course was quite a revelation to me. As it happens, I was the last of the 64 to qualify for the matchplay!"

In hindsight, by scraping into the matchplay stages, he knew that he couldn't rest on his laurels and focussed hard on playing clever golf in order to prolong his holiday! Three days later he advanced to a place in the Championship decider over 36 holes, as it was then, against a wily old campaigner in Johnny Duncan from the Belfast club, Shandon Park. Duncan had recently claimed the Irish Open Amateur title at Royal County Down, so his form was excellent, not to mention his intimate knowledge of the course.

"I played Johnny in the final and he fairly trounced me in the second 18. The weather conditions were pretty awful and I had no wet wear, but to be honest, I wasn't geared for bad weather, psychologically or physically. Duncan was a fitter in Harland and Wolff in Belfast - small in stature but a strong player. He also knew the course extremely well, but it was more my lack of experience and proper equipment that put paid to my chances."

"I only ever played in certain championships in a year and prepared thoroughly for them and said to myself that I'd put my melt into it. It proved to be a very successful policy."

Sheahan was also out of cash, having covered all of his expenses, including a caddy. He hadn't planned on being in Portrush until the end of the Championship, but through the kind generosity of Tom Montgomery of the Ulster Branch of the GUI, he was driven back to Belfast and stayed at Montgomery's house in Shandon Park. He took the train home to Dublin, with a loan from his host, which was duly paid back.

His experience at this level gave life to new-found ambitions in the game. Dreams of a Championship win were now uppermost in his mind. His medical studies were always going to be the priority however but in golf, Sheahan had clearly found a newer form of expression. It wasn't until the following Easter, when he made it as far as the quarter-finals of 'the West' at Rosses Point that his golf received official recognition. He got the nod to play for Leinster in the upcoming Inter-provincials and this saw his elevation up the ranks of the game's playing hierarchy.

Over time, Sheahan came to favour the "West" and the "East" over all other Championships, playing in the South only twice in his illustrious, if short, golfing career. The championships in Baltray and Rosses Point were a great deal more sociable than most, which added to their regularity on the young medic's calendar; *"there was always a great time to be had at those two events, even if you didn't do to well!"*

It's been said of David that he displayed great maturity for his years when it came to working out the nuances of performing well in big-time golf. Having figured out the critical importance of having a tip-top short game in his earliest days, he drew parallels from his success as a student to his preparations for big competitions. *"I only ever played in certain Championships in a year and prepared thoroughly for them and said to myself that I'd put my melt into it. It proved to be a very successful policy."*

Although practising when he could on the course at Grange Golf Club, Sheahan readily admits to giving greater precedence to psychological preparation, being of an academic disposition. *"The whole concept of playing in the championship that I was preparing for would be rolling around in my mind for several weeks beforehand. Say I was in contention for a Championship, I couldn't even sleep at night. I'd be quite nervous and edgy and irritable before I got on the first tee. Once I hit the first ball though, I'd be away and felt in charge."*

Sheahan is presented with the Carlow Scratch Cup, alongside runner-up Tommy McAleese of Portmarnock/UCD

The Good Years

There was a noteworthy victory in the prestigious Carlow Scratch Cup, but it was in 1961 that the 21 year-old student demonstrated his undoubted pedigree.

Having under-performed at 'the West' at Easter he did however have the good fortune to meet his future bride, Maureen Casey, at a dance one evening during the Championship at the Yeats Hotel!

In returning that summer to Rosses Point for the country's premier Championship, the Irish Close, he wasn't exactly brimming with confidence as far as his game was concerned. However, he made the trip back to County Sligo, knowing that he had put in a lot of concentrated effort into his preparations for a tilt at the national title.

At the business end of the Championship, from the last eight on, he was thankfully starting to feel very good about his game, and when he accounted for Paddy Leydon of Lahinch (who had been a West finalist there two years previously) in their quarter-final encounter,

There was a noteworthy victory in the prestigious Carlow Scratch Cup, but it was in 1961 that the 21 year-old student demonstrated his undoubted pedigree.

his expectations of a possible outright victory began to grow, as did his poise, both on and off the course.

Monkstown's Tom Egan, the Irish Champion in 1952 (and the recently-crowned 'East' Champion) was the next big name to fall to the Grange-man in the semi's. Ironically, the man who lost to Egan at Craigivad (Royal Belfast) in that '52 final, was to be Sheahan's opponent over 36 holes in the deciding match for this Championship.

Joe Brown of Tramore Golf Club in County Waterford clearly had pedigree, and he also had the notable distinction of winning 'the West' at Rosses Point nine years earlier in 1952, beating no lesser a figure than Norman Vico Drew, who himself would go on to claim the unique honour of gaining representative honours at Walker Cup, Ryder Cup and Canada (World) Cup levels before that decade was out. Brown had in more recent times won 'the South' at Lahinch in 1958.

The Enniscorthy native was now 53-years-old however, when squaring up to the pencil-thin 21 year-old Sheahan. Despite Brown's advancing years, he remained one of the best swingers of a golf club in the amateur game, with a beautiful action and a great pair of hands. In many respects, he was very similar to Christy O'Connor in his ability to pick the ball so cleanly off the fairways with his woods.

A large group of supporters from the Grange travelled to Sligo for the final and famously, Philip Love, the patron of the Grange Golf Club, led his troops to the first tee and announced, 'Mr Starter, you can commence the final; Grange has arrived!'

Sheahan was suitably boosted by the support and massively determined to win the title: *"Joe was not to be underestimated, but my confidence in my own abilities was growing all the time and as the old cliché had it, nothing succeeds like success. If you start*

A large group of supporters from the Grange travelled to Sligo for the final and famously, Philip Love, the patron of the Grange Golf Club, led his troops to the first tee and announced, 'Mr Starter, you can commence the final; Grange has arrived!'

Sheahan pictured with Tramore's Joe Brown ahead of the 1961 Irish Close Final.

Sheahan's distinctive putting style during 1961 final at Rosses Point, "it served me well I can tell you!"

winning more often than not, you walk onto the tee a more confident man and consequently, you make decisions in a more confident way. Instead of questioning yourself about the type of shot or what the club could be, you now don't have any of the second-guessing. You become very decisive." So decisive that he contrived to win the match in a canter, by the margin of 5 & 4.

Soon after, he played again for Leinster in the Interprovincials and came up against the aforementioned Johnny Duncan, the man who had taught him a lesson in his first ever final two years earlier in 'the North'. *"I gave Johnny a dousing around Lahinch and proved to myself, most importantly, that I had improved a great deal."*

Despite such a resounding success in the country's premier Championship, Sheahan was never really in the reckoning when it came to Walker Cup selection that year. Joe Carr was the lone Irishman on the side to take on the Americans in Seattle, who numbered a young Jack Nicklaus amongst their team. While it was too late for the 21 year-old student to force his way into the reckoning, a spot on the Irish team was assured, which was just the tonic.

Given that he was now the National Champion, his sights were firmly set on making the next Britain and Ireland side in 1963. *"It was always my Mecca to get on that team from a very young age. It was a target that I had set early on, but I knew that in those days, you needed to do something really special to make the final selection."* Little did he know that something extra-special was just around the corner!

1962-A Golden Year

The year began as it always did with a visit to Rosses Point over the Easter Bank Holiday for the annual West of Ireland Amateur Championship. Playing well and once again highly focussed in his approach towards maximising his chances, he found himself in the last four. Instead of marching boldly towards another title however, he stumbled at the second last hurdle, blaming himself totally for the loss against a player he knew he had the measure of.

Sheahan and Carr at the 1961 Home Internationals in Wales

Barney O'Beirne's name was to make international headlines exactly six years later, in the saddest of circumstances. On the 28th of March, 1968, O'Beirne captained the Aer Lingus Vickers Viscount plane that mysteriously crashed over Tuskar Rock in County Wexford, while flying from Cork to London. In the Easter of 1962 however, he was a 29 year-old pilot who had just joined Aer Lingus after 6 years in the Irish Air Corps and also happened to be a good-swinging scratch golfer of some note, who was a keen competitor, playing out of Portmarnock Golf Club.

Sheahan was full sure of beating O'Beirne but readily acknowledges that mentally, he slipped completely out of gear, giving more thought to that afternoon's final, where he was relishing the prospect of stopping JB Carr's relentless gallop towards an eleventh title!

"I suffered from a severe case of over-confidence against Barney. I was three up after eight and cruising.

"I gave Johnny a dousing around Lahinch and proved to myself, most importantly, that I had improved a great deal."

I was really looking forward to having a crack at JB, who was actually going for a hat-trick of wins, never mind eleven in total. I switched off midway through my match against Barney and started thinking about playing JB. In the end I lost on the 18th and I was as sick as a dog." It was a serious lesson learnt and Sheahan took it as no more than that. It was, in effect, one that got away. In the end, it was yet another championship for Carr, winning easily by the margin of 7 & 5.

"I was really looking forward to having a crack at JB, who was actually going for a hat-trick of wins, never mind eleven in total. I switched off midway through my match against Barney and started thinking about playing JB. In the end I lost on the 18th and I was as sick as a dog."

In hindsight, much of Sheahan's life was starting to fall into place. He was now in fourth Med at UCD. Although in no way reluctant to enjoy university life and all its social possibilities, he kept his studies on the straight and narrow, which is a credit to him, although Ita Sheahan's watchful eye should also be commended! His relationship with Maureen was really blossoming and his golf was showing undoubted signs of more great things to come.

The lesson of that semi-final defeat to O'Beirne had been painfully learned, so it was time to move swiftly on to fresh challenges. Surprisingly, given the demands of upcoming exams, Sheahan decided to add a new tournament to his limited schedule, in advance of the upcoming East of Ireland Championship over the Whit Weekend.

The predecessor to what became the European Tour was known loosely in those years as the British Tour. There were tournaments on the continent, namely the National Opens of France, Italy, Portugal and Spain and Belgium, but they were never part of any centrally organised fixture list.

The Jeyes Tournament was an event on the British circuit that was in actual fact the forerunner to the modern day Pro-Am. However in this case, the amateurs were all of a scratch standard. In the early sixties, tournaments were held over three days, with 18 holes on Friday and Saturday, concluding with 36 holes on the Sunday. It was also an era in which there really was no such thing as a full-time Tour player. The vast majority of professionals held down club jobs and played the tour as a way of earning extra cash. It also allowed them to temporarily escape the monotony of club repairs, rubber shoe and ball sales, and gave them the opportunity to show off their respective talents!

Official programme cover of Jeyes Tournament

The venue for the Jeyes International Pro/Am Tournament was Royal Dublin, the links on the Bull Island at Dollymount on Dublin's northside. For David B.Sheahan, as Irish Amateur champion, it represented nothing more than a valid way to further his learning curve in competitive golf. Being a Dublin resident clearly made it a very practical decision to commit to entering, and with the East of Ireland taking place the following week at Baltray, it was a perfect opportunity to sharpen up his strokeplay game.

"If your handicap was a certain level, you could enter a tournament like the Jeyes and to be honest, I never really fancied my chances. It'd be like the Irish Cricket team winning the World Cup, so I was about a 1,000 to 1!" This was very much a pro tournament, with good money on offer and he was up against players of the calibre of Dai Rees, Peter Butler, Harry Weetman and our very own Christy O'Connor.

O'Connor, who was by then the club professional at Royal Dublin, was aware of Sheahan, but as nothing more than a good amateur. Given UCD's association with the Dollymount Links, the pair had often played together, in challenge matches between the University and the club, *"but that week, very few of O'Connor's colleagues would have ever considered me as a threat!"*

It was no more than a fanciful notion to think that 'the Walking Pencil' had any chance of contending against these battle-hardened campaigners, so he focussed on making the cut and contending for the amateur award. *"I was utterly fixated that week with beating JB Carr in the amateur section."*

On that fateful Friday in June his day of reckoning finally came, and with it all the usual anxieties. Sheahan's outstanding memory is of standing on the first tee on day one, alongside the South African Cobie Le Grange, waiting for the third member of their group to show up. He was an English pro and in the end he never did show up, which was something of a relief for the student, as it meant one less person to worry about trying to impress! Reality bit very quickly though, when the Champion amateur of All-Ireland topped his opening drive!

There was hardly time to gather himself as he arrived up to his ball and he hurriedly shanked his approach into the rough near the second tee! That he managed to then compose himself quickly was admirable, but the fact that he contrived to pitch the ball from the hay onto the green and hole the putt for an outrageous par points to an altogether different class of competitor.

It didn't take him long to get into his stride thankfully, and with no heavy burden of expectation weighing him down, he dusted himself off in no time and managed to get round in a highly impressive total of 69 shots, four under par (which at the time was 73).

Sheahan's march was very much up-and-running. After the opening round, he was most certainly in contention, but he didn't receive any great scrutiny from the media, other than it being 'a fine Corinthian effort in august professional company'. In other words, four rounds would find him out, as it tended to do, when boys tried to mix it against the men of the Tour!

Although clearly in the hunt after the opening 18, he was blissfully unaware of his overall position because he wasn't looking at the professional's scores, instead focussing on the efforts of his fellow amateurs!

The 22-year-old remained very much in the mix after three rounds, carding rounds of 72 in rounds two and three and was at six under. *"I was very relaxed throughout the tournament and to be honest I was lucky in that respect. Even as I started the final round after having 72 (on the Sunday morning), I wasn't even thinking of winning. I knew that I was well ahead of JB in this one and that's all that really mattered to me!"*

In the all-important final 18, an extraordinary coincidence occurred on the par-five eighth hole. Sheahan, using a pitching wedge for his short

"I was utterly fixated that week with beating JB Carr in the amateur section."

Sheahan watches an approach shot during the final round at Royal Dublin

approach, contrived to hole it for an outrageous three! Walking to the elevated green, he suddenly remembered that when he first played Royal Dublin as a fifteen-year-old, alongside his late father, he had also managed to eagle the eighth! It's at moments like this that a player can easily lose focus, or, if they have the ability to stay in the present, they can build on the new momentum.

Thankfully, that elusive eagle was followed by a perfect 6-iron to ten feet and a birdie two on the short ninth which brought him to 8 under for the tournament and just one off the lead held by Denis Hutchinson of South Africa.

It wasn't until he turned for home, with the wind at his back, that it first occurred to him that he could win the overall tournament. Walking up the fairway at the par-five 11th, he overheard the booming voice of Philip Love, in between puffs on his ever-present cigar, exclaiming to all within earshot, *'I think our man is going well to beat these pros!'* Love, as previously mentioned, was the patron of the Grange Golf Club, an exceedingly wealthy man who owned much of Marlay Estate, where the club is situated, and was also well known as the breeder of Larkspur, who won the Epsom Derby that very year.

'I think our man is going well to beat these pros!' - Philip Love

"There were very few comments that I remember from people during the four rounds, but that one sticks out. It dawned on me then that it was a possibility. Of course if I started to think in those terms, then it would make the amateur prize much more achievable, because I'd be raising my standards and expectations."

Another jolt to the senses wasn't long in coming however. Failing to get up and down at the par five 14th, Sheahan carded an untidy six for a bogey and in so doing, loosened his grip on the title. Playing partner Bernard Hunt was having a nightmarish day, which completely went against the grain, as he was always so steady (having played in five Ryder Cups). On the fifteenth tee, Hunt was completely out of the reckoning and, recognising that his young amateur playing partner had a real chance to win the tournament, chose to offer a kindly word of encouragement, telling Sheahan to steady himself and make sure of a par at the hole. In the end, he did one better, holing out for a birdie three and jumping right back into serious contention. The game was still very much on.

As often happens, there was a hold-up at the driveable par-four 16th. Sheahan reasoned that it was as good a time as any to have a smoke and attempt, in some way, to keep his emotions in check. Perching himself on a bench, he nervously lit a Sweet Afton, and while gathering his thoughts he was approached by a familiar face. It was Teddy Firth, who was a Leinster team-mate from the nearby Sutton Golf Club; he sidled over and couldn't resist informing the 22-year-old of his assessment of the situation: 'you need three-four-four to win!'

Sheahan was having none of it: *"I chose to dismiss it, knowing that there was a fair chance that Ted could get it wrong! I knew that I was within a shot or two of the lead, so it really was in my hands alone, as to what I would do."*

Having cracked his trusty two-wood onto the heart of the green, a second successive birdie was marked down when he got down in two putts. He was now three under par for the round, but had two very demanding holes yet to come. The regulation par four was achieved on the penultimate hole without too much difficulty and as he walked to the final tee, a place in the history books was firmly within his grasp. As he stood on the final tee, inexplicably, a previous assessment of his game by club pro Christy O'Connor was, for some bizarre reason, ringing in his ears: 'Sheahan, your irons are alright, but you're hopeless off the tee!' What a time to remember such a quote!

In those days, the 18th at Royal Dublin was a par-5 with the infamous out of bounds 'Garden' lurking all the way down the right hand side. 'The Garden' has lured many a stray fade in its time and its very presence could un-nerve even the most confident of straight hitters. With so much on the line, Sheahan admits to feeling extremely nervous on the tee. *"Not pleasant at all. My over-riding thought was to whang it away left off the tee, avoiding the garden at all costs. I was going to make sure that I was in play!"*

Sheahan's natural shot in those days fortunately was a high draw. Thankfully it didn't desert him on the 72nd hole. After finding a decent lie in the left rough, he initially considered firing a three-wood over the corner of 'the Garden' and took a few swings with it. With the wind into him, another fortuitous moment occurred. Larry Gunning, a stalwart of Royal Dublin for over sixty years now, was in charge of communications that day and was operating the public address. Noting how Sheahan had taken out a three-wood, he announced via his microphone to the clubhouse spectators that this was unwise and that an iron was more favourable. With the wind into him, Sheahan may have heard Gunning's wise words, but remembers only that he was in a cocoon of concentration. Nevertheless, he proceeded to take out a four-iron, which he manoeuvred around the corner of the dog leg into a perfect position for a simple pitch and putt.

Forty-five years later, he admits to slightly miss-hitting his approach with the wedge. *"I didn't quite hit the pitch perfectly, which is a bit of a secret – but to the naked eye, it probably looked a lot better than it felt!"*

David Sheahan is carried on the shoulders of Sean Cannon, a UCD Golf Society colleague, surrounded by delirious friends and supporters from University and Grange Golf Club.

"I didn't quite hit the pitch perfectly, which is a bit of a secret, – but to the naked eye, it probably looked a lot better than it felt!"

Nevertheless, it drew a huge cheer from the assembled spectators as it checked up and came to rest no more than four feet from the cup. After a few deep breaths, the putt was confidently holed. Having finished three-four-four, as Teddy Firth had rightly predicted, the title was his and David Sheahan was greeted by an outburst of applause and cheering that wouldn't be seen again for twenty years until the Ballesteros/Langer era came to Royal Dublin at the Carroll's Irish Opens of 1983 to 1985.

Rounds of 69, 72, 72 and 69 gave Sheahan a 10-under par total for the 72 holes and as if to further emphasise his remarkable play that week, he had six nines of 36 shots and two of 33. It doesn't come much better. South Africa's Hutchinson finished second overall, to take the professional prize and five Ryder Cup players were in the student prince's wake, namely Christy O'Connor, Dai Rees, Harry Weetman, Ralph Moffatt and his playing partner Bernard Hunt. Recalling the Jeyes from his home in Johannesburg forty-five years later, Hutchinson, (who had himself won the South African Open as an amateur in 1959): "I said at the prize-giving, I used to think it was funny when you could beat the pros, but I didn't think it was so funny when David beat me that day!", he laughed.

"I said at the prize giving, I used to think it was funny when you could beat the pros, but I didn't think it was so funny when David beat me that day!"
- Denis Hutchinson

It was life-changing in many respects, for it brought Sheahan's name into the mainstream as an amateur winner of a main Tour event. His photo was splashed across every newspaper and as he himself puts it, *"on Friday morning nobody had heard of me, but by Monday morning, I couldn't get the press out of my mother's house in Rathdown. They (the photographers) were getting me to sit this way, that way, take a book down from the shelf and look as though I was reading it, it was unreal!"*

How he managed to enthuse himself for the East of Ireland Championship the following weekend at Baltray is a credit to him. Opening up with a course record 67, he tailed off over the remaining three

Denis Hutchinson

rounds as his hectic golfing schedule caught up with him and finished fourth in the end.

He was fêted by all quarters in the weeks following his win at the Jeyes, yet he still had to keep an eye on his studies. The reaction amongst his tutors however, was mixed. *"Some of my medical bosses were very keen and enthusiastic, others less so, but that's life."*

A semi-final defeat to Michael Edwards (who won for a second time) in that summer's Irish Close may have been disappointing, but he bounced back to claim the Boyd Quaich Trophy at St Andrews as the overall winner of the British and Irish Universities'

Championship. 1962 would bring further rewards with a place on the Britain and Ireland team to face the Continent of Europe in the St Andrews Trophy, which was an indication that he had every chance to realise his ultimate golfing dream of winning Walker Cup honours the following year.

As previously outlined, those Walker Cup matches in 1963 at Turnberry gave Sheahan much to be proud of. Obviously, he was disappointed to feature on a losing side, but his winning singles performances clearly showcased his undoubted ability in that most pressurised of situations.

Although focussing more on his medical career from that time onwards, Sheahan continued to shine on his less-frequent outings to the domestic Championships. Some weeks later, he was runner-up to Michael Guerin in the final of 'the South' at Lahinch. In 1966, he regained the Irish Amateur Close title when it was played at Royal Dublin...a happy hunting ground indeed!

Sheahan's most notable international successes were as a member of the Irish team. He figured prominently on the historic European Championship-winning sides of 1965 and 1967, and as if to prove right the old adage 'horses for courses', he delighted the members of the Grange Golf Club when he completed a hat-trick of Irish Amateur titles in 1970 over his home track. After the Home internationals that year, he called it a day at the top level, playing only for Leinster for the next six years, and giving more of his valuable time to his growing family and his GP duties in the Terenure area of Dublin.

In the 1990's David Sheahan was a prime mover in the establishment of the Golf Scholarship programme at his alma mater. University College Dublin is currently the only University in the Republic of Ireland in receipt of R&A funding. **In 2003, Peter Lawrie, the 1996 Irish Amateur Champion, who benefited from the scholarship programme there, was presented with the Sir Henry Cotton Rookie of the Year Award on the European Tour by Ernie Els.**

In 2001, Dr. David B. Sheahan was honoured by the Irish Golf Writers Association with their Distinguished Services Award, to recognise his massive contribution to Irish amateur golf. These days, he continues to practise medicine from a surgery at his home in Rathgar in Dublin. Although now playing off a handicap of five at the Grange, he remains well capable of shooting in the sixties, when the mood is right.

As Sam Snead once said: 'You have to think like a winner to win!' Dr David B. Sheahan not only thought it, he did it and in so doing, became a genuine legend, in his spare time.

Dr. David Sheahan at home in Rathgar, October 2007.

Sheahan's most notable international successes were as a member of the Irish team. He figured prominently on the historic European Championship-winning sides of 1965 and 1967.

CAREER HIGHLIGHTS

Name: David (Bernard) Sheahan

Date of Birth: 25th February,1940

Family: Wife Maureen, 3 Children: Leonard, Darren & Lisa

Occupation: General Practitioner

Club: Grange Golf Club

Lowest Handicap: +1

CHAMPIONSHIP HIGHLIGHTS

Irish Amateur (Close) Championship:
Winner in 1961, 1966 & 1970
Semi-finalist 1962

Jeyes Professional Amateur Tournament:
Winner 1962 at Royal Dublin

South of Ireland Amateur Open Championship:
Runner up to Michael Guerin in 1963

North Of Ireland Amateur Open Championship:
Runner up to Johnny Duncan in 1959

West of Ireland Amateur Open Championship:
Semi-finalist 1962

East of Ireland Amateur Open Championship:
Fourth overall in 1962. (broke course record with 67 in Round 1 (a week after winning Jeyes Tournament)

British Universities Championship (Boyd Quaich Trophy)
Winner in 1962

Leinster Boys Open Championship:
Runner-up 1956

REPRESENTATIVE HONOURS

Walker Cup, Turnberry 1963 (Won both Singles, Lost both Foursomes)
St Andrews Trophy, GB & I v Continent of Europe 1962 & 1964
European Amateur Team Championships: Irish winning team in 1965 & 1967
Home Internationals: 1961-1967 & 1970
Interprovincials: Leinster Team from 1959-1976

INDEX

D

E

N

O